PROFESSIONALISM MATTERS

Practical ways to enhance credibility & reputation

Dr Cheryl E Whiting

PROFESSIONALISM MATTERS

Practical ways to enhance credibility & reputation

ISBN: 978-1-909929-95-1

Note that the advice and strategies in this work may not be appropriate for every situation. This book is sold with the understanding that neither the author nor the publisher are held responsible for outcomes resulting from actioning the advice herein.

First published by Tantamount August 2023

tantamount

CONTENTS

DEDICATION

To those committed to developing themselves and others around them.

ACKNOWLEDGEMENTS

I want to start by thanking members of the business community who accepted the invitation to be interviewed and appear in this book. Without their willingness to candidly share their stories, thoughts, and ideas, it would not have been possible to present such a comprehensive overview of the subject. The richness of their insight undoubtedly shaped the book's content and transformed my perspectives and vision of what it means to be a professional.

Throughout the book, I discuss the need to develop a robust professional identity and engage with a supportive community. My journey into authorship would not have been the same without the friendship, advice, and support of those who have gone before me. Here, I extend my thanks to Deborah Klee and other members of the #FriSalon writing community who have embraced me as one of their own, taught me so much, and inspired me to keep going. Nor would I have made it without the support of John Eaton and Dan Harris, who took the time to listen to my ideas and read and comment on my earlier drafts. Their intellectual companionship has been instrumental in helping me carefully explore professional issues in such detail.

Of course, if you write a book on professionalism, it must be professional. I am incredibly grateful to my book coach Gwyneth Box and her publishing team at Tantamount. Together, they have demystified the art of writing and publishing. Their expertise and precision have driven the quality of this work, helping refine my writing skills and craft a book I hope you enjoy reading.

I offer, too, a big thank you to family and friends. I owe much to those who have lived and breathed this experience alongside me. Through their fortitude, I found the strength to fulfil my writing ambitions. Last but by no means least, I would like to thank you, the reader, for your shared interest in pursuing professionalism. Together, we can do this and make the world a better place for all.

FOREWORD

Professionalism Matters, the title of Dr Cheryl Whiting's excellent book, is very apt for today's business world and life in general. Professionalism is a much admired and valued attribute, not only because it signifies so many positive attributes of performance and behaviour, but also because it plays a significant part in defining one's personal brand, or what used to be called in bygone days, reputation. Achieving and maintaining a high level of professionalism has an intrinsic value like a golden coat of armour protecting you as you advance through your career. The consequences of losing the shine of this highly valuable attribute are dire and always make for a sad and unfortunate tale. *Professionalism Matters* helps build that armour and keep that shine every step of the way.

I've been interested in this book since its beginning and have discussed it on many occasions with Cheryl. It's been a three-hundred-and-sixty-degree exercise in the good, the bad and the ugly of professional life and has increased my appreciation of the value that professionalism provides to the individual and his or her colleagues. Cheryl's decades of professional experience, writing, researching and lecturing on the subject have come to fruition in this book, and we are fortunate that she has covered it so competently and comprehensively. If you want to build a promising future for yourself and the organisations you work for, internalise and practise what this book preaches. Cheryl's writing is accessible, so you can easily understand and implement her message. In a sense, she embodies the inner voice of the professional, providing insight and knowledge to build your skillset, slalom past obstacles and be the consummate professional you want to be.

From a macro perspective, faith in professions and institutions has been rocked over the decades by scandals and a decline of standards. Examples of institutional malpractice and corrupt behaviour of the police, government officials, religious organisations, corporations and an inexhaustible list of other professions seem to be increasing at an alarming rate. One would not be remiss for thinking that we're fulfilling Nietzsche's theory of 'will to power' where, arguably, professional ethics and standards are merely superficial concepts and our more basic instincts prevail. Hopefully, a book like *Professionalism Matters* will help lead us to more exemplary behaviour and performance from both individuals and institutions.

The perception of diminishing professional standards may be a grumpy malcontent point of view, but it is a challenge facing both business and society, nonetheless. How individuals perform their jobs and organisations conduct themselves is a greater concern than ever before. Professionalism, for instance, is a significant factor when analysing a nation's productivity and for good reason: productivity is a key indicator of the strength and health of an economy, and elements of professionalism such as values, attitudes, work environment, working practices, and well-being play an important role. Since the turn of the century, productivity in the UK has been struggling relative to other industrialised countries. After a series of major events including Brexit, government instability, the Covid-19 pandemic, and the war in Ukraine, the UK is desperate to improve its middle-ranking level of productivity and competitive position among the leading economies. The teachings provided in *Professionalism Matters* are, therefore, vitally important to helping improve the productivity and performance of the UK and any nation's economy.

Having worked at various levels of corporate life in the USA and Europe for some of the biggest names in high technology, government, and finance, I've seen great examples of consummate professionalism, as well as dreadful behaviour and performance. It's a daily challenge to maintain and develop your professional skill set, especially in organisations whose values aren't rock solid. In those circumstances, it's difficult to maintain, let alone grow, that skill set when some of your colleagues don't adhere to the same high standards. What really matters, however, is not the profession, but the values and attitudes each individual holds, regardless of job title. This is brought to light throughout *Professionalism Matters* and will help anyone in any profession achieve high standards and capture the intrinsic value of being a true professional.

There's also something special about seeking a higher level of professionalism nowadays. It's basic economics that when a precious commodity is scarce, its value usually goes up. Given diminishing standards and values, being recognised as a person with high professional standards will make you a valuable asset, a provider of high customer satisfaction and enable you to differentiate yourself in a competitive workforce, as promoted throughout this must-read book.

Even if you are a good, positive, hard-working individual, challenges in working life are ever present and that's why *Professionalism Matters* is so valuable. Read it, enjoy it, and keep it close to hand throughout your career.

Dan Harris

Vice President, Cheltenham Chamber of Commerce
Podcast Host, *Over Here, Over There.*
Director, HymnSheet Ltd.

May 2023

INTRODUCTION
BE BETTER, NOT THE SAME

Welcome to *Professionalism Matters* – so called because it is about matters of professionalism that matter to our clients. If we want to be professionally admired, these matters must also matter to us. As you are reading this book, the chances are you already take professionalism seriously and are proactive in delivering excellent service. The good news is that you have found yourself in great company because, like you, those who have contributed to this book have been inspired to be better professionals. Together we are all on an aspirational journey. We each have a vision of the professional we want to be and are ready to make it happen. This book is here to help us all achieve just that.

We each have our own ideas about the meaning of professionalism. What that looks and feels like and how it manifests in practice varies for everyone. We may already adopt best practices and meet the standards and expectations others demand of us. Nevertheless, times change, no one is perfect, and there is always scope for improvement. As a book, *Professionalism Matters* aims to keep us on the path of personal development. It is intended to raise our sights and standards and enable each of us to enhance our reputation, achieve success, and be the person everyone admires.

Professionalism Matters is a self-help guide with a difference. Almost everyone we meet in business has a wealth of knowledge and experience that we can draw on and share with others. As I started to write this book, I soon realised there was a potential for others, not just me, to be holding the pen. As a result, I chose to tap into the thoughts of others, interviewing over 60 people from a range of business sectors: solo entrepreneurs, freelancers, small to medium-enterprise employers, those new to the business world, and those who have been in the game longer than they care to remember. Because whatever we think we know about professionalism, our peers and contemporaries can offer insight and words of wisdom, which will change how we think and feel about ourselves as professionals, what we do, and how we do it. Hence, much of the content of this book comes from the hearts of people who aspire to deliver a quality service and be their professional best.

As we progress through the book, we discover, through discussions and illustrative examples, what is required of us as professionals, and how we can become better equipped to continuously act with professionalism. Regardless of career path, there is something useful and appealing to anyone with a client-facing role. There is valuable advice for business students and those considering setting themselves up in business, who want to be sure of starting on the right footing. Equally, the book offers support and validation for anyone with experience. Whether you are a business owner, team leader, mentor, or coach, it serves as a resource to stimulate ideas and revitalise existing perspectives.

Naturally, a great deal of emphasis is placed on self-improvement. The book is designed to challenge our assumptions, inform, illuminate, and inspire. It offers a framework that will change how we think about ourselves as professionals. It is important to note that this book is not about persuading us to imitate others and follow the crowd. Instead, it aims to ensure that, in our own unique way, we each measure up to what others expect of us and what we expect of ourselves. Professionalism has no set template or mould we should conform to. With this in mind, the book serves to help us arrive at a point where we can be our authentic selves, leveraging our talents to good effect and making full use of resources, experiences, and opportunities so that each of us shines bright and stands out as someone who is professionally distinctive in every way. All being well, through reading, we will understand ourselves better and be more appreciative of our existing professional traits and practices. Furthermore, as we look to the future, we will do so with a clearer understanding of the self-improvement opportunities that will make us distinctive and exceptional.

Over the following ten chapters, we will gain a comprehensive overview of critical professional principles, issues, and personal qualities relevant to us, no matter our work or position. Within each chapter, we explore several pertinent issues alongside the challenges these generate. The positive and negative consequences of different actions are examined and guidance is offered on how to avoid pitfalls, weak strategies and inappropriate attitudes that potentially destabilise our capacity to act with professionalism. With this, we discuss approaches to upholding standards and building and sustaining our credibility and reputation.

Each chapter is designed to stand alone, allowing the opportunity to read aspects of particular interest or dip in and out of the book at various points. In addition, each chapter is divided into manageable sections, making it easier to absorb and read at leisure. As well as a concluding summary of the key issues identified in the chapter, there is a short closing section entitled 'Hold that thought'. Here, we are encouraged to take a moment to pause, reflect, and self-evaluate our thoughts, activities, and strength of character. Within some of the later chapters, a great deal of emphasis is placed on self-discipline to self-nurture and self-regulate. Each 'Hold that thought' allows us to do just that as we question and examine the extent to which we live up to various professional ideals and are situationally responsive such that we are confident of leading by example.

By the end of the book, we should be confident of who we are and how we need to grow. The concluding chapter draws together various themes, threads, thoughts, and ideas. In doing so, we consider their collective impact on professionalism and where we, as individuals who aspire to be the best, need to go from here. In a moment, we will look broadly at what each of the chapters has to offer. Before this, it is essential for us to consider what we know and understand about professionalism and appreciate why it matters so much that it constantly needs to be nurtured.

IT IS ALL TOO DEEP FOR WORDS

Almost everyone we come across in business wants to be perceived as a professional. And why not? After all, everyone admires a professional. Being admired is good for our self-esteem and good for business too. If we are highly thought of and respected, there is every chance people will want to do business with us. Great! Not only do we get their business, but we acquire all the personal and financial benefits of being sought-after.

When it comes to professionalism, seeing ourselves as a professional is different from acting like one. Our self-image may be that of a professional, but it cuts no ice unless we understand what it is to be one. Failure to display the right attitudes, values, and behaviours is catastrophic for business. We should not underestimate people's expectations. Fall short of standards of safety, conduct, and proficiency, and people soon notice. Word soon spreads, and, as clients vanish, so does our reputation. Maintaining public and client confidence is essential to be held in high regard.

Never has there been a greater need to be admired for our professionalism. The advent of consumerism and media coverage of high-profile cases of misconduct means the wider public and our clients are critical of our actions. Greater access to information and more freedom of choice necessitates higher levels of accountability to meet the demand for quality and client satisfaction. All of this emerges when people are increasingly sceptical and the business world is awash with initiatives to measure and improve economic productivity and benchmark performance. Technological advances also intensify the demand for new roles, knowledge, and skills. To say nothing of the post-Covid era that has changed how we work and engage with colleagues and clients.

To stand up and be counted as a professional, we need to understand all that this entails. So, it is appropriate to start by asking that age-old question, what is professionalism? It might seem like a small question, but it is one without a pocket-sized answer, hence this sizeable book! The thing is, professionalism is not a word that can neatly be defined. There is a lot of debate and ambiguity about its meaning and what it 'looks' and 'feels' like in day-to-day practice. How we view professionalism is essential because our understanding of what it is, and what it is not, is central to shaping our attitudes, values, and behaviours. Our sense of professionalism gives meaning to our actions and drives our commitment to pursue the things that matter most to our clients and ourselves.

People use the term professional in many ways. We only need to listen to how people introduce themselves at business networking events to understand this. For example, Frank introduces himself as 'a professional musician', to portray proficiency and distinguish himself from amateurs or those who play their instruments for pleasure and do not make a living from it. Niamh describes herself as 'an HR professional', revealing her dedication to serving the interests of others within a particular sphere of practice. Then there is Ben, who explains he is a 'professionally accredited financial advisor', signifying external recognition of his expertise and quality of standards.

Underpinning each of these introductions is a desire to gain recognition and respect. In describing ourselves as a professional, we hope to create feelings of confidence and competence, thus generating the trust needed to gain business and receive the financial reward that comes with it. In these examples, the word professional illustrates how Frank, Niamh, and Ben see themselves. This is in no way a criticism because, as we shall see later in Chapter 1, self-identity as a professional positively influences our professional actions.

Yet what about those who present themselves without using the word professional, like Simone, who introduces herself as 'a social media communications manager'? Are we to assume she does not see herself as a professional or has no desire to gain similar recognition or respect? Although, in Simone's case, she feels 'every bit the professional', she does not feel the need to characterise herself in this way. She is confident that she has gained sufficient recognition and respect, evidenced by her years in business and the number of clients she has. Cameron is of a similar mind, preferring to 'keep it simple' and describe himself as a 'heating engineer' because it reflects the true nature and reality of his work. Simone and Cameron show us that we do not have to openly declare we are a professional in order to feel like one. That said, there will always be some who will never subscribe to this self-image, which is somewhat worrying because it is the feeling that motivates us to subscribe to a range of professional ideals and principles.

THE LIGHT IS ALWAYS ON GREEN

The main reason people do not see themselves as professionals is that they have yet to permit themselves to be seen and appreciated as such or because they have not been encouraged to do so. Over the years, I have met people who hold on to the idea that they are from the 'wrong social class' based on their level of education, income, and whether the job they do is physical or not. Some consider that what they do is not important. In such cases, they often downplay the value of their work and their contribution to society and the economy. Others consider that their job sector has little notability and is insignificant relative to other occupations. None of us should ever undervalue what we do, and all perceptions of status and exclusivity must be cast aside if we want to get on and succeed.

In the past, professionalism has been linked to professional status, a position conventionally reserved for doctors, lawyers, architects, and members of the clergy. This view gives prominence to power, prestige, advanced knowledge, and principled standards above all other occupations. To me, this is an outdated and somewhat egocentric perspective. It assumes a clear distinction can be made between roles and responsibilities, educational accomplishments, skill sets, and the values underpinning working practices.

Traditionally, society has revered professions. Hence, attaining professional status is intensely desired. Back in the 1950s, sociologists and academics attempted to identify the distinguishing features of a profession. This led to the adoption of a trait approach and several criterion-based frameworks sprang up. Each lists a series of 'ideal' characteristics, forming the basis for the judgement and distinction between an occupation and a profession. This, in principle, seems straightforward. However, since no two frameworks are the same, it soon becomes apparent that each criterion ultimately includes or excludes certain occupational groups. In short, it is all very subjective and relies upon personal judgement.

Essentially, these frameworks ascribe a level of value to different occupations. In essence, if what we do does not fit the framework or meet the discrete benchmarks, then it is not worthy of being considered a profession. This only perpetuates the idea that distinctions can be made between professions and occupations when, in fact, they cannot because nothing is ever that clear cut. For many years I worked as a radiographer in the National Health Service. On talking to Cameron, a heating engineer, our discussion turned to training and career pathways. Noticeably we had studied for higher-level qualifications with hands-on training. We achieved standards of competence and developed a broad skill set. Our practice benefited society in ways that maintained and secured health and well-being.

Our work involved the application of specialised knowledge. We acted autonomously, often solving problems in emergency situations. For both of us, our work also involved dealing with hazardous materials. For me, this was ionising radiation. For Cameron, it was flammable, poisonous gas. We both worked according to operating procedures and legislative frameworks. In the interest of public safety, we had to be registered to practise. We were both accountable to a professional body with requirements to follow codes of conduct and ethics, regularly update our knowledge, and prove ongoing competence.

Whilst our work may have been different, for each of us it meant we met many of the criteria sociologists use to define time-honoured professions. Over the years, radiography and engineering, like so many other occupations, have evolved to meet the criteria. However, this does not automatically enable occupations and sectors to fully claim professional status. This aspect relies upon public acceptance and recognition as a profession. Society needs to be convinced that an occupation can, over time, sustain its professional characteristics. Obtaining such validation can take several decades.

It is evident that professions are developing more rapidly than the criteria used to define them. If we fast-forward from the 1950s (when these criterion-based approaches began to materialise) to the present day, we find that the criteria remain essentially unchanged. In the meantime a whole range of different jobs have emerged across a wide range of sectors. Technological innovation, the growth in consumerism, and recognition of its impact on the environment have led to the advent of specialists in automation, cybersecurity and artificial intelligence, green energy consultants, and customer experience managers, to name but a few. These jobs within private and public sectors did not exist back then.

In today's world, such criteria no longer seem fit for purpose. We would be hard pushed to think of a job or commercial operation that does not benefit someone, or society and the economy, in some way. The emphasis the criteria-based frameworks place on qualifications, training, and governance arrangements is bureaucratic and conveys functional arrangements. Arguably they do provide a supporting infrastructure that aids the pursuit of professionalisation. However, they fail to capture the physical and intellectual activities required to carry out our work, or the associated attitudes, values, and behaviours that underpin and strengthen professionalism. So why am I saying all this? Well, I believe it is time to move away from such archaic classifications. Not only are they potentially divisive, but they also serve as a distraction from the real issue of what it means to be a professional.

Being a professional is an aspiration that is open to all. It is not an exclusive club. We do not need to neatly fit into someone else's box. We do not require anyone's permission to be a professional. Nor do we need a golden ticket to reap the rewards, benefits, and opportunities professionalism brings. Being a professional is not about who we are or what we do. It is about how we do it. The nature of our work is immaterial, as are our qualifications. It has nothing to do with our job title, length of service, or seniority within an organisation. We do not have to wait to be a professional. The green light is always on 'Go!' Professionalism is about the values, attitudes, and behaviours that underpin our actions. Professionalism is about the way we conduct ourselves, perform our tasks, and fulfil our responsibilities. Although we all have our own opinions of its features and characteristics, professionalism is something we can all accomplish. If we take away perceptions of status, we discover that we are on a level playing field. Whether we run a restaurant, drive a taxi, volunteer for a charity, or manufacture soap, each task can be performed in a professional manner.

Professionals are everywhere, and we can be one of them. When it comes to professionalism, no one occupation, trade, or appointment ranks above another. Regardless of whether we are employed, self-employed, between jobs, or volunteering, we each have the capacity to be our professional best. However, reaching our professional best relies upon our understanding of professionalism.

CONTEXT IS CRITICAL, YET CONSENSUS IS IMPOSSIBLE

To understand professionalism, we must appreciate what it is and what it is not. However, this depends on what we do! Professionalism is very much context dependent. Each business is unique and varies in nature and complexity, offering different services or products to different client groups. The type of work we do defines our responsibilities, who we are accountable to, and how we manage and organise our work. This influences the tasks and methods by which we market, sell, and interact with our clients. Even businesses in the same sector will function and operate differently. In many ways, the realities of our work account for the lack of consensus on the meaning of professionalism.

The varying nature of business activity adds to the complexity of defining and understanding professionalism because no one perceives it in the same way. We all have our own idea of the professional standards we aim to give and wish to receive and what is or is not acceptable. What we do influences the values, attitudes, and behaviours that we consider central to professionalism.

To Patrick, a Methodist minister, professionalism is about 'ensuring our inner values are always reflected outward'. For Poonam, a funeral director, it is about 'doing it right and acting with integrity, sensitivity, and authenticity.' Nancy, who supports vulnerable adults to access health and social care services, considers it to be 'valuing clients enough to give support without judgement.' Adam, who repairs computers, relates professionalism to 'reliability, dedication, and competence.' In contrast, heating engineer Cameron sees it as 'doing a good job no matter how tough with a positive frame of mind,' a view also held by electrician Iain.

In these few examples, it becomes apparent that context guides our patterns of thought. It is easy to see the personal significance of the views held. What is also interesting is that, across these opinions, the spotlight falls variously on knowledge, skills, attitudes, principles, behaviours, outcomes, and outlook, demonstrating just how multifaceted professionalism is. Yet these are the opinions of just a few people. Whilst we might have similar thoughts, our perceptions of professionalism may differ significantly, not just between individuals who work in a different sector but between those who work in the same industry.

I have for many years delivered workshops that focused on helping businesses and organisations generate a shared understanding of professionalism and foster a positive company culture. In one of my activities, I would ask individual participants to list the five most critical professional characteristics. Naturally, one would expect some variance in thought, but the extent of the difference always amazed me. It was common to get 100 different responses from 20 people in a similar line of work. This shows that the range of expected professional characteristics and behaviours is extensive and by no means exhaustive.

In the second part of the activity, I would ask participants to form small groups and reach a consensus on the five most critical professional characteristics. This was challenging and typically generated some lively debate. Indeed, for some groups, it proved impossible to do. Why? Because in business, we are accountable to the many people with a vested interest in our company or organisation.

This means that for each of us, there are a multitude of competing professional expectations from a range of stakeholders, be they our clients, employers, board directors, financiers, the Government, those we collaborate with, or those who license and accredit us. Hence, professionalism demands the commitment to fulfil these multiple obligations.

Professionalism is about more than just serving the interests of our clients. It is also about our relationship with society, colleagues, associates, and ourselves. For example, while our clients expect quality, confidentiality, and competency, society demands that we pay our taxes and comply with health and safety laws. Likewise, our colleagues and associates expect interactions that foster collaboration, fairness, and trust.

In addition, we also have a responsibility to ourselves to ensure we are fit to practise. By this, I mean that we are prepared and able to meet such expectations through continual assessment and development of self. We each have a duty to remain competent and keep abreast of change by learning and updating our knowledge and skills. So too, must we look after our well-being by taking care of our health needs and responding appropriately to stress if we are to remain in top form and ahead of the game in these competitive times.

Each of these multiple obligations is of equal importance, which presents us with the challenge of adopting an approach that enables the expectations of all our stakeholders to be met. There is no picking and choosing and no option to side-step when it comes to professionalism. Were we to focus on competence and attention to detail at the expense of respectful communication, client numbers would soon diminish along with our reputation. The ultimate professionals out there are those who pay attention to every requirement.

TIME CHANGES EVERYTHING

Not only is professionalism grounded within a particular context relating to the type of work we do and the stakeholders we serve, but it is also very fluid and dynamic. It changes over time and is influenced by many things. Our roles and responsibilities and our level of experience are significant. In the early stages of our careers, some aspects of professionalism were probably not immediately apparent or, at the time, seemed unimportant. For example, on qualifying as a computer repair technician, Adam thought the only thing that mattered was his technical competence. His view of professionalism equated to rapid problem-solving and clear understanding of various hardware, operating systems, and software applications. Now older, with more experience, in an age of vast technological advancement, Adam has come to appreciate the interdependent relationship between people and their computers. To be professional, Adam recognises the need to take account of the human side of his role, in which his emotional intelligence becomes significant.

Christine, the owner of a printing company, notes how, as a former print production employee, her professional focus centred around quality and maintaining client relationships. Now an employer, she has moved away from project management to managing people, processes, and performance. It is a different type of management where professionalism includes the need to personally value quality and clients, and the duty to develop an organisational culture that values quality and clients.

What is also interesting is that social and political agendas, culture, research, and development influence professionalism. For example, heating engineer Cameron observes how the issue of climate change has created a need for him to develop what he describes as 'green skills,' so he can appropriately encourage the use of low-carbon fuels and technologies. For Cameron, professionalism now includes mitigating the effects of environmental impact.

Successive generations also influence professional ideals. Different values penetrate and transform the focus of our professional activities. For instance, generally speaking, Generation Y values diversity and social responsibility much more than Generation X, whereas, for Generation Z and Millennials, attention is turned to lifestyle balance, well-being, and personal development.

Educational trends such as self-reflection or mindfulness, which originate from Buddhist traditions, have transcended their sources to be embraced as professional virtues. Elsewhere, misconduct prompts changes to the law or codes of conduct that transform expected professional standards. For example, in recent times, through the General Data Protection Regulation (GDPR), there have been changes to how businesses handle, process, and protect personal information. With this came a duty to adopt principles of consent, ensure privacy, and enhance levels of transparency.

These changes help characterise professionalism. Consequently, the meaning of professionalism and our understanding of it constantly needs to be reconsidered and negotiated. The ever-changing nature of professionalism means it is not a point we can ever truly reach. In many respects, it is transitory, and we must continually navigate our way through, often at pace, knowing we can only aspire to be our professional best. There is no better example of this than the global Covid-19 pandemic, which saw the need to quickly adapt and comply with legislation and guidelines to uphold standards and protect our staff, our clients and ourselves.

DEFINITIONS MAY VARY, BUT EXPECTATIONS DO NOT

The fluctuating, contextual and multifaceted nature of business practices makes it difficult to present an all-inclusive definition of professionalism succinctly. However, whilst professional attitudes, values, and behaviours are variable and subject to transformation, there is one constant. This is the continued commitment to their application in our day-to-day working practices.

Regardless of which attitudes, values, and behaviour we identify with and relate to, we must uphold and adhere to their application in practice. This requires us to think, decide, and act. It is not enough that we know what the right thing to do is. It is about ensuring we carry it out in a recognised way and that it becomes a regular part of all we do. Of course, we can all imitate professional actions. Still, we would only, with any genuineness, be considered a professional if we had an appropriate state of mind and a diligent devotion towards applying the standards others expect.

In business, two clients are rarely the same. No two situations are either. The diversity, complexity, and uncertainty of each new situation and the need to meet each client's unique requirements bring the need to apply our knowledge and skills in different ways. Not only do we need to have the right mindset, we also need to possess skills that enable us to solve problems, make discerning judgements, and evaluate our performance. This brings the need to think critically, reflect on what we know, and apply it as the situation demands.

Sound judgements allow us to adjust our actions, make right and fair decisions, and ensure that the quality of our work and excellence in service is not compromised. Reflection allows us to look back on our actions and is the basis of self-regulation. It acts as a mechanism by which we can adjust to the realities of our work, evaluate, and manage our actions, thoughts, and level of competence. Considering there are few checks on our competence once we have gained our qualifications, self-regulation is an essential feature of professionalism.

I started by asking: what is professionalism? Having said that it is almost impossible to define, it does not prevent a conclusion from being drawn as to its meaning. Professionalism has two contrasting features. There are the variable values and behaviours, and the static core subtext that focuses on how we apply these during business activities. If we keep in mind the underpinning aim of professionalism, which is to fulfil our obligations in a principled way and achieve positive outcomes for ourselves and our stakeholders, then we can gain a sense of what it entails.

Professionalism is a habit founded on a particular way of thinking, such that it becomes a customary and integral part of our daily thoughts and actions. This professional mindset prompts us to commit to acting in ways that build trust and enable us to live up to the required standards and expectations. When our mindset incorporates natural tendencies towards making well-judged actions and we have the capacity to engage in personal reflection, we are well equipped to uphold appropriate attitudes, values, and behaviours, whatever they may be.

UNPROFESSIONALISM IS WITHIN US ALL

We cannot talk about professionalism without discussing what it means to be unprofessional. By and large, professionalism is understood to be an explicit activity, something visibly apparent within our words and actions. Our failure to display what are deemed appropriate values, attitudes, and behaviours is regarded as unprofessional.

It is evident that unprofessional behaviour surrounds us and presents itself in many ways. For every professional characteristic that can be identified, there is a matching unprofessional characteristic and many more besides. Unprofessional behaviour is all-encompassing. Whether it is deception, ineptitude, abuse of systems or people, or downright bad manners, one thing we can be sure of is that unprofessional behaviour is detrimental to business. You name it, we can all recognise it, simply because we have experienced it, moaned about it, and even, to some extent, been guilty of it ourselves!

Collectively, people have a more unified understanding of what it is to be unprofessional, generally recognising it as something contrary to meeting expected standards and behaviours. Unprofessional behaviour often arises through inactivity, omission, and opportunism and is created out of self-interest, a lack of integrity, or self-discipline. It is instantly recognisable, primarily because we feel it when we see and experience it. Incompetence leaves us feeling frustrated, dishonesty leaves us feeling violated, and rudeness and insensitivity offend. Unprofessional behaviour generates intense emotions in ways that professional behaviour does not. What is more, the unprincipled behaviours of others often directly inconvenience us and have consequences.

We tend to see those who are unprofessional as having lost their moral compass and lacking a sense of right and wrong. Admittedly there are some shady characters out there: we only need to watch televised consumer programmes to appreciate that fraud, poor-quality craftsmanship, and poor customer service are real. Thankfully, most of us in business have integrity and strive to achieve excellence. Unfortunately, a few bad apples can leave a bitter taste in the mouths of those of us who might be in a similar line of work. Their unscrupulous actions and dangerous practices can generate scepticism and distrust amongst our potential clients, which we need to work hard to overcome to gain their business.

More generally, unprofessional behaviour arises from less acute misdemeanours. As a rule, people do not deliberately set out to be unprofessional. Instead, it is more of an unconscious action: taking one's eye off the ball, being ignorant of expectations, overstepping the mark as to what is acceptable, or a temporary lapse of judgement, rather than outright trickery or law-breaking. Nonetheless, each is potentially detrimental to business.

This book is not about calling out unprofessional behaviour. It is about helping everyone – and I include myself here – to be better professionals. The world needs better professionals, and this book is about raising the bar. We can all name people in business whom we greatly admire and perhaps we are even mildly envious of those who are seemingly well-liked, charismatic, and ooze gravitas. If we look more deeply, we will find that they are all flawed in some ways, and so are we. No one is perfect. When it comes to professionalism, we are all work in progress. The people we admire will not always have been the professional they appear to be. They will have made mistakes, let standards slip and offended people as they journeyed along. As each new business day dawns, they will face the same challenges we each face. The difference is that when it comes to integrating professional ideals, they have mastered the art of navigating their way through the professional maze.

Those we admire will not have passed through these often confusing and complicated passages alone, that is for sure. Professionalism is far from an individual pursuit. It is built upon co-operative engagement. Their employers, peers, and members of the professional associations and networks to which they belong will have collectively supported their pursuit of professionalism, such that they transmit and breathe the professional qualities we have come to admire.

The reality is that even with help, those who have gone before us have had to unravel the complexities of professionalism without the aid of this book. This is not to suggest they have done so without understanding. Far from it. They will undoubtedly have read widely because many of the professional issues and ideas explored within this book are individually well-documented and written about elsewhere. However, in the business world, the market is not saturated with books on the topic. Indeed, few books exist that consider professionalism as a composite whole in a way that exposes connections we would otherwise need to make for ourselves. Nor, in any conceited way, am I suggesting that all the answers are here or that the book will instantly revolutionise our working lives and bring us highly acclaimed success overnight. On the contrary, this book is all about keeping it real.

The content will, however, challenge our assumptions of what we know about the subject and ourselves as professionals. As we go about our business, we will still have to navigate the professional maze, but at least we will do it with a better sense of direction and a plan to get us to where we want to be far more quickly. If we can use the book to move somewhere beyond where we are now, we are making good professional progress. So, let us briefly get a flavour of what lies in store.

EVERYTHING YOU NEED TO KNOW (FOR NOW, AT LEAST)

In Chapter 1, we explore professional identity. When thinking about professional characteristics, this does not immediately spring into people's minds. Yet our professional identity profoundly affects how we feel and how committed we are to making various professional values, attitudes, and behaviours a visible and integral part of our practice. Here we consider the need to feel like a professional in order to be one. Hence the chapter focuses on building a positive self-image and developing an awareness of how others see us as professionals. We discover how we can capitalise on our passion, experiences, and networks in ways that connect us with professional issues, people, and resources that shape and affirm our identity and aspirations.

The significance of values and attitudes as predictors of personal conduct and our approach to business is explored in Chapter 2. The spotlight falls on remaining authentic by adopting values with personal meaning while understanding the practical implications and commitment required to live and breathe them. Acting in line with our values requires a congruent set of attitudes. So, here we direct our attention to developing a positive, caring, can-do attitude to enhance productivity, sustain relationships, and get the best outcomes for ourselves and our clients.

In Chapters 3, 4, 5, and 6, we consider what most people regard as the central tenets of professional integrity. Trust, honesty and transparency, reliability and consistency, and dignity and respect, respectively. As we read on, it becomes apparent that all four topic areas have strong interconnecting relationships. In combination, they influence the extent to which we, as individuals, are considered credible, reputable, and trustworthy. Fail to display any of these, and we do ourselves out of the right to call ourselves professional.

Chapter 3 considers the overarching issue of trust as a foundation for building relationships and a thriving business. Here we learn why trust is necessary for society and what it represents to clients. We come to observe what a fragile, complex, and multi-faceted process it is to earn and secure trust. With this, we consider how we can constructively work to strengthen relationships, inspire confidence, and protect our reputation by eliminating suspicion and preventing violations. As we move on to Chapter 4, the trust issue resurfaces as we consider the requirement for honesty and transparency. The need to accurately represent ourselves, speak the truth, and accept the truth is considered paramount when building trust. So here, the focus falls on our internal struggles when explaining our actions and on being authentic, open, and candid. This leads us to examine the skill set required and the resources, systems, and practices we can use to cultivate honesty and transparency and raise our level of accountability.

Since people expect professionals to deliver on what they promise, Chapter 5 explores the issue of reliability and consistency. We get to examine why clients value these and the consequences for all parties when we fall short of acting on our promises. Delivering both an equitable and excellent service time and time again is essential if we want our reputation to be based on quality and commitment. Our attention centres on the need to take control of personal actions, collaborative opportunities, and business growth, such that we build client confidence and remain reliable and consistent, even in times of change and uncertainty.

The dignity and respect we extend to others influences how much we are admired and trusted. So, in Chapter 6, we consider the factors that influence the impressions we make, alongside the need to convey respect for others in equal measure through our sincere words and actions. We explore how a personalised service, combined with sensitive, courteous interactions, helps create an atmosphere of dignity and respect. Acknowledging the negative emotions brought to bear through disrespect, we examine issues around developing our emotional intelligence, setting boundaries, and affording ourselves self-respect by maintaining our dignity and professionalism even in the most challenging situations.

Our decision-making potential comes under the spotlight in Chapter 7. How we make decisions is critical to the success of our business. As we explore the complexity of the decision-making process, we examine the dilemmas alongside the factors influencing our choices. To assume responsibility, we must diligently manage the decision-making process in the interest of business sustainability and client care. Hence, our thoughts turn towards developing a systematic approach that enables us to think critically and evaluate objectively, so we can quality-assure our decisions and maintain accountability. Finally, notwithstanding the need to act on our choices, we explore how we empower ourselves and our clients to be principled and autonomous in achieving our goals and aspirations through competence, courage, and self-discipline.

Chapters 8 and 9 focus on professional excellence and professional development, respectively. If we are to innovate and exceed client expectations, we must continually refine our expertise and make learning and development a top priority. Chapter 8 focuses on the need to display professional excellence, continually raise our standards, and improve our level of service. Here we examine the relationship between quality, innovation, and client satisfaction and how this helps to build business excellence. This chapter considers the impact of complacency and how it can be avoided through self-improvement. We learn how excellence is built on co-operative engagement with the need to capitalise on the wisdom and experience of others to achieve a competitive edge. Furthermore, we discover that by adopting a fearless approach, remaining humble and developing a growth mindset, we gain the strength to persevere and become pioneering trailblazers capable of inspiring others.

In Chapter 8, emphasis is placed on the need for self-improvement. In Chapter 9, we expand on the importance of personal development. As we consider a series of self-directed learning strategies, we examine how these influence our self-awareness, our understanding of professionalism, and our practices. Here we get to see how our experiences and the people we are surrounded by potentially enhance or erode our professional ideals. We consider the need for self-regulation through reflection to ensure we effectively manage our personal development in ways that allow us to pursue professional excellence.

Lastly, Chapter 10 explores the need for passion and purpose, a theme that threads through most chapters. Together, our passion and our purpose motivate us to learn, develop, and give everything our best effort. We explore how caring for things that matter creates satisfaction, promotes excellence, and adds value to our lives and those of others. We see that by appreciating our professional skills and attributes and furthering our interests, we can find a fit for our talents and harness our passion in ways that better serve the greater good of society through professional citizenship. We learn that being a passionate professional requires energy and resilience without self-sacrifice. We discover that peak performance requires optimum physical and mental health. As we explore ways to retain our self-belief and remain fit for practice, we discuss the need to reduce stress and support our well-being by nurturing our energy through self-care.

The book ends with a series of concluding thoughts. The dynamic nature of professionalism and variability in perceptions means that no definite conclusion can ever be drawn. Even after reading each chapter, we will still hold very different views. Our interpretation may have changed, but it will not necessarily conform to the ideas of others. So rather than make any presuppositions, attention is turned towards the coherent application and seamless integration of personal characteristics and professional virtues discussed throughout the book. While there are many factors that we cannot control, here we focus on those we can. We explore how integration and positive momentum are sustained by effectively utilising professional-orientating social and cognitive processes that help us remain situationally responsive and accountable.

As we consider how we might develop going forward, we examine the concept of self in achieving our aspirational goals. We discover the powerful impact a combination of self-discipline, self-determination, self-awareness, and self-regulation has on change, development and success. As we look back, we are encouraged to create our professional future by continually reflecting on our experiences, actions, attitudes, and strength of character as each 'Hold that thought' at the end of each chapter prompts us to do.

Without wishing to ruin the surprise, when it comes to professionalism, it is down to us to make it happen. We must continue to expand our understanding of what it means to be professional and develop ourselves accordingly. With any luck, by the end of the book, we will aspire to new heights. Consequently, we will each have one mighty to-do list. Not that it matters, because professionals are plucky people, unafraid of a challenge, which is why they cannot wait to read on.

1

PROFESSIONAL IDENTITY

FEEL IT; LIVE IT; BREATHE IT

Being a professional might not be inherent in our genes, but furnish us with the right values, attitudes, and behaviours, and we are primed for success and admiration. Professionalism is not so much predetermined as it is self-determined. As individuals, we are each a master of our own professional destiny. We each have it within us to become the professional we aspire to be. If we direct our efforts towards self-improvement, apply some sound practice principles, and set our standards high, we are likely to achieve our goal. However, the success we yearn for will be much harder to achieve if we do not consider ourselves to be a professional in the first instance.

Before we can think and act like a professional, we need to define ourselves as such and be conscious of our professional identity. A strong professional identity is a powerful force and one which is likely to set us apart from those in a similar line of work. If professionalism is to be an integral part of how we think and act, we must adopt a professional mindset and a positive self-image. These are the things that help us relate to the values and behaviours others expect us to observe, and prompt us to commit to acting in diligent and principled ways. Without either, we are unlikely to succeed or be regarded as professionals.

In the introduction, we saw how musician Frank, HR manager Niamh, and Ben, a financial advisor, included the word 'professional' when introducing themselves to others. Their use of the word illustrates how they see themselves and encourages others to see them in a comparable way. Defining ourselves as a professional is certainly a step in the right direction when developing a professional identity. However, any self-declaration on our part is unlikely to convince others that we are who we claim to be. We can claim to be anything we want, but unless we can provide evidence or proof, those we are trying to win over will remain unconvinced and become suspicious of our credibility.

Professionalism is built on authenticity, so we must act genuinely in ways that are compatible with our beliefs and values. Words can be meaningless without action, and appearances can be deceptive. Fortunately, professionalism is not something that can easily be feigned. Faux professionals who do not share and live up to professional ideals are soon exposed. We cannot realistically be a professional without having a solid professional identity. This identity reflects the level of connection we have with the work we do; it is only when we truly embrace our professional identity that we become capable of giving our best, building trust, and inspiring confidence.

Hence the reason why this is the first chapter. Professional identity is the cornerstone on which professionalism is built, for it is our professional identity that transforms the way we think and act as a professional. The stronger our professional identity, the more steadfast our professional commitment will likely be. However, building a strong professional identity has its challenges. Many things affect how our professional identity is formed. Some relate to our internal ways of being, others to our external environment, and our connections with others. Throughout this chapter, we will gain a sense of the significance of these aspects, how they influence, strengthen, and reinforce our professional identity, and ultimately our professional values, attitudes, and behaviours. More importantly, we will see the role we have to play in building and maintaining our identity so that we feel it, live it, and breathe it, such that professionalism sits at the heart of who we are and all we do.

FIND MEANING AND CREATE COMMITMENT

We each have distinct characteristics based on our genes, sex, race, and ethnicity. We have many identities and take on different personas in different situations. We progress from children to adults, from students to qualified wage earners, and indeed to business owners. We have multiple relationships that define us as a parent, a partner, a cousin, or a friend, for example. Through our working activities, we may also be an employer, a colleague, or a mentor. We may even belong to different associations and networks or be members of several social and community groups. All these collectively influence our identity and give us a sense of what it is to be who we are, the type of person we are, how we relate to others, and how they relate to us.

Professional identity exemplifies how we see ourselves as a professional within the context of our work and how we express this through our words and actions. It characterises the extent to which we define ourselves as a professional and how we internalise this by aligning ourselves with the attitudes, values, and behaviours our clients and others expect to see.

Professional identity arises when we feel emotionally connected to our work in a meaningful way, such that it becomes the very essence of us. Take Dominic, a chef who describes himself as a 'food nerd.' Passionate about food and keen to ensure people eat healthily, he is not just carrying out the work of a chef; he is a chef. There is a clear distinction. Dominic is not just cooking a meal; he is preparing delicious food for people to enjoy. He is creating nutritious dishes that appeal to all the senses. His heart is on making them look, smell, and taste good. Dominic's passion drives his commitment to doing a professional job, making everything about his dishes stand out. As a result, he is motivated to learn new things and experiment with ideas and culinary techniques. He is part of a professional network for chefs and reads specialist magazines. He puts effort into sourcing the finest quality ingredients, cooking them to perfection, presenting them well, and adding a decorative finishing touch. All because he wants his clients to delight in the food and enjoy the experience of eating and eating well.

It is clear that Dominic loves what he does. From an early age, he had ambitions to own his own restaurant. To him, 'food is amazing,' and he wants others to hold that opinion too. He is proud to be a chef, and a chef is who he is. It runs through his veins. Dominic does not perceive himself to be 'anything else but a chef.' How he views himself drives his commitment to be his professional best and do whatever is necessary to create the tantalising food he is so passionate about.

Having an emotional connection to our work makes a substantial difference. It moves us from a state of doing to a state of being, and with this comes a shift in our mindset. The connection we feel alters how we view ourselves, our business, and our clients. What we feel on the inside is significant. This helps us define the person we believe ourselves to be and establish what we believe in. Our emotions make us appreciate what matters most and push us to act accordingly. The deeper they become, the more they guide us to automatically think and act in professional ways.

Our professional identity helps us find meaning in all that we do and has the potential to transform us. It is like owning a pair of glasses we might wear to improve our vision. Except that this pair helps us see the world in a different light and allows us to focus on things that matter, raising our sights in another way. Our professional identity helps us clarify our responsibilities, purpose, goals, and ambitions. It influences our relationships, attitudes, values, and behaviours. This, in turn, motivates us and shapes the way we work, and drives our commitment to meeting the highest standards and expectations. Professional identity prompts us to make better judgements, continually learn, and respond to change.

Professional identity is, therefore, the foundation of professionalism. We forge our professional identity when we become emotionally connected to what we do and know what we value. The standards we expect of ourselves become integral to who we are, how we perform, and how we behave. Without a strong professional identity, we limit our personal growth, mindset, and aspirational focus. Moreover, we limit our capacity to live up to the expected professional ideals.

FORM TO TRANSFORM

Whatever sector we are in, whatever our line of business, how we perceive ourselves as a professional is important. Our perceptions guide our behaviour and influence our sense of purpose, self-efficacy, drive and enthusiasm, and commitment to upholding standards. However, we can never separate our personal identity from our professional identity. Who we are outside of work invariably influences who we are in business and vice versa: each identity builds and shapes the other. Our professional identity, therefore, represents the integration of our personal selves within our professional roles. Yet it is not in any way fixed because, like many things in life, there is change and deviation.

As time passes, we form various relationships and acquire new knowledge and skills. We broaden our experiences, and with this comes the opportunity to improve our competence and deepen our insight. We enhance our appreciation of what matters most to us and why. Life is unpredictable, so our personal circumstances will inevitably change at some point. We will find ourselves in new situations, taking on new roles, veering off in a different direction, or even changing careers. As circumstances change, so too does our professional identity. At any one moment, it is being eroded, challenged, or strengthened. This means our professional identity is dynamic and something we constantly need to navigate and negotiate. As situations shift and vary, we need to adjust. Developing and retaining a sense of who we are and what we value requires a continual process of self-appraisal to direct and refashion our professional selves.

Many of us will have entered the world of business following a successful career in another industry or commercial sector. I, for one, had a long career as a university lecturer. I like to think I was a credible and proficient expert in my field, with a good reputation, portraying the standards and behaviours expected of someone in my position. Like many others, I leapt into the business world believing I knew everything, naïve to the fact that running a consultancy business requires a different skill set entirely from that needed to teach. Suddenly, I shifted from a state of competence to incompetence without the support of people I once knew and could rely on. My daily routine changed, and so did my role and responsibilities. There were new things to learn and things I needed to unlearn. All of this brought about a temporary state of angst and confusion while I worked out who I was and came to terms with what it meant to be a self-employed consultant.

Rose recounts a similar experience when she left her job as an administrator to become a life coach. By her own admission, she initially struggled to forge her professional identity as a coach because she clung to her identity as an administrator. Rose likens her experience to a caterpillar that metamorphoses into a butterfly. For a while, there was a bit in the middle where she was 'in a chrysalis', caught between two identities, feeling like she was neither one thing nor the other. If she was to become that butterfly, she needed to work at it. This meant adopting strategies to help her shake off everything holding her back and give her the energy to move forward and materialise as someone new. For Rose, it was all very well being excited and ready to take on a new challenge, but if she could not relinquish her grip on her identity as an administrator, she felt she would never have the confidence to put herself out there as a coach.

Rose's strategy focused on gaining more clients and putting herself amongst other coaches. She realised that until she started to 'walk like a coach,' she would not see herself as one, so she sought to build a network that connected her with others in her field. As we will see later in this chapter, this was a good tactic, as those we associate with have the capacity to influence and reinforce our professional identity. By putting herself amongst people who did similar work, Rose gained access to people she could learn from and model herself on. She wanted to see what they did, what they were currently reading or talking about. She created opportunities to connect, explore best practices and ask questions about how they got to be where they were today. By learning something about their journey, Rose could change her own journey and follow a path that led her towards recognising herself as a coach, just as other coaches did.

The biggest shift in Rose's identity came when she gained more clients. Rose's identity was conflicted until she physically started to do what she had trained to do. Without practising, we have no appreciation of our ability to perform or how others perceive us, and with this comes self-doubt. Only when the clients kept coming, and Rose gained evidence of her abilities, did she feel confident enough to define herself as a coach. The most notable thing about Rose's transition was that once her identity started to shift, everything else began to slot into place. It clarified the things she valued, her coaching interests changed, she was more focused on her business, and she started to think and behave in a way that matched others in her field of work. Over time and through her own determination, Rose managed to build a new professional identity. Interestingly, her new identity as a coach is now so strong that it has completely changed her way of thinking. From time to time, she still undertakes administrative work. However, now, Rose sees herself not as an administrator but as a coach who trades her time with an organisation and gains an income by using the administrative skills she previously acquired.

This illustrates that without a strong identity, achieving the level of success we hold out for is difficult. Any change in our career will inevitably disrupt the relationship we have with ourselves and others. Before we can build a new identity, we must detach ourselves from our current identity. We must deconstruct it before reconstructing it, which will not happen overnight. Feeling conflicted and disconnected is a natural part of that transitional process. Whilst it might be uncomfortable, forging a new identity is within our control if we adopt a strategic approach like Rose. She sought to draw on other coaches' confidence and strong identity to strengthen her own.

Although the change may disrupt our sense of self, it does not necessarily disrupt our sense of professionalism. Being able to relate to professional attitudes, values, and behaviours certainly gives us an advantage. However, professional identity is founded on our understanding of what it means to be a professional in the context of a particular area of practice. The process of transition leads to cognitive and behavioural reorganisation. In building a new identity, we gain a better appreciation of the values, attitudes and behaviours needed to meet our current roles and responsibilities. As our new identity develops, our sense of professionalism becomes heightened and refreshed. In the transition, we come to understand and appreciate what professionalism looks and feels like in our new working environment. This furnishes us with a fresh outlook that guides our standards of behaviour and professional identity.

PERSIST WITH POSITIVE PERCEPTIONS

Our self-image is a principal factor in how we see ourselves as a professional. What we think of ourselves and what we think others think of us is critical to developing our professional identity. We each have a mental picture of ourself as a professional. As a virtual assistant, Sarah sees herself as approachable, organised, and courteous. As a graphic designer, Neil considers himself to be a dependable, creative, and conscientious individual who goes the extra mile, while Alannah, a make-up artist, judges herself to be clued-up and level-headed, with good foresight. How favourably we feel about ourselves affects our self-esteem and self-efficacy. Notably, Sarah, Neil, and Alannah all have a positive self-image, which is the prerequisite to being a confident professional.

Such a high level of self-esteem is energising. It boosts our confidence and improves performance and productivity. It strengthens our belief that we can succeed in business and are indeed capable of embracing professional ideals. A positive self-image inspires professionalism and affects how we perceive and respond to situations. It motivates us to act in certain ways and empowers us to take a particular course of action and pursue our goals. Only when we value ourselves and appreciate our qualities can we give our best and strive to be our best.

In our heads, many of us will hold an image of what an ultimate professional should look and act like. Interestingly, many of us also recognise that our self-image does not always match our ideals and we feel we fall short in some way. We each have an aspirational identity: deep down, we all know the type of professional we wish to be. We all have a particular someone implanted in our minds whom we admire and want to resemble – someone who has achieved immense success or has qualities and talents we can only dream of emulating.

Tom, who provides clean air systems, admires Jeff Bezos, executive chair of Amazon, for 'his innovative vision and ability to explain complex markets.' Karyl, a social marketer, respects Richard Branson, the founder of the Virgin Group, for his 'humble entrepreneurial spirit and the courage to continue when ventures do not go according to plan.' However, no one needs to be famous the world over to be admired for their professional attributes. Seemingly, those we are in awe of live and walk amongst us. We tend to marvel at those we are close to, like Andreas, a freelance journalist who is in full admiration of a former colleague, a person who remains composed in a crisis and is totally unfazed by deadlines. For Rose, family members have been her inspiration. She used to think her husband Orpheus, a builder, was an ordinary guy doing an ordinary job. More recently, she has come to appreciate just how extraordinary he is. She admires how he focuses on safety and stays organised, cares for and stores his tools, and leaves home in a clean set of workwear each day. To Rose, Orpheus's actions remind her that professionalism should be embedded in every aspect of her work.

Although we may not always feel we live up to our own perceptions of what it means to be the 'ultimate professional,' it does not mean we should feel ashamed or deterred from developing and claiming our professional identity. We have it within us to raise our sights and be equally admired. It is only natural to want to compare ourselves to others and see how closely we measure up. When making comparisons, it is easy to feel inadequate, less successful, or even a fraud. We can easily be swayed into thinking we lack something based on how wider society sees us or how the media stereotypes us.

Imposter syndrome can affect us too from time to time. This leaves us feeling we have no legitimate right to enjoy success or be where we are, despite achievement through our own efforts. Too often, we allow nagging self-doubt to creep in. We end up telling ourselves we are not good enough, are incapable of meeting others' expectations, or do not fit in. We can soon create a distorted view of ourselves as we stop appreciating our strengths and focus on all that we are not. This diminishes our confidence and self-worth and, before we know it, we give up on ourselves, our goals, and our ambitions.

Self-doubt can prevent us from developing a strong professional identity and the hope of becoming the professional we aspire to be. Although we may not be close to our ideal, it does not give us a reason to have a negative self-image. We are inclined to be self-effacing and prone to playing down our strengths and magnifying our weaknesses. A central part of developing a professional identity is accepting ourselves for who we are. We should not dismiss how far we have come in being the professional we are today. It does not matter where we are; it is only a reference point for future refinement. There is every reason to feel positive about ourselves, silence our inner critic, and be confident in our abilities. Although it may be hard to believe, it is worth remembering that, just as we admire certain qualities and abilities in others, we undoubtedly possess something others do not, which leads people to admire those qualities and abilities in us.

As individuals, we are a combination of our traits, knowledge, and experiences. Aspects of this will set us apart from others. Our uniqueness is something to celebrate, for we each have special talents and attributes. We can fool ourselves into believing we must conform and be like everyone else, but this is not true. It is OK to be different and break the mould if we remain authentic and true to ourselves. An unfavourable self-image will only hold us back, so rather than being envious or comparing ourselves to others negatively, we need to see those we admire as role models. Sadly, there is no perfect role model. Like us, everyone has flaws, but we benefit more when we feel inspired by others. If, like Tom, Karyl, Andreas, and Rose, we can identify with other professionals who exemplify the values and behaviours we want to display, we can learn from them and better ourselves. We can use their inspiration as a source of motivation for self-improvement, fuelling our passion, unlocking our potential, reinventing our professional selves, and building a more robust professional identity.

STOP, LOOK, AND LISTEN

Professional identity is developed through self-awareness. We all like to think of ourselves as a professional, someone who is competent, trustworthy, dependable, etc. The truth of the matter is that others do not always see us in the same way. The image we want people to have of us as a professional is not necessarily the one they hold.

To be a professional, we must understand ourselves and how others see us. This requires us to observe reality and deal with whatever stares back at us. If not, we will never come to know the extent to which we deliver and behave in line with professional expectations. And unless we know this, we cannot own it, live up to it, or do something about it.

Evaluating our own behaviour and characteristics is fraught with difficulties. Not least because it relies upon self-perception, which can be wrong. We are prone to overestimating or underestimating our capabilities and attributes. In company, we all try to paint ourselves in a positive light, even if this is not the reality. For most of us, this is not a conscious or deliberate deception. To think we are better than average is just a way of protecting our self-esteem. However, self-deception often creeps in if our competence and confidence do not equate. We have all encountered self-confident individuals who believe they are talented but are nothing more than incompetent. In contrast, we come across individuals who lack confidence and are full of self-doubt. In front of them stand many people in admiration of their exceptional qualities, yet they do not see it.

What is interesting here is that both the propensity for self-deception and self-doubt unconsciously obstruct our self-view. If we are oblivious to our traits, attitudes, and behaviours, we cannot close the gap between how we see ourselves as a professional and how others see us. When it comes to developing our professional identity, this gap is significant. Our ability to recognise ourselves as a professional is based on knowing how capable we are and how closely we measure up to our aspirational identity. Inaccurate assumptions on our part will affect our capacity to fully develop our professional identity.

Self-assessment is not something most people are particularly good at. Personal reflection is a flawed process. It comes with the assumption that we can, without bias, use our own eyes to see ourselves as others would see us through their eyes. Those glasses we wear to raise our sights also have the habit of inadvertently becoming rose-tinted. It is hard to be objective, avoid self-deception and fully detach ourselves from our personal perspectives. To avoid unnecessary discomfort and protect our feelings, we are often selective in what we deal with when examining how we think, feel, and act.

I, for one, remain a mystery to myself. I do not believe I have a creative bone in my body. I joke that there is no beginning to my talents. My attempts to draw or sculpt always turn out to be more tat than Tate. My self-perception rarely matches that of family, friends, students, colleagues, and business acquaintances. To them, I am witty, full of ideas and insight, resourceful and inventive. They invariably arrive at a more accurate judgement of my personal characteristics and are far better at highlighting my strengths and weaknesses than I could ever be. It is the same for Nicala, who provides private health insurance, and for virtual assistant Sarah. Neither of them feels confident presenting in public, and each is regularly surprised by the positive feedback they receive. On the other hand, Andreas always thought of himself as a straight-talking type of guy until a colleague recently told him he has a sharper edge, with the propensity to be blunt.

What this demonstrates is that external opinions are essential to our self-view. Gaining insight from others is vital if we are to evolve as professionals. This is our reality check. In business, our reputation is based on what others think about us. The judgement of clients, stakeholders, associates, and fellow networkers carries weight and generates consequences. People talk, which affects how others see us and determines the extent to which we gain business or obtain recommendations and referrals.

KNOW IT FOR SURE

We cannot determine for ourselves how people view us. When we interact with others, we can only surmise how they might feel about us from the responses we get and the way they act towards us. What we are observing here is their behaviour. What we deduce from this is only our interpretation, which is also open to misinterpretation. What we fail to get from this is a sense of how people really perceive us. To understand how we are perceived, we need to hear it from people personally and honestly.

Not everyone is comfortable asking for feedback. The fear of negativity can hold us back, coupled with the fact that learning an ugly truth will require action on our part to remedy any shortcomings related to ourselves or the service we provide. The truth is that no matter how good, bad, or ugly the truth really is, it brings us closer to building our reputation and developing our professional identity. Feedback is a powerful thing. Through it, we can draw inferences about ourselves as professionals. It helps us to define who we are, assists us in disposing of self-limiting beliefs, and raises our sights.

There is no shortage of ways to gain feedback on our qualities, attributes, and behaviours. Many communication channels are open to us, each one a valuable source of information. Whether feedback comes from clients, stakeholders, or mentors, via testimonials, online reviews, emails, or conversations, it allows us to see ourselves through the eyes of others. The more sources we use, the more insight we gain. With this comes a higher level of self-awareness. We can never guarantee that the feedback we receive will be honest, but some people will always be more candid than others. This potentially levels up any bias, enabling us to appreciate that there is some accuracy, and that thoughts and comments represent reality.

Through feedback, we come to know ourselves more and gain a sense of how well-rounded a professional we really are. Feedback alters how we see ourselves and evaluate ourselves by providing an objective starting point for reflection. It gives us the ability to recognise the type of professional we truly are.

Whether we live up to our aspirational identity or not, feedback helps us secure our position as a professional in the world of business. Our identity as a professional is legitimised and strengthened when our self-view compares favourably with the opinions of others. Our spirits are raised if what we learn about ourselves is confirmed and reinforced. Such positive affirmations encourage us to continue in the same way. Recognising our strengths is a boost to our self-confidence. It permits us to become our own cheerleader and take credit for the qualities we possess.

Recognising our best qualities helps us more readily embrace our flaws and deal with the undesirable aspects of ourselves that others have highlighted. This, of course, requires a willingness to respond to what we discover about ourselves and engage with the issue in a self-directed way. If we start with a strong professional identity, we are more likely to embrace opportunities for self-improvement. In our bid to improve ourselves, we examine aspects of ourselves that we were previously unmindful of. As a result, we grow and develop. Our analysis helps strengthen the choices we make and the actions we take. Discovery allows us to broaden our horizons, seek new experiences, expand our skill sets, adopt different values and behaviours, and set new goals. Feedback offers us a chance to reappraise our self-perception and self-esteem. Whether it reaffirms or disaffirms our personal views, we can use it to improve, acquire a stronger identity, and reposition ourselves more confidently in the professional arena.

PROFESS THOSE VALUES, LOUD AND PROUD

Part of our professional identity is linked to our awareness of what we stand for and believe in. Our values, philosophical outlook, and attitudes guide our professional actions and play a key part in building our reputation. Values and attitudes are discussed in detail in Chapter 2 but require a mention here, as professional identity is linked to how in touch we are with them. Our work roles and responsibilities provide context to our actions, add meaning, and strengthen our sense of purpose. This leads to the formation and adoption of corresponding attitudes and values. The values we hold give us a sense of direction. They structure the way we think and act. Our professional identity is reinforced when we consciously know and live by our values. If we cannot articulate what we value, we lack a sense of what we expect from ourselves. Having clarity guides our actions, shapes our decisions, and intensifies our commitment to adopting and upholding specific standards and behaviours.

The nature of our work often determines the values we hold. Whatever is important to us and our clients, whether honesty, reliability, or sustainability, for example, our values and professional identity are closely connected. Our desire and ability to define and live by our values arises through our professional identity. There is something cyclical about it. Whatever our values, our identity strengthens our commitment to applying them in practice, and in doing so, we become more readily engaged and actively associated with them, strengthening our identity.

We saw earlier how chef Dominic values the use of high-quality ingredients. He looks to source fresh, natural produce because he believes they have more flavour and improve the taste. Over time Dominic's experience of procuring food of the right standard has led him to develop a sustainable mindset. By making a commitment to his core values, Dominic has developed a set of secondary values. Not only does he value quality ingredients; he now values sourcing quality ingredients in a way that minimises environmental damage. Using a localised supply chain, and using whatever fruit and vegetables are in season, has become increasingly important to him. It is similar for Nancy, who supports vulnerable adults to access necessary health and social care services. Nancy values independent decision-making and respectful, courteous client communication. She has also come to appreciate the need for inner peace and works to reduce her clients' emotional stress and anxiety throughout the various stages and processes that must be followed.

Dominic and Nancy show us that our experience strengthens what we believe in. We become more in touch with our values and discover other principles that shape our beliefs and behaviour through them. All the things we come to appreciate take on a new meaning. They become an internalised and inherent part of us, which in turn strengthens our professional identity. Our identity is, in part, created through our values, and the values we hold reinforce our identity. The deeper our association with a particular set of professional values, the stronger our identity will likely be.

So, if we do not know what we value, what we believe in, or where we stand on certain professional issues, we must question what is at the core of our identity and whether we are sufficiently equipped to meet our professional expectations. To survive in the business world, we need a strong professional identity constructed in line with our work and the clients we encounter. A strong set of values enables us to develop a strong professional identity. As Nancy says, 'if you have the strength and courage to live by your values, you can hold your head high and be proud of being the professional you are.' Professional pride brings out the best in us. We become more immersed in what we do; we invest our time and energy in doing our best and adding value to the experiences and lives of others. Pride motivates us to think and act as a professional and identify as one too.

FIND IT IN GADGETS AND GIZMOS

It is not just our understanding of self and the values we use to guide our thoughts and actions that influence our professional identity. Our identity is also constructed through tools, symbols, and our relationships with others.

Our personal experiences of doing the work we do and carrying out various activities give us a sense of purpose. The tools we use to carry out our tasks, and the activities we undertake when using them, help define or accentuate our professional identity. The physical equipment and computer applications we use, the manuals we refer to, and the paperwork we produce are tools of our trade; all have practical relevance. Naturally, they enable us to perform effectively but are also significant in shaping our actions and interactions. All the tools and equipment we use are a tangible indication that what we do is real. They influence the nature of our work and how we do it. Through their use, we come to appreciate what it means to be a professional within a particular context. The practical use of these tools in the real world also authenticates our endeavours and influences our self-image. This transforms and assures us of our professional identity.

To carry out his work as a corporate video producer, Sam uses various pieces of technology. By all accounts, it is quite an impressive kit. Each piece performs a different role and function, allowing Sam to apply sophisticated cinematic and editing techniques. In Sam's profession there is a certain amount of posturing, but for good reason: as Sam says, 'if you want to be seen as a professional in this line of work, you cannot be seen to be a hobbyist.' It is true that if we have the visual look of a professional, clients are more likely to be convinced of our credibility. Higher-grade, higher-quality equipment with advanced features is reassuring to those clients anticipating outstanding quality and performance. Of course, it is not just the type and volume of equipment that defines us as a professional. It is how competent and effective we are in using it. If we have 'all the gear with no idea', we are unlikely to be up to the job. Nonetheless, all the tools, equipment, applications, and gizmos we have at our disposal play a part in forming and preserving our professional identity.

When Sam started out in business, his equipment gave him a sense of identity. In his perception, the brand and quality of the equipment he had purchased were a step towards putting himself on the same level as others in his field. As his business developed, Sam invested in more equipment. The more he got, the more professional he felt. It is easy to see why, because there is a psychological element to possessing equipment. Having the right equipment gives us self-belief and boosts our confidence. Internally we feel less of an amateur and more of a pro.

Sam certainly could not be a video producer without any of his equipment. However, looking back, Sam notes how, initially, he depended on the ownership of the equipment to define him as a video producer. Now, though, his identity is tied to the outcomes of what is produced when using that equipment. For Sam, the turning point came when he became more skilled at using each piece of equipment and more appreciative of their capabilities. Knowing the equipment could do what he wanted it to do took away some of the guesswork. Being more adept at using it made his work easier. With greater self-confidence, better skills, and a portfolio of showreels, Sam no longer relied on the equipment to create a convincing impression or seal his professional identity. Sam is a video producer not because he owns video-producing equipment but because the equipment enables him to produce videos. It is no longer the equipment that defines Sam as a professional but his competence and achievements.

What we can observe from this is that our professional identity becomes strengthened by how we use the equipment, rather than by mere ownership. The tools and equipment we possess act like stepping stones. But instead of helping us cross a stream, they help develop a more robust professional identity. Each piece of equipment, like each stone, provides us with security. It gives us a sure footing and helps us control our professional identity. In appearance, stepping stones sit in isolation, yet collectively they form a continuous path. It is only when we use them that we advance our journey. It is only when we become more familiar and adept at using the various tools of our trade that we arrive at the next level. The tools and equipment we are surrounded by are a good foundation for establishing our professional identity. However, unless we use them with good effect and gain meaning from them, we end up misleading ourselves. We can fool ourselves into believing we are a professional just because we have something in our possession, not because of what we do with it when it is in our hands.

INTERPRET THE SIGNS

Aside from our tools, we are surrounded by physical objects and visual materials that symbolise and reinforce our professional ideals. These are powerful stimuli. Each tells a story that impacts how we think of ourselves as professionals and how we correspondingly behave. We derive meaning from their presence, and their significance validates our sense of professionalism.

Jamil's college certificates hang on his wall, each demonstrating the knowledge and skills he has acquired that enable him to work as a photographer. They serve as a reminder of how he has moved from being a student and complete novice to being a qualified expert in his field. For Iain, an electrician, his records of ongoing training and compliance with statutory requirements prove his commitment to self-development, working within the law, and developing public trust. The membership badge attached to his van window signifies his association with a professional business organisation; it is a symbol that conveys unity and engagement with peers and a wider professional community. The mug on his desk bears the logo of a recent exhibition he attended, and the words underneath – 'my heart belongs to health and safety' – serve as a daily reminder of the need to protect others.

Our identity can similarly become reflected through the work we have done, the evidence of which carries meaning. Cathryn, a public relations consultant, surrounds herself with pictures of clients and materials from marketing campaigns she has led. It is a way of reminding herself that she is sociable, determined, proficient, and talented. In her case, images of activity, people, places, and events symbolise her unique strengths. The pictures create a sense of satisfaction that reinforces Cathryn's love of the job and deepens her desire to keep doing what she does. Through symbols and imagery, we can get to know ourselves. They remind us of our authenticity, abilities, and commitment to delivering the best for our clients. Alone, they might only provide a small indication of who we are, but collectively they are symbols that clarify and reinforce our identity.

There is nothing more symbolic than the way we dress. Dress is a significant factor in how others see us and how we see ourselves. Our clothes define us as a professional and influence our mindset, mood, our level of confidence, and behaviour. Whether we dress in a suit, wear a uniform, or arrive armed with the latest accessories, if we 'look the part,' we will act the part. This is why Nicala puts on a smart dress and shoes even when she is working at home. Because when she does, something magical happens. It transforms her mindset. It puts her in a positive frame of mind and focuses her on the task at hand. Clothes have a positive impact on our self-image and set the tone. They play a significant role in building self-confidence and psychologically preparing us for our roles and responsibilities. We return to the issue of dress in Chapter 3, when we explore how it influences trust. The point here is that if we look professional, we feel professional. If we feel professional, we are in a better position to execute our duties with professionalism.

BUILD A NETWORK AND GET INVOLVED

Our professional identity is also developed through our association with others. We saw earlier how Rose used this strategy to build a new identity. By connecting with other coaches, she shed her identity as an administrator and developed her identity as a life coach. The relationships we form with individuals or organisations influence our professional self-image. As we discover in Chapter 9, personal development is not always influenced in a positive way, but let us not dwell too much on that for the moment. It is best to take an optimistic approach and have faith that our social interactions and experiences serve to reinforce rather than diminish our professional identity.

The world of business can, at times, be lonely and isolating. Being visible and active within a network or professional community provides a vital support system. We tend to think of membership in sector-specific organisations and networks as a space or place to meet new people, obtain support, raise awareness of our services, and gain access to those we want to do business with. What we often fail to appreciate is that networks are a pathway to legitimising our professional identity. Being part of a wider community of people within and outside our occupational sector brings opportunities to prove our professional credibility, build our reputation, and establish ourselves as a professional in the eyes of others. The mere act of gaining membership, turning up, and engaging can make us feel professional. However, nothing boosts self-esteem and self-efficacy more than being accepted as a respected member who displays professionalism. This feeds into and sharpens our self-image.

Any manner of membership of a wider community brings formal and informal opportunities for learning and development, together with access to a wide range of resources. We might take delivery of their newsletters and magazines, have access to a repository of subject knowledge, or participate in interactive online forums and seminars with others who share similar interests. Through this activity, we hear about existing professional issues related to the nature and subject of our work or business. How we actively engage with the issues, people, resources, and pursuits of the organisations of which we are members influences how we build our individual identity. We cannot afford to be passive, as this will lead to a slow transformation process, in which we have little control over our professional destiny, not knowing who we are, where we fit in, or what is expected.

Taking the initiative allows us to get down to business literally. Active involvement enhances the transformative effect, and we get to where we want to be much faster. Through participation, we acquire knowledge and develop our expertise. We gain a better understanding of our roles and responsibilities and the standards expected. We learn from other people's wisdom, foresight, and hindsight. We hear their ideas and opinions and gain an opportunity to share our own. These experiences have the capacity to influence our mindset and inspire us to act. They also enable us to reconsider our own understanding of what it means to be a professional in the context of our work. From all of this, we often gain a better sense of the extent to which we meet professional expectations, where we stand on issues, and where we sit amongst the wider professional community. This helps shape and affirm our professional identity and prompts us to feel and act in more self-assured ways.

When we are part of a group, there is often a sense of fulfilment, particularly when we feel the group is supportive, has an excellent reputation, and fosters a culture of professionalism. The extent to which we are proud of our association rests on whether the organisation or network we belong to has a positive image externally. This, of course, depends on its members' collective energy and drive to promote and uphold professional attitudes, values, and behaviours.

There are two important aspects to being a group member: one is a sense of belonging, and the other is a sense of unity. Both influence our professional identity. We recognise we are in the right place when we feel accepted and in the company of like-minded people who share our interests. The feeling of being a professional amongst professionals can change our internal perception of what it means to be a professional. We refashion the beliefs we hold about ourselves, and our motivations change. We even self-present as professionals and play out the role with greater intent. We do the accepted things and conform to group values and norms. This is not necessarily to look good, but because we are proud to be part of something and want to protect and nurture the professional ethos and ensure it lasts.

Pride spurs us towards excellence. We feel inspired to do our best and positively project our sense of professionalism. If we are fortunate enough to be part of a group where members are of the same positive mindset, a respected collective identity is formed. Together, through various activities and pursuits, members proactively commit to ensuring professional standards are upheld.

Not only does this reinforce our identity and shape our future professional selves, but it can also influence our peers and wider society, nurturing a culture of professionalism. Whilst this might seem a bit ambitious, it illustrates that if we do not conceptualise ourselves as a professional and cannot positively construct our own identity, we stand little chance of assisting others to do the same.

KEEP THE BALL ROLLING

Until now, we have not explored how a strong professional identity arises when harmony between key influencing factors exists. This is not easy to establish because identity has a large psychosocial dimension. Our identity comes from our internal thought processes, experiences, and legitimised acceptance amongst a community of like-minded people. These factors are variable. We are not always cognitively prepared to challenge our own perceptions of ourselves. Nor are we always emotionally and psychologically ready to embrace our professional identity. We might be overflowing with confidence and ready to accept the next challenge, yet the world and the people within it are not always ready to support us. As Rose showed us earlier, we stand a better chance of forming our identity when the internal and external conditions are positively aligned. Only then will everything begin to fall into place such that we can create the meaning and connections needed to secure our professional identity.

We can only be influenced by things that exist and where there is continuity. Whether by choice or circumstance, without the right mindset, a positive self-image, regular work, feedback, access to tools, resources, or role models, or participation within a community, we are unlikely to fully appreciate what it means and feels like to be a professional in the context of the work we do.

Each of these factors influences our identity in their own way, but also through the complex relationship that exists between them. Moreover, two very different activities and courses of action can lead us to the same outcome. For example, the mere act of writing a business plan gives us a sense of past success, where we have been, and where we are heading. It is just one element of business practice. Nonetheless, this strategic process helps us internalise what we stand for and helps us see where our future lies. We might not particularly relish the prospect of writing or reviewing it, but we learn so much about ourselves and our professional capabilities and competencies when we do. Still, there is every chance that other things, such as conversations with a mentor, would similarly lead us to appreciate our personal abilities and business potential. Either path can have a powerful impact on our self-esteem and our identity.

Their direct impact is, however, hard to measure because our professional identity does not stem from one thing alone. It accumulates through a series of activities, events, and stimuli. There is often a cascading effect. For example, many of us give out business cards as a way of connecting with potential clients and members of our network. They are a visible reminder of who we are and what we do, and are a powerful way to communicate this to others. When we hand them out, we feel good. It reinforces our self-image as a professional. It signifies that we are making valuable connections with people we want to do business with. By themselves, business cards influence our identity, yet when we give them out, something else often happens. For example, some form of interesting conversation develops: one that enlightens us and prompts us to discover more about a subject. With our interest piqued, we might listen to a podcast or do some research to learn more. Suddenly we have the confidence to try it out and put it into practice. The positive feedback and the outcomes we see motivate us to reflect on our experiences and share this with others. The entire process of talking, listening, reading, applying, evaluating, and sharing consolidates our understanding. It helps us pull it all together. We arrive at a point of knowing our professional selves. But, in this case, it has come through a broad range of intrapersonal and interpersonal interactions and stimuli. We see here that one self-affirming act can open opportunities for us to gain a broader view of ourselves.

In any combination, various actions, interactions, and stimuli will help form and maintain our identity. They do not have to exist concurrently in equal measure. We build our identity in diverse ways. It is not so much about what method we use to gain insight; it is about how proactive we are and how continually engaged we are when using these methods to determine our self-view.

Whilst we might feel very sure of our identity right now, assuming this will always be the case would be wrong. Developing our professional identity is not a past or future activity. It is very much a present-day activity. Not only must we forge our professional identity, but we must also continually reinforce it. To keep our identity fresh and at the forefront of our minds, we must supply ourselves with constant physical and social interactions, intellectual and visual stimuli to expand our insight and fuel our passion and commitment.

It is no surprise, therefore, that a shortage of influencing factors, or personal indifference towards them, negatively impacts the formation, strength, and continuity of our professional identity.

Not only does it change how we relate to ourselves, our work, our clients, and others, but we also risk becoming disconnected from the professional sphere we once knew. Instead of being immersed in it, we find ourselves sitting on the periphery, a place that sees us isolated from the activities, practices, people, and issues that underpinned our sense of self and drove our commitment to achieving high standards of professionalism in the first instance.

Professionalism demands that we take ownership of our professional identity. We must look to become engaged in the process of developing, adapting, or maintaining our identity by making effective use of all the things that potentially influence our identity. When we do, we increase our chances of positive interactions and experiences. These help us understand ourselves, learn and develop as professionals. By being proactive, we exert a bigger influence on ourselves. It prompts the cognitive, behavioural, and emotional changes required to wholeheartedly identify as a professional and meet the demands of being one.

FEEL, LIVE, BREATHE, REPEAT

Developing a professional identity is part of the dynamics and processes of becoming a professional. A strong professional identity is at the heart of professional growth and success. It gives us confidence and momentum to meet standards, live up to our professional ideals, and achieve our aspirations.

This chapter has explored internal and external factors that influence and intensify the complexity of developing and sustaining our professional identity. We started the chapter by exploring how passion is a catalyst and plays a big part in unlocking our potential and forging our professional identity. The love of the job and our passion for what we do helps build emotional connections. We feel it within us: the strong beliefs we have in ourselves as a professional drive us to do all that is necessary to do a professional job. Our internal emotions make us conscious of our professional identity. This motivates us to act in professional ways. It determines such things as the type of activities we engage in, the clothes we wear, and the choices we make in the interest of our clients. The physical act of doing what we do, with the equipment we have, for the clients we encounter, helps us find meaning and shapes the associations between our role and identity. This influences our values and attitudes and our commitment to applying them. This moves us beyond simply feeling it to living it, for our commitment to upholding standards and meeting expectations keeps professionalism alive. It is almost impossible to forge a professional identity without these building blocks. The connection we feel with our work and the meaning we derive from it act as our point of reference. Together they shape our thoughts and processes and serve as the foundation for our actions. All that we feel we put into practice.

Whilst our experiences and feelings put us on a path that leads us towards recognising ourselves as a professional, the journey does not end there. There is a uniqueness in our professional identity. There is no smoothness or logic to how it develops. It is a non-linear process. We do not progress along a continuum with a definite start and end point. Our professional identity develops in distinct ways, at various times, through different activities and stimuli. It fluctuates, evolves, and changes according to how we feel, the work we do, and our roles and responsibilities. We have seen how forging an identity can be a bit of a rocky road, confounded by the need to readjust our existing identity or let go of our old identity to build a new one.

Nonetheless, whatever course it takes, it remains a process of transition. One that transforms how we think and behave as a professional and how others see us. To journey on, however, we need new ideas, differing insights, and physical and emotional energy to enlighten and empower us to pursue our goals, raise our sights, and be our professional best. We get these when we are proactive and constantly engaged with the world around us. For example, when we take time to focus on personal development, read, practise, listen, interact, and reflect on what we feel, see, and hear about ourselves. New ideas, insights, and energy all play a vital role in strengthening and sustaining our professional identity. They are a form of fresh air that we inhale and exhale. This moves us from living our identity to breathing it. Moreover, they revitalise us, incite the passion needed to extend the life of our professional identity, and allow us to carry it with us. Through our enthusiasm, knowledge, and actions, we exude our identity. It helps us make visible all that we are and that we stand for, which can positively influence and strengthen the professional identity of others.

Building a professional identity does not come without effort on our part. We have seen how we must work at removing self-doubt and creating reasons to feel positive about ourselves. Therefore, it is important that we take steps towards being more self-aware and actively engage with a wider professional community, using this as a springboard to develop our identity and cultivate professionalism more widely. If we do not have a sense of who we are, we do not feel a sense of duty. This creates a barrier to engaging with professional issues. Without constant social and physical interactions and visual stimuli to fuel our passion, we become ignorant of the expected values and standards.

The communities to which we belong, the material we read, the training we complete, the feedback we receive, our tools, and acquired memorabilia remind us of who we are and what is expected of us. All these factors help us develop, adjust, and retain our identity, allowing us to move with the times and according to circumstances. They add force to what we do, why we do it, and how we do it. All of which validates our sense of our identity and keeps us accountable. This constant reinforcement allows us to feel, live and breathe our professional identity, keeping us connected because when we are disconnected our identity weakens. And, as it weakens, so does our commitment to our values, standards, and behaviours. This compromises our level of professionalism.

HOLD THAT THOUGHT

The strength of our identity comes not only from how we seek to build it, but from how we seek to sustain it. To be admired as a professional, our identity must be visible and integral to who we are. We must value ourselves and the processes by which we form and sustain our identity.

Our professional identity evolves through a process of development in an ever-changing world. To keep pace, we must remain self-aware. If we want to feel, live, and breathe a professional identity that guides us towards being our professional best, we must regularly explore how events, our mindset, passion, values, and associations with others, enhance our sense of identity. We must also check the accuracy of our assumptions and understand how our self-perceptions align with the views of others. Furthermore, we must ask ourselves, to what extent do we evaluate our level of intellectual engagement? How effective are the strategies we adopt in building and reinforcing our identity, and cultivating our sense of belonging? These are important issues because we can never truly appreciate or be assured of our professional identity until we question them. Only then can we manage our identity in a way that allows us to feel, live, and breathe it.

2

VALUES AND ATTITUDES

BRING THEM INTO LINE, BRING THEM TO LIFE

Hands up! Who wants to be popular, successful, and prosperous? Right now, it is not hard to imagine a giant sea of hands all waving about. Simply because, if we are all of these things, we know we have built ourselves a thriving business. There are two ways of achieving this goal. We can either cheat our way to the top, trampling over others to get what we want, or we can work diligently, knowing that through genuine effort and the right approach, one day, our aspirations will come to fruition. The path we choose rests on our values. We all want to feel we have made it in life. Yet many of us want to feel the satisfaction that comes from being true to ourselves and doing business by fair means. Therefore, we choose to prioritise values like honesty and responsibility over making a fast buck. We do this because we have created a set of values that carry meaning and represent all that is important to us. These values shape our behaviour and give us the self-confidence to do what we believe to be right in the interest of our happiness and well-being, as well as that of our clients.

In Chapter 1, we explored how by defining our values, we strengthened our professional identity, strengthening our commitment to applying these values in practice. When we do, they become tangible entities instantly recognisable through our words and actions. We show them to be an active part of our being. We bring them to life. In doing so, we validate the extent to which we uphold our values. Alongside our technical competence, living in alignment with our values is central to building our reputation.

When there is a positive alignment between our actions and the values we profess, we are perceived as someone who is both honourable and professional.

Our actions are also driven by our attitude. How we see the world and the people within it affects our motivation to adopt behaviours and practices congruent with our values. Our values represent our intent and all that we aspire to be. They guide us towards making the right decisions. Our attitude determines the extent to which we carry out our intentions with professionalism. Sound values do not signal sound actions. For our efforts to encompass all that we value, our attitudes must reflect a determination to succeed and prompt us to act in principled ways with the interests of our clients at the forefront of our minds.

We start this chapter by exploring how our values and attitudes, over and above our competence, distinguish us from our competitors and influence the bond we forge with our clients. Emphasis is placed on establishing a set of core values that have personal meaning and reflect the true nature of our business activity. Examining this, we see how our choices influence business growth and development opportunities. Mindful of the need to uphold values, we consider the commitment required to consistently deliver on them, alongside the professional attitudes we need to portray, to be sure of leading by example and generating client satisfaction.

Despite our best intentions, there is always the potential to drift off course. To prevent a decline in our standards and overall attitude, we explore what it takes to stay focused and maintain a healthy perspective such that we add value to our clients' experience. Additionally, we consider how our outlook and approach affect our level of emotional and physical investment in the work we do and the clients we do it for. As we delve into the potential effects of our thoughts and actions, we explore the significance of the alignment between our values and attitudes and how this breathes life into our level of professionalism.

COMPETENCE COUNTS, BUT VALUES AND ATTITUDES COUNT MORE

Our ability to perform with a high level of proficiency is vital if we are to be considered an expert in our chosen field. We achieve mastery through our in-depth knowledge and advanced technical skill sets. When it comes to obtaining business, it certainly helps to have a good command of a speciality. Yet competence does not equate to professionalism. Indeed, we might be a computer coding whizz-kid, a screenwriting genius, or a champion beekeeper, but that does not automatically make us a professional or ensure we behave like one. If we are looking to be admired and respected, no amount of talent will eclipse our behaviour. This is not to say that competence is not essential, because it is. Without the proper knowledge and skills to perform tasks associated with our line of business, establishing credibility will be hard.

The defining thing about competence is that it is observable and easy to judge. We only need to watch reality television programmes, such as those in which amateur cooks' and celebrities' baking skills are tested, to learn that competence is represented in the outcome. We do not have to tune in for long to know it takes more than enthusiasm and a fancy spatula to make a cake worth eating. To us, it is entertaining. We sit back and laugh at the ineptitude as cakes collapse, biscuits burn, and meringues melt. Back in the real world of business, the reality is harsher than any television programme. Incompetence is something rarely tolerated and certainly not a laughing matter. No one trusts or believes in the incapable. In fact, people will do everything they possibly can to avoid them: incompetent people spell danger and are bad news.

Competence relies upon having sufficient experience and understanding of the expected standards so that we can perform tasks effectively. No matter what business we are in, we must possess a distinctive combination of capabilities that enable us to lead, manage, fix, craft, and create a favourable outcome for each one of our clients.

Through education and experience, we will have acquired and enhanced our knowledge and proficiency, perfected our techniques, and honed our attributes. As a result, we have developed various skills and abilities and advanced our way across a continuum, moving from novice to expert. However, to be considered competent, we must draw from our range of skills and abilities and make appropriate judgements about various situations and tasks. Competence is thus grounded in our capacity to repeatedly integrate and directly apply these skills and abilities to our work. Unless we know what to do, how to do it, when to do it, why it needs to be done, and under which circumstances, we will not be deemed competent.

Developing and sustaining competence requires commitment. Later on, in Chapter 9, we consider the need to adopt effective strategies to facilitate continuous learning and development. For now, let us focus on the fact that competence represents progress and personal development that we will have worked hard to accomplish. When it comes to developing competence, there are few quick wins. Our journey will not have been easy. It will have taken years of study, hours of practice, considerable financial investment, and a few personal sacrifices for good measure.

Naturally, when we have such great talent, we want to tell people about it. Without a doubt, we would be doing ourselves a great injustice by keeping it hidden, particularly when competence represents a positive feature of our professional self and a good way of marketing ourselves. Unsurprisingly, we look for ways to publicly profess and persuade others of our competence.

Having furthered her proficiency through qualifications from the Chartered Institute of Insurance, Nicala, who provides private health insurance, places the letters Dip CII after her name. It is a direct way of getting across her credentials and bringing clarity to the minds of people she communicates with or those who might come across her online profile. For similar reasons, Jamil, a photographer, includes the logos of his awards and accreditations on his website, business card, and email signature.

The display of competence is everywhere. We see it on merchandise and promotional materials. It appears in communications, brochures, and on social media. Displaying it is undoubtedly to our advantage because in doing so, we create an opportunity to make known our expertise and distinct skill set.

From an early age, we are directed towards thinking that competence and experience are everything. Parents, carers, teachers, recruiters, and employers often reinforce the idea that any amassed knowledge and experience will ultimately culminate in professional success. Previous experience and high levels of competence will certainly help us to get along in business. However, no matter how adept and proficient we are, competence does not instantly define us as professionals. Competence allows us to function as a professional rather than characterising us as one. We do what we do because we can and because we have the know-how.

However, we are not alone in this quest. Whatever we are doing, many more are doing the same. Some might even be doing it better.

Our competitors are numerous. The difference between whether clients come to us or fellow networkers recommend and refer us is not a matter of competence. It is one of values and attitude. On its own, competence is not a good benchmark. It is an attribute every client expects. By all accounts, competence is the minimum requirement. We need to go beyond the minimum if we want to set ourselves apart.

MEANINGFUL VALUES, MEANINGFUL PURPOSE

Faced with a choice between two people equally competent and offering the same service, the final decision is likely to be made on the values and attitudes portrayed. They each significantly impact the relationships we form and the level of trust that ensues. As individuals, we warm to people who share our values and attitudes. There is something comforting about being around others who appreciate and exemplify what we consider important. There is an element of certainty attached to knowing someone is like us. It inspires confidence. Hence, our values and attitudes are the very things that attract or deter clients and define the level of support and goodwill we are likely to receive from them and others.

Values and attitudes tend to guide our actions. To those on the outside looking in, our attitudes and values are a good predictor of the behaviours we are likely to exhibit and how we are likely to approach and manage our business. Primarily, our values and attitudes symbolise where we stand regarding professionalism.

Our values are based on things important to us in life and business. They represent a personal collection of principles and standards that tell a story about who we are. They reflect our personality, our professional identity, and what motivates us. As individuals, we have different values, mainly because values tend to develop through socialisation. Our family and friends, education, personal experiences, and religious or spiritual beliefs all play a significant role in determining our values. So does the nature of our work and the clients we serve.

Poonam, a funeral director, values compassion and dedication to duty. Since she attends to grieving families at all hours of the day, it is easy to see why these values take on such significance. Anneke, a civil engineer, values quality and safety because she monitors operations on construction sites daily. Jonathan's sense of community is important because he runs a business network that brings people together. Emma, an accountant, values comprehensibility, making facts and figures easy to understand. Like Diana, a financial advisor, Emma values honesty and integrity. Perhaps this is not so surprising since both have roles and responsibilities associated with managing finances and taxes.

This list of potential values is by no means exhaustive. Undoubtedly, some of these values will be equally important to us and may sit alongside other principles we value. Some values, such as honesty and integrity, for example, are almost universally shared and will resonate with most of us since they help build and maintain trust and public confidence.

But it matters not if we hold different values from others. Indeed, it pays to be different in business and we can purposefully use our distinctive values to differentiate ourselves from others. What matters is that we have established a set of core values that are the heart and soul of our business and capture the very essence of what we are about. For it is these core values that provide meaning to our work. They provide a reason for being and drive our commitment towards doing what matters most to ourselves and our clients. Values represent a framework that guides our business activities. To be a professional, we must be in touch with our values. If we do not know our own values, we have nothing to steer us in the right direction.

PINPOINT THOSE CORE VALUES

If we want to be known and remembered for our values, we must first find the time to determine what they are and understand them. This is by no means a lesson on arriving at a set of core values; I simply wish to emphasise that our core values must be authentic and have personal meaning. Without personal meaning, they offer little by way of direction and purpose. To gain trust, our values must be an integral part of us. Clients will want to see them reflected in everything we do. Therefore, we must establish values we are passionate about and can openly advocate. If we do not do this, then the chances are we will not be sufficiently motivated to act in line with them.

If we are in business with others, our core business values must resonate with partners, team members, and associates. The success of our business depends on everyone being able to channel their energy into the same things with the same level of enthusiasm. This means we must find ways of creating a shared value system that everyone feels connected to and cares about.

Following a period of business growth, recruitment consultants Steve and Georgina, along with their team, took time to critically reassess what they saw as the company's core values. A group discussion generated 50 possible choices, which they narrowed to four. Since they work directly with people, Steve, Georgina, and the team decided on a set of client-focused values: honesty, integrity, reliability, and relationships. These were values everyone could relate to and ones that would optimise the opportunity to gain and retain clients, grow the business, and enhance its reputation. These were also values that, if upheld, would strengthen the team, and create a positive working environment. This is a double plus because when we see the benefits of such values, it deepens our personal association and reinforces their significance.

As Steve and Georgina point out, connections are always a two-way process. The values chosen also reflected the type of clients they wished to attract and do business with. In the past, the team has found that clients who do not share their values are often more challenging to work alongside. As recruiters, Steve and Georgina's clients are mainly employers. However, for them, in any recruitment process, there is always a third person in the equation: the candidate looking for employment. Although it is an indirect relationship, Steve and Georgina consider it unethical to recruit someone knowing they could potentially be working for an employer who is likely to treat them badly. For Steve and Georgina, their values ensure they place themselves amongst the right people to protect themselves and others. Defining their values makes it easier to identify the type of people they wish to work with.

We learn from Steve and Georgina that our business values are much more than a marketing exercise. Values help us build sincere relationships, make better-informed choices, set quality standards, and progress our business goals. Our success and reputation rest on the values we choose to adopt. Hence, they need to reflect our business identity and aspirations in terms of how we wish to behave personally, how we expect ourselves and our clients to be treated, and how we do business. If our values genuinely mean something to us, we are more mindful and deliberate in our intent to uphold them.

MATCH ACTIONS TO VALUES

It is one thing to put time and energy into defining our core values and another to live by them. On the surface, our values may look and sound good, but if they are hollow, lacking sincerity and substance, they do not count for much. We can spend all the time we like repeatedly promoting our values, hoping people will believe in us. But, if we do not own, live by them, and hold ourselves up to them, we are not being true to ourselves or others.

Our level of professionalism will be judged on the extent to which we honour and espouse our values. There must be a match between the values we profess and the values we deliver consistently through our activity day in, day out. For example, it would be no good valuing excellence and innovation if we were not prepared to invest in research and development in a way that enriches and transforms the services we offer and improves the outcome and experience for our clients. Claims of valuing a prompt and accessible service may seem an obvious client winner. However, ignoring incoming telephone calls and emails will only provoke a negative response. It is never wise to profess values simply because we think it is what clients want to hear.

Cathryn, a public relations consultant, reminds us that there are plenty of companies out there greenwashing – falsely encouraging people to believe they are environmentally friendly and sustainable, and claiming to be socially responsible to improve their public image and grab everyone's attention. Cathryn encourages companies to hold back on what she describes as 'marketing puff' unless they have substantial evidence that they are making a difference to the environment and society. Our values need to be visible. If we want to tick the box, we must deliver at all costs without compromise. In Cathryn's words: 'Once we claim it, we have to maintain it, and then keep pedalling along the same path.' Her point is that in order to live by our values, there needs to be a high level of commitment and a deep understanding of what is required for us to deliver on them consistently. We might have a vision, but that does not necessarily lead us to act accordingly.

If we consider that our values distinguish us from others, we must establish what is expected of us regarding the professional attitudes and behaviours we must portray. If we add to this their role as guiding principles, then we must be prepared to harmonise our operational, financial, and strategic decisions if we are to put our values into practice and stay on course.

Living and breathing this rhetoric is easier said than done. No one appreciates this more than Kriss: motivated by his passion for diving and marine conservation, he set up a sustainable travel company. Kriss provides a niche service for people who are equally passionate about protecting the environment and who want to see the world while limiting their carbon footprint.

Through his travel and working experiences, Kriss knows first-hand how travel and tourism negatively impact the environment, local communities, and indigenous wildlife, and how unfeeling tour operators can be. Knowing how difficult it is to offset carbon emissions attributed to air travel, Kriss focuses on ensuring responsible tourism. To provide value for money, cater to the needs of his clients, and remain competitive, Kriss directs his energy towards ensuring he works with the companies that share his ethos. Staying true to his values means establishing clear location criteria to avoid popular polluted tourist destinations and opting for tours in places like Costa Rica and Argentina, where governments have legislated to protect the environment. In addition, to ensure carbon neutrality on the ground, Kriss must do much research to ensure companies are eco-certified, not just greenwashing.

As Kriss says: 'You can always find companies to work with, but finding ones that share your ethos is difficult.' However, Kriss has demonstrated that this is possible. He has managed to work with companies across the globe that are committed to protecting resources and investing profits in animal, land, and marine conservation, as well as companies that support local community projects and ensure fair wages and continued education for those working within his business supply chain.

For Kriss, doing what he sees as right is a labour of love. The combination of passion, an optimistic outlook, and a determination to preserve the planet and make the world a better place to live, fuels his unrelenting commitment. To backtrack or compromise on his principles does not sit well with Kriss. Staying true to his values spares him any emotional turmoil. The small actions we take today will have a big impact on tomorrow. If we drift away from our values, we are heading towards disaster. To clients, professionalism manifests in our ability to walk the talk by continuously aligning our actions with our values and not compromising our principles. If we do not wholeheartedly embrace our values or bring them to life through our efforts, we fail to achieve our goals. We also unwittingly compromise our well-being and our integrity and potentially do ourselves out of business.

REASSESS ONCE IN A WHILE

We must remember that our clients come to us based on what we stand for, yet they stay because of our behaviour. Our core values define and differentiate us, but we only stand out as professionals when we stick to them. Staying true to our values certainly requires a great deal of stamina. When business is good, and everything appears to work in our favour, it is easy to stay on track and commit to them. When pressure from others mounts, circumstances change, challenges intensify, or when we find ourselves amongst the wrong people, our mindset changes too. Rather than using our values to guide us in the right direction, we are often tempted to give in to others or deviate from our standards. We are all susceptible to this.

Our ability to remain connected to our values comes through continual reinforcement. This arises through daily actions and choices, and the systems, processes, and frameworks that we use to hold ourselves accountable. We fundamentally deliver on our values through patterns of behaviour. Change the pattern, and we change our course. We are not always aware that we have drifted away from our values: our behaviour can subtly change, such that our values slowly erode over time.

To ensure our values remain at the heart of everything we do, we need to regularly check in with ourselves and reaffirm our values, like, for example, Steve and Georgina, who make it part of their annual business review. The world evolves; time does not stand still and we do not operate in a bubble. As our business grows, we as individuals change, and so does the context and nature of our work. As we experience new situations, adopt new ways of working, take on new clients, or work collaboratively, our original core values may no longer seem as imperative as they once were.

This by itself should lead us to question and explore three things. First, are we out of touch with our values and need to work to bring ourselves back into line? If so, we need to examine the factors that have led to this and what we need to do to restore the situation. Second, is it that we have drifted so far away from our values that we need to seriously question whether, in all sincerity, we ever held those values in the beginning? If so, we must devote time and thought to discovering our values. Finally, is it that our core values no longer serve as a foundation for our business activity simply because the strategic direction of our business has changed? Whatever the answer, something needs to alter, be that we ourselves, our core values, or a moderate amount of both.

This is not to suggest that we entirely abandon our values. Instead, it is to emphasise that we need to reconnect, adjust, or evaluate them occasionally. It is a way of holding ourselves accountable. With values representing the reality of our current business activities, we are steered in the right direction to achieve what we want for our clients and ourselves. As a result, we achieve greater success all around.

BE A CHAMPION OF CHANGE

In committing to our values, we show ourselves to be a professional. This certainly strengthens the relationships we have with clients and deepens their level of trust. When we live by our values, we lead by example. If we act responsibly and with integrity, we gain credibility. Through this, we become the type of person others wish to emulate. Our role-model status allows us to make an impact and inspire others to adopt similar values.

Earlier in the chapter, Cathryn reminded us that we need substantial evidence before declaring that a particular value is central to our business activity. We may have core values embedded in all we do, but that does not preclude us from adopting secondary values. Progressing with what we value and care about will help us grow and shape our future vision and practices. It is better to ease ourselves in and understand what is required of us and grow from there, rather than profess a tokenistic core value that we cannot fully commit to. Over time, we may have progressed such that our secondary values are now so integral to our business activities that we recognise them as core values. By taking small steps, we act responsibly. We show ourselves to be professional when preparing to meet clients' expectations and standards, and avoid false-hearted superficial attempts that fool no one.

We all like to champion a cause based on what we value. When emotionally invested in something, we often aim to facilitate positive change in others. We look to reinforce different ways of thinking and behaving, allowing clients, associates, and fellow networkers to identify with the standards and principles close to our heart. As Kriss sees it: 'Business gives us the power to provide. It also gives us the power to influence.' If we are credible and live by our values, people will listen, and we can make an impact. Through conversations, Kriss has discovered that other companies want to do their bit for the environment. He uses his knowledge to educate others and has encouraged companies to make small incremental changes. Persuading tour operators to provide clean sources of water in metal rather than plastic containers is a small change, but it is a positive start, nonetheless. Steve and Georgina recount similar experiences. They advocate for special educational needs and disability employment support. Often, the fear of the unknown prevents employers from engaging in this aspect of the inclusivity, equity, and diversity agenda. Through their passion and insight, Steve and Georgina have successfully encouraged employers to consider alternative candidates and create pathways into work.

To make an impact, we must live by values that genuinely correspond to who we are. If we are to adopt the values we profess, a clear understanding alone is not sufficient to consistently deliver on them without compromise. The 'living' part has to be a way of life. It requires high levels of commitment. Having an appropriate set of attitudes and a visionary outlook is essential. Without these, it is all an act. Our attitudes and perspectives allow us to bring our values to life. This makes us even more interesting. It is hard to inspire others by simply going through the motions. Our values might awaken people, but our professional attitude stirs them.

ATTITUDE IS EVERYTHING

Bad attitudes are bad for business. They are not so great for our professional reputation either. We may be experienced, highly credentialed, and competent, but we are unlikely to earn anyone's respect if we are rude and belligerent. Poor timekeeping, a pessimistic outlook, or shoddy work will only alienate clients and associates. Our business and profits will decline if we do not have the right attitude. People will not want to work with us, and we will struggle to build and sustain relationships, missing out on opportunities for growth and development. After all, who wants to hang around with those who appear apathetic, continually vent their anger, blame others, and sap everyone's energy with their 'no can do' defiance and incessant moaning? We have all encountered people like this, and no doubt borne the brunt of their undignified behaviour.

In business, attitude matters. It sounds obvious, but if we want success and admiration, we need to embrace all we do with the right professional attitude. Making an excellent impression requires more than a smile, a cheerful greeting, and the propensity to be polite.

For clients, finding the right person with the right attitude can make a big difference in achieving their desired outcome. Our internal perspective influences our behaviour and that of our clients. Sarah, a personal stylist, recalls the time she sought financial advice. Sarah describes how difficult it is to lay out how successful we are to others and how relieved she was to find someone who was empathetic and not condescending. Finding someone approachable restored Sarah's confidence to speak honestly without fear of judgement.

When Frank, a musician, was looking to buy a house in a new area, he found himself warming to organised estate agents who had good local knowledge and made an effort to keep in touch. To Frank, the difference was clear. Those with a proactive attitude and a strong work ethic made him think they could be trusted and relied upon to help him purchase the right property. Frank notes how their attentive attitude significantly reduced the time he took to relocate.

On the other hand, Christine, the owner of a printing company, recalls how, on a night out with friends, the unwelcoming attitude of the restaurateur left her feeling disappointed. Although the meal was enjoyable, the atmosphere was uncomfortable. As a result, she feels reluctant to return or recommend the venue.

From these examples alone, we can see how personal attitudes towards others provoke an emotional and physical response in others. We can also see that our attitudes have the potential to make or break clients' experiences and that, at the very least, clients expect us to approach them with an affirmative attitude.

An affirmative attitude provides reassurance of human connection. Positive acceptance and thoughtfulness leave clients optimistic about the possibilities of a positive outcome. When we display affirmative attitudes, it is not just our clients who benefit. Being amenable, empathetic, non-judgemental, and responsive, for example, helps to make the process of doing business less stressful and the experience more pleasant for all. It creates opportunities to get the outcome clients are expecting. Feeling at ease, Sarah was willing to freely share information about herself with her financial advisor. This led to her getting appropriate advice. Frank was prepared to trust the estate agent and, in doing so, found a new home quickly.

There is a personal satisfaction to be had in knowing we have satisfied clients. However, how we make our clients feel influences the extent to which we benefit and how we feel about ourselves. Adopting the right professional attitude builds stronger client relationships, solves problems, and creates an enjoyable experience. All of this feeds the heart and soul of ourselves and our clients and allows us to reap the benefits. For it is on the back of our well-regarded attitudes that we secure money in the bank, customer loyalty, a good reputation, and the respect of others. Such rewards are the gift we get when we embrace attitudes that help us build positive connections, fulfil our clients' needs, and create feelings of satisfaction. With the right attitude, we get the right results.

CHOOSE POSITIVITY!

The people I know and admire the most all have one thing in common. It has nothing to do with the job they do, the roles they have, the positions they hold, or how successful they are. While each has a different personality, they all appear to share the same outlook on life. They are all upbeat, energetic, and enthusiastic about what they do. They remain confident despite the challenges they face. They are kind-hearted people who believe what they do is worthwhile. They each seek to do their best, help others, and improve the world. These people have a vastly different attitude from many others I know. They stand out because they exude positivity, are optimistic, and have a growth mindset. Their attitude is their biggest asset. The way they think, feel, and act has a powerful impact. How these people have chosen to see and respond to the world makes a difference.

Attitude is a choice, and they have chosen to make positivity their trademark. As a result, they have grown to be more fully-rounded professionals. As we explore later, adopting a positive attitude has many benefits, including strengthening our professionalism. What is evident is that those who choose to adopt a positive mindset and optimistic outlook are provided with a toolkit that enables them to make the right choices, build better relationships, grow their business, and be successful.

Business is never without its ups and downs. Yet when we choose to go about our business with a positive frame of mind, we can deal much better with uncertainty and unpredictability. Positivity enables us to remain confident, deal with stress, overcome challenges, and generally be more productive and hopeful about the future.

For Rose, a life coach, having a positive mindset prevents her from giving up on herself and the task at hand. Staying positive gives her the confidence to achieve her long-term goals. Rose believes in the laws of attraction. If we give off positive energy, good things will come to pass. This helps her to be brave, fearless, and self-assured. She strives to do her utmost and firmly believes she can be whatever she wants. A positive attitude enables Rose to 'stick with it' when problems arise. Staying positive fuels her curiosity and helps her think differently. Rather than seeing the problem as a stumbling block, her mindset leads her to see it as a problem for which there will be a solution. Rose's view is that there is always a way. It is simply a matter of thinking about what we can do to improve the situation. For Rose, the secret lies in being confident and open-minded to all the potential possibilities.

Jake, a business development manager, holds a similar view. Jake believes negative thoughts create cognitive barriers that reduce our capacity to think straight, and interfere with productivity. He notes how the more positive he is, the less likely he is to worry. To Jake, worry is a distraction that takes away the ability to be grounded in the present. He feels his positive state of mind allows him to 'come across well and handle things better.' It leads him to focus on building client relationships and getting the proper outcomes. This is a view shared by personal stylist Sarah.

Sarah considers how a negative attitude would prevent her from doing her job properly. Many of Sarah's clients seek her services because they are dissatisfied with their outfits and ensembles, shape, or appearance. Sarah aims to make her clients feel positive about themselves. If she were to give off negative vibes, it would only make things worse. To be able to turn things around for her clients, Sarah must maintain a positive perspective because a positive outlook allows her to communicate positive, uplifting thoughts that counteract the negative opinions her clients might hold about themselves.

Just as Sarah promotes the use of positivity to overcome negativity, so too does Jake. Jake believes his positive outlook helps him bounce back from adverse events more quickly. Bad things are never as bad as they seem. A negative mindset can be a distorting factor. We end up overlooking success and blowing things up out of all proportion. Jake believes his positive attitude helps him add a positive twist when things go wrong or take an unexpected turn. This has allowed him to be kinder to himself. Rather than dwelling on mistakes, he reframes what has happened as an opportunity to learn. In Jake's words, it allows him to 'move on and not beat myself up so much.'

Through Rose, Jake, and Sarah, we learn that we see ourselves, our clients, and the situations we face differently when we adopt a positive attitude. It influences our approach and the outcomes we will likely get. A positive outlook lets us be enthusiastically committed and focused on our clients' needs. Seemingly positive energy creates a level of composure that allows us to rise to the challenge, make better decisions, and, as Jake says, 'give it our all.' It also helps us to learn, develop, and be more resilient. It strengthens our faith in our ability to achieve and be successful. With a positive attitude, we can love who we are and love what we do, such that we do it well. Collectively, we see that positive attitudes lead us to act positively in ways that help define us as professionals.

CONQUER NEGATIVITY!

Staying positive takes effort. As we each try to stay ahead of the markets, meet deadlines, find new clients, manage existing ones, deal with our finances, and resolve IT problems, our capacity to stay positive is often tested. There is no doubt that a positive mindset diminishes daily tension. The last thing we want is stress. It wears us down and affects our health and general well-being. However, being a professional is not about being in a perpetual state of exhilaration. We cannot always be happy, and trying to be so can be surprisingly stressful and self-defeating. We are, after all, only human. Things will come along that will frustrate and irritate us and leave us full of self-doubt. Whether it is a curt email, a contract that falls through, or a mislaid receipt, we can soon find our mood suddenly shifting from contentment to despondence.

We might be unable to control our feelings, but we can seek to cancel out our negative thoughts and build resilience quickly. This is not to suggest we completely repress our negative thoughts, since this, too, can be bad for our mental and physical health. In preference to this, we should make a conscious effort to develop a positive frame of mind that helps limit our negative thoughts so that we can personally progress and develop and extend positivity to those around us.

A negative outlook that endures creates barriers to success. Negative thoughts weaken our confidence. We focus on all that is wrong rather than all that is right. We can be over-critical of ourselves and others. Everything and everyone becomes a source of irritation, and we play the blame game when things do not go as planned. We perceive problems rather than solutions. We procrastinate, avoid taking risks, and accept defeat before we have even started. Before we know it, we have undermined our professionalism and sabotaged our goals and aspirations, destroying relationships and our self-esteem in the process. Positivity is far more likely to keep us on track regarding personal and professional success. To sustain a positive attitude, we must be conscious of our negative feelings and take steps to reinforce positive ways of thinking. There are many strategies that we can adopt that assist us in the shorter and longer term.

Nicala predominantly works from home. She notes that, if not careful, 'isolation can see you slipping into a black hole.' To remain in a buoyant mood, Nicala surrounds herself with motivational quotes. She also keeps a diary and consciously writes down everything she is grateful for at the end of the working day. For Nicala, mindful gratitude, personal contemplations, and external inspirations stimulate and encourage her to be spirited and determined. When feeling low, Yasmina, an interpersonal therapist, regularly uses affirmation cards to shift her thinking and reframe her self-perception. Likewise, Cathryn uses her vision board and photos of past business success to harness positive energy. She describes how when she feels 'chewed up and dumped on,' a short walk in the park and a cup of coffee re-energises her and gets her back into the right frame of mind.

Here Nicala, Yasmina, and Cathryn show us that every day, in small ways, it is possible to self-manage our outlook. We can, however, draw on the support of others to sustain a positive mindset. For example, Phil, who runs a cleaning company, counts on those he classes as mentors. When frustrated and overwhelmed, he knows he can always 'rely on the wise and experienced to yank me out of the doldrums and see that there is a silver lining to be found.' Similarly, Steve and Georgina take time to explore their thoughts and feelings with their business coach. Their business expansion means Steve and Georgina are in unfamiliar and uncharted waters. With many unknowns, they must keep their mindset in check so it has a beneficial impact. Steve and Georgina liken it to therapy that helps them put things in perspective. The questions posed by their business coach guide them towards finding answers. The reflective discussions that arise are often illuminating. Steve notes that through these sessions, they have become aware of the successes he and Georgina had previously overlooked because they were too focused on negative aspects that were unimportant in the grand scheme of things.

It is easier to stay motivated when we focus on our wins. When we are so bogged down in the detail, we forget to see the bigger picture, which often reflects our confidence and capability. Phil, Steve, and Georgina demonstrate that sometimes we need help and support from others to reframe our perceptions and dispense with our unhelpful thoughts. Encouragement helps us to maintain a healthy perspective that brings clarity and keeps us focused. There is no better way to stave off negativity than to be amongst those who exude positivity because, in time, it will rub off on us.

We often forget that we can choose whom we associate with. Negative individuals can sap our energy in no time. Devoid of vitality, we are left ill-equipped to reconcile our emotions, and before too long, we are as miserable and unproductive as they are. However, a group of cheerful people can soon fill a room with an energy that we can feed off. It becomes transformative, and just as others' positivity affects us, so will our positivity affect others. It is pleasantly infectious.

With a positive attitude, we can change our world and that of our clients and the people around us. However, if we want to feel good and do good by delivering a top-class professional service, the best thing we can do for ourselves is to keep a tight rein on our negative mindset.

ADOPT A CAN-DO ATTITUDE

As well as a positive attitude, we must possess a can-do attitude. In business, things do not get done by doing nothing. So, a can-do attitude is essential if we want to see satisfied clients and take pride in a thriving business. As clients seek our services, they anticipate that we are both willing and determined to get the job done. Having previously explored how a positive attitude influences our inner drive, it follows that a can-do attitude is much easier to adopt if we feel cheerful, confident, and optimistic.

The problems and issues clients bring to us will never fit neatly into a box. We will always need to accommodate personal preferences and match our service to different situations and circumstances. Clients will expect us to find a legal, ethical, and creative solution and make things happen, no matter how challenging it may seem. A can-do attitude provides reassurance of our belief that nothing is impossible and that we can persevere until the desired outcome is achieved. If we do not have a can-do attitude, clients are sure to perceive us as someone who cannot be bothered to try, does not want the hassle, or lacks the skills and insight necessary to do all that is required. Anything suggesting our unwillingness is a red flag, a warning to steer clear.

Having a can-do attitude allows us to build trust and prove our competence. As we progress through this book, we find that trust and credibility predominantly stem from our actions, not words. This said, our initial interest and enthusiasm put us in the game. No potential client wants to hear us complaining about their problem, finding excuses to cut corners, or stalling decisions. When we hum, haw, waver, or say no, we immediately close communication channels and work opportunities. Everything comes to a dead end.

For clarity, a can-do attitude is not about saying 'yes' to seek approval or be polite. Nor is it about promising our clients the moon on a stick. Chapter 5 shows how counterproductive this can be, since it affects the capacity to be reliable and consistent. A can-do attitude is about being mindful of an opportunity to help others, and opening ourselves up to them by showing we are wholeheartedly ready to listen, deliberate, and follow through with an appropriate course of action. A can-do attitude enables us to keep the flow of conversation open and pursue a positive outcome for our clients and ourselves.

All problems need to be approached from different angles, considering the level of need for intervention, situational circumstances, and budget. There can indeed be any number of solutions to the same problem and variations in how it can be approached and managed. We are unlikely to know how to get there unless we know the expected outcome. A can-do attitude demands that we are equally visionary, analytical, and resourceful.

Andy, a marketing consultant, considers that anything is achievable. However, to achieve the achievable, Andy believes our can-do attitude needs to be constructed on the basis that we are prepared to work outside normal conventions, question perceived wisdom, and look to innovate while retaining a sense of realism. These things enable us to reframe the problem, adopt an out-of-the-ordinary approach, and work more creatively and collaboratively with clients to achieve their goals.

Andy explains that many of his clients are keen to use state-of-the-art technology to enhance their processes and procedures. Something that comes with whistles and bells, and all the trimmings, might help businesses do more, but the cost can be prohibitive. Andy's view is that clients want to see progress. Although we might not be able to deliver what our clients ideally want, that does not stop us finding an alternative solution. Sometimes there is a need to find a middle ground, maximising functionality in accordance with affordability. Andy believes that when we possess a can-do attitude that centres on inquiry and practicality, we add value to the client's experience. He explains that by investing time in critical thought, he is better positioned to establish his clients' priorities and negotiate the most favourable outcome for now. Andy's point is that by showing a can-do attitude, we can progress with what is practically possible under the circumstances and outline what can be achieved in time as the situation changes. Even if we have to divide the task into manageable phases, we can help clients make a start. By proving we can achieve one end goal, we generate faith in our capacity to make even bigger things happen for our clients in the next stages of the process.

In navigating our way around a client's problems, we progress towards our own goals. Professionally we can break new ground if we are prepared to approach the challenge and move outside our comfort zone. It is something that Jake has come to appreciate.

He notes that in adopting a can-do attitude, he has developed new skills and become more aware of the talents and abilities he never knew he had.

As Jake sees it, a can-do attitude allows us to put ourselves out there. He believes that we will only know what we are capable of if we go out there and attempt to do it. It is a good point that links to Andy's thoughts on adding value. If we are ready to solve a problem and take time to see and do what others are not prepared to see or do, we have something extra to offer our clients. Our frame of mind sets us apart and leads us to be more advanced in our knowledge, skills, and ways of thinking. Only through a can-do attitude can we stretch ourselves and demonstrate what we can actually do. With each experience, we learn and develop, making us better professionals. We explore how we optimise personal development through experience in Chapter 9. The point here is that, as we become more adept, we have more of ourselves to give and more to offer clients by way of service. As a result, we can provide a personalised, better quality, and wider-ranging professional service. There is much persuasive merit in this, particularly when promoting our business.

DEMONSTRATE CARE AND CONCERN

Every one of our clients will want to feel appreciated and valued. To clients, the level of interest we show in them indicates the importance we attach to their patronage. They want to feel we value them more than we value their money. Clients want to feel loved and cared for because in order to trust, they need to feel a close bond and believe they are in safe hands. They want to feel confident in their decision, knowing that any involvement with us will have a positive impact on their life or business in some way.

Reassurance comes when clients sense how passionate we are about our work and the people we do it for. This is even more the case when they feel we are equally as keen as they are on getting to the right outcome and achieving success. From beginning to end, and at all stages between, clients want personal attention as we attend to their needs, issues, and affairs. Therefore, to be confident in giving the best service and enriching our clients' overall experience, we must adopt a caring attitude and be concerned about the outcome.

Care and concern are reflected in how we communicate and act. We can do this in many ways beyond some of the examples we are about to see here. However, to do it in a way that adds value, we need to be sure of building social connections and a deeper level of understanding. Caring requires an active level of engagement in which humanistic values are reinforced. How we sensitively listen, show gratitude, respond to emotions, and treat people with respect and dignity, reflects how much we care for our clients. Upholding relationship-based values positively affects how people perceive us and the outcomes that can be achieved. Caring attitudes help build a trusting bond that enables us to work in partnership with clients. Caring brings us closer to solving their problems and enhancing their overall experience.

The extent to which we are proactive in addressing our clients' needs, keeping them informed, or reaching out when problems arise, demonstrates our level of concern and interest in their feelings and the job at hand. If a job is worth doing, it is worth doing well. The amount of personal satisfaction we feel invariably arises due to our more profound and sustained level of concern. Client satisfaction is derived through actions that manifest because of our level of personal concern, actions that almost certainly lead to an outcome that unburdens our clients and eases their worry and stress.

To be appropriately concerned, we must be emotionally and physically invested in achieving a positive outcome. Furthermore, we need to understand what that investment might look and feel like within that process. As Jake, a business development manager for a company that provides printer services, says: 'A broken printer is not a matter of life or death, but it is a matter of livelihoods and reputation if not quickly fixed.' Many of Jake's clients are business owners. He notes how: 'At the end of the day, we are all trying to achieve the same thing and fighting the same battles, so you have to see their issues as equal to your own.' Jake's point illustrates that to show concern, we must be able to empathise and perceive things from the perspective of our clients. So too, must we be able to anticipate the impact of our actions and inactions on the outcome, and be willing to act in ways that enable others to achieve the kind of outcomes and the peace of mind we desire for ourselves.

To Sarah, a personal stylist, that sometimes means trying harder when things are not working. Sarah is determined to leave her clients feeling happier within themselves. She sticks at it and extends her effort if the signs indicate they are not. Sarah aims for consistency: she wants all her clients to be at the same point, no matter how long it takes. She shows us that, to get the right outcome, we must be prepared to go above and beyond to bring about satisfaction and closure.

Yet so many factors can influence an outcome. It is impossible to mitigate against them all. Andy believes that our concern needs to be born from curiosity. He points out that our efforts and thoroughness in the early stages of a project are wasted once we become unconcerned with progress. If we are blasé about analysing and tracking developments, we cannot see the extent to which we are making headway with intended plans. To Andy, curiosity is what keeps us focused on the objective. As he explains, when we are concerned enough to gather the evidence and data, we can intervene as required, even if that means coming back to the table with a fresh set of ideas and a plan B.

An unconcerned attitude is a negative attitude. Concern represents getting involved with the things that matter most to our clients. It is an investment of our time and thought on their behalf. Our enthusiastic can-do attitude might have put us in the game, but if we are not prepared to make a concerted effort, we are not playing fair and are arguably infringing the rules. We can never expect to act in the full interests of our clients where there is disinterest or a superficial level of engagement. Without a more profound concern for the outcome, our efforts will be half-hearted at best. Without showing care or concern, we come across as indifferent. To clients, this signals an apathetic state of being. We are perceived as lacking respect and commitment. As a result, we get labelled as someone who could not care less. If we cannot relate to our clients or we detach ourselves from their main goals and aspirations, our clients feel unappreciated. With this, the only thing they will have come to appreciate about us is our third-rate level of professionalism. If we want to step up a level or two, we need to care enough to discover our clients' concerns and be concerned enough to make them less of a concern.

BE SURE TO SYNCHRONISE

To deliver an excellent service with all the hallmarks of a professional, we have to be so much more than technically competent. Our extensive knowledge and wealth of practical skills may mean we are very good at what we do. However, this is not enough to distinguish us from the competition, generate satisfied clients, or make us successful in business. Whatever our business activities happen to be, without the right values and attitudes we can soon compromise our goals and aspirations and fall short of meeting client expectations.

As individuals in business, we have a great deal of autonomy. However, this freedom comes with responsibility, particularly if we want to stand out as professionals who serve their clients well. When it comes to values and attitudes, we can choose. But to be seen as credible and exceptional, we must choose wisely. From the outset, we must define and safeguard our values through attitudes, words, and actions.

This chapter shows that core values are so much more than a symbol of our inner beliefs. They represent our strategic vision and provide a roadmap of standards that give meaning to our work, guiding how we carry out our business. Establishing values requires conscious consideration. Through the illustrative examples, we see how essential it is to personally connect with our core values and take them to our heart. Vehement proclamation alone does not inspire client confidence. Trust comes when we commit to making our values an integral part of our practice. For this, we must have a deeper understanding of our values and be fully prepared to do all that is required to uphold them without compromise. When we truly relate to our values and harmonise our business activities and personal behaviour accordingly, we create more robust cohesive interconnections. Each aspect reinforces the standards by which we operate. We discover that the more they are reinforced within our practice, the easier it becomes to live by our values, lead by example, and inspire others to value what we value.

None of this is possible without the right attitude. We might have nailed down our values and pledged to commit to them, but we need a congruent attitude to implement them. Strong values with an affirmative, positive, caring, can-do attitude make for a good combination when it comes to getting the best outcomes for our clients and ourselves.

An affirmative attitude creates a human connection that facilitates open communication and strengthens trust. A positive mindset boosts our confidence and limits our fears. A can-do attitude prompts us to rise to the challenge, push the boundaries and finish the job. When we act with care and concern, we become physically and emotionally invested in providing a quality experience, working more proactively in partnership with clients to achieve the desired outcome. Our affirmative, positive, caring, can-do attitude gives us the energy to live by our values. Perspectives of this nature boost our professionalism. In adopting these attitudes we act in ways that add value to our clients' experience. What is more, they help us learn, develop, grow, maintain our standards, and build resilience.

It is clear that to be professional, values and attitudes need to align. Our core values connect us to our work and drive us towards our goals and ambitions. Our attitudes influence our approach to that process, particularly when building relationships and getting things done. Appropriate attitudes with the wrong values potentially see us floundering without a sense of purpose or direction. Strong values with bad attitudes potentially lead to disappointing outcomes and alienation from clients and collaborators. Misalignment weakens the significance we attach to our work, business, clients, or ourselves. Whichever way we look at it, we are professionally out of sync.

We must remember that even if we manage to synchronise our values and attitudes, there is always the potential for deviation. Within this chapter, we see how circumstances can shift our thoughts and actions such that we lose sight of our values and drift away from our standards. Life events and the stress and strains of business can drain our energy and enthusiasm. As time passes, we need to bring ourselves back in line. We refrain from deviating from our course by regularly evaluating the situation and adopting strategies that ensure we adjust or realign our values and reorientate our mindset.

Alignment is vital. It is the thing that gives us the momentum to act professionally. The combination of meaningful values and positive heartfelt attitudes gives us the get-up-and-go needed to make things happen. This allows us to define ourselves and stay true to all we believe in. It raises our professional consciousness. Through this, we come to life: it prompts us to do what we must to get where we want to be. In serving the interests of our clients, we are driven to be our professional best. As we live by our values professionally, we come into a league of our own. Here, we increase our chances of popularity, success, and prosperity.

HOLD THAT THOUGHT

To develop authentic values we can live by, we must be 'alive.' That is, responsive to the needs of our clients, suppliers, and other stakeholders and business associates. A thriving business comes when we are of a mindset to be of service. So whatever else we value, we must ask: how much do we value people?

When we value people, we are much more physically and emotionally engaged in building relationships and become increasingly mindful of the opportunity to help others. Being responsive generates care and concern that helps us find our true purpose. It awakens us to the vision of our core values. Without valuing people, we cannot realistically expect to translate our core values into meaningful actions that bring about excellence in practice. Nor can we expect to bring about excellence in practice unless we also consider the extent to which we value accountability. The key question is, are we taking responsibility for how we integrate our core values into practice and align and manage our attitudes and behaviours?

By valuing people, we create a foundation on which all other values are constructed and brought to life. In valuing accountability, our values and attitudes are brought into line. We have a filter that helps us make responsible choices, making it easier to consistently uphold our values and maintain an optimistic outlook. If we are not sufficiently motivated to value people or the notion of accountability, we disrupt the potential for synchronicity. Without these underpinning professional values, we cannot expect to harmonise and apply our core values, retain satisfied clients, or grow and develop our business in a state of contentment.

3

TRUST

VALUE IT AND RESPECT IT

Professionals are those who inspire trust. In business, trust is a game-changer. It changes the course of action and marks the point at which a potential client becomes our client or someone else's. Trust is the basis on which relationships are built. If we can build trust, we can build a reputation, which is vital for growing a successful business. Most people would agree that trust is synonymous with being a professional. It is centred on the confident expectation of others that we will adopt specific standards of behaviour. If our intentions are not honourable, or we are perceived to be unreliable, dishonest, with a propensity to mislead, then people will default to a position of distrust. Where we display such flaws within our character or conduct, we are considered to be without a moral compass and lacking in the very characteristics that define us as professionals. In this situation, few will want to do business with us or be associated with us.

Just as we would not want to extend trust to those who do not deserve to be trusted, the same can be said for our clients. If we expect clients to trust us, we need to understand what trust represents and what we must do to secure it. Establishing trust can be a challenge. First, it must be built and then continually reinforced. Building a good reputation and assuring others of our integrity and trustworthiness takes time and effort. Violate that trust, and we instantly damage our reputation and heighten public cynicism.

In this chapter, we explore the valuable role that trust plays in forging strong interpersonal relationships and the benefits it brings to ourselves, our clients, the occupational sector, and the organisations to which we belong, as well as to society in general. Trust is largely intuitive and not without personal or financial risk to our clients. Hence, this chapter explores why people might initially view us with scepticism. We see how trust manifests through a chain of events and explore the processes by which clients and others judge the quality of our character and capabilities. This sits alongside a discussion in which we learn about influencing factors and the actions we must take to prove ourselves credible and trustworthy. Notwithstanding the need to maintain trust and secure our reputation, we consider the impact on ourselves, our clients, others, and wider society when trust is broken. We explore how professionalism influences trust and generates higher levels of trust. As a final point, we explore our role in that process and how professional accountability helps to reinforce and validate our commitment to establishing and preserving interpersonal and public trust.

TRUST UNDERPINS EVERYTHING

To achieve anything in life, we must place our trust in others. It is the foundation on which relationships are built and maintained and it underpins how we engage and co-operate with others. We tend only to trust those who act in lawful ways, conform to societal norms, and live up to our own expectations. As a matter of course, when we first encounter people, we analyse their characteristics and behaviour. Fundamentally, we are looking for evidence that assures us of their integrity and trustworthiness. By the same token, we, too, are under scrutiny, as others seek to ensure that their trust in us is equally well placed.

If we are to survive and be successful in business, gaining the trust of others is imperative. Proving ourselves trustworthy is essential if we are to benefit from our endeavours. People will only buy from and sell to, recommend, or collaborate with, people or organisations they truly trust. So not only do we need to prove ourselves trustworthy to potential clients, but we also need to prove ourselves trustworthy to members of the business community, the professional associations, and the networks to which we belong.

Trust is an invaluable asset that underpins our reputation. In the world of business, a good reputation is a priceless commodity. When we gain trust, we gain much more than work and income. We gain better outcomes for both ourselves and our clients. We each become personally better off because of the constructive way trust influences our attitudes and actions. Financial advisor Diana is aware that when it comes to making investments, people are naturally cautious. It can take a lot for people to trust her. So, when Diana has gained a person's trust, she feels: 'It is both a real privilege and confidence booster.' This energises and motivates her to do her best and expand her skill set because, as she says: 'The last thing you want to do is undermine that trust by letting someone down.'

Once people have faith in our integrity, they are more inclined to invest in the relationship. To Yasmina, an interpersonal therapist, this facilitates meaningful interactions. When clients feel they trust her, they are less guarded and more willing to share information and disclose their thoughts openly. When this happens, she can be more helpful in empowering clients to overcome the challenges they face.

As well as strengthening connections and creating healthier communication, trust generates honesty. For graphic designer Neil, trust boosts participation and gives people the confidence to express themselves. Clients become much more proactive and candid in stating their preferences, which, for Neil, makes the whole design process much easier, more efficient, and more enjoyable. What we see here is that trust adds value. It is a form of social capital. It not only makes a difference in generating profits, but it also brings a range of benefits. It enhances customer satisfaction, the level of service we provide, and the quality of our interactions, making all we do seem much more attractive and worthwhile.

Trust needs to be valued and deeply respected. It is not given freely and should not be taken for granted. It can take many years of hard work to build and establish trust. We should see it as a prized possession. Once we have acquired it, we must work hard to maintain its present state, knowing it is incredibly fragile. Drop our guard, and the chances are trust will be shattered in an instant. Violations come with consequences, and the damage to our reputation is likely to be costly and irreparable. If we are considered untrustworthy, people are unlikely to want to interact and work with us. That means fewer business opportunities and fewer chances to demonstrate that we are sincere, honest, and upright citizens and business owners. It becomes a vicious circle that is hard to break out of. Trust does not happen by accident; it is driven by us. If we are to succeed in business, we must value trust by exhibiting regard for its importance and respect it by being committed to establishing and maintaining it.

GOODWILL CREATES CONNECTIVITY

In life, we are all givers and receivers of trust. In the same way that we expect others to put their trust in us, so we must extend our trust to others. Trust governs all our interactions; without it, society would not function. To live our lives or achieve our goals and ambitions, we must engage in a process of co-operative exchange. With each transaction, we must commit to an interaction, in which information, money or possessions are exchanged. Such exchanges occur many times a day with others, many of whom are strangers. We often do this without a second thought.

As we pay our fare to the bus driver, we trust they will get us to our destination safely. When we hand over our parcel at the post office counter, we trust it will be delivered to the correct address. Having ordered a gift of flowers over the phone, we trust those taking our order will keep our debit card and address details secure and not share them with others.

We do so because, as members of society, we depend on others in order to live our lives. Consequently, we anticipate that those we encounter will adopt and comply with social norms and demonstrate integrity and sincerity as they go about their work. These social norms provide a framework for behaviour. It is this which enables us to extend our trust to unfamiliar people. Everyone gains from this type of trust; it creates goodwill and keeps society connected. Without it, there is the potential for wide-scale distrust. Imagine how inharmonious, unsociable, and unproductive our society would be if we constantly thought everyone was out to deceive us. Such paranoia would almost certainly deprive us of emotional connections and lead to a very unfulfilling and unhappy life indeed. Generally, it is in our best interest to trust others, since trust functions to safeguard our own personal well-being and that of society, because it creates social harmony and economic productivity, which we, as individuals, benefit from. This, however, does not mean we should automatically trust everyone we meet. If we go about trusting the wrong people, we can soon find ourselves in difficult situations. To mitigate against this, we almost certainly need to exercise caution and perceptive discernment.

BEING CAUTIOUS IS NO BAD THING

Trust is a very variable entity, and context is key. In an emergency that calls for immediate action, we might have no choice but to trust others. Should we suddenly fall critically ill in the street, for example, time does not allow us to deliberate. If our life depended on it, we would doubtlessly be happy to trust anyone who came to our aid. Emergency situations aside, it is prudent to be cautious and take a more considered approach before we decide who we are willing to trust. Being initially wary has its benefits, not least that of protection. It helps us to safeguard our own interests, assess risks, and avoid deception, harm, and exploitation. Rarely do we trust instinctively. More often, we come to a decision gradually over time as we become more familiar with a situation and get to know people better. As you would expect, there are people we come to trust and those we do not. The division is, however, not so clear cut because, of those we do trust, we might not trust them completely and in equal measure in all situations.

I, for one, have a friend who cannot be trusted to arrive on time, yet I would wholeheartedly trust them to look after my house and feed my cat when I am away on holiday. I have worked with people whose competence I have doubted, and although I might not have trusted them to perform a particular task, I have trusted their word, knowing they were honest, upright citizens. The fact is, we all have small cracks in our personality and proficiency, but their existence does not mean we are entirely untrustworthy. At no point have I ever felt that my friend or colleagues were out to harm, deceive or exploit me, so it is easy to look beyond their individual flaws. The extent to which we are prepared to overlook, compromise, or accept someone's shortcomings depends on situational context, the relationship's quality and what we value. What we know of people in other ways, our strength of feeling in relation to certain characteristics and behaviours, and the personal impact we anticipate because of their absence, all influence the degree to which we trust others.

Trust is a complicated thing and difficult to capture and explain. Like the word professionalism, it means different things to different people. Trust is a unique feeling and choice that is based on past experiences, personal perceptions, and internal emotions. It is often intuitive and not necessarily something we can pinpoint. So, how do we know someone is trustworthy? As Alison, a network marketer, told me: 'You get a gut feeling inside.'

This internal feeling is not as random as it seems. Although we might not appreciate it or consciously be aware of it, that 'gut feeling' results from a great deal of thought processing. When we meet each other for the first time, we scan for clues, analyse evidence, and monitor the emotional connections we feel. Rachel, who runs her own legal marketing company, describes it as 'peeling the layers of an onion.' The interactions assist in exposing the 'inner layers,' and with this, we discover more about the other person and their motives. Quite typically, each person is looking for evidence of the quality of the other person's character, competence, intentions, values, and behaviours.

Everyone has their own expectations about the attributes and behaviours they wish to see in others before they extend their trust. Our expectations can vary depending on the situation we find ourselves in. Only when we are satisfied that what we see or feel is what we expect, do we begin to place our trust in others. In essence, trust represents the level of confidence we have in someone's character and behaviour and a belief that, given our circumstances, they will act in our best interest. Ultimately it represents how comfortable we feel and how positive we are that they have honourable intentions and can be depended on to do what is right.

It is sometimes difficult to know whom we can trust, but our observations and feelings act as navigational tools in a sea of uncertainty, like the radar and compass on a ship. What we observe reinforces our perceptions and provokes emotions. Our eyes and ears act like a radar providing us with an early warning system that detects and identifies potential dubious standards and actions. Our feelings, like the compass, are the things that guide us in the right direction, away from harm or towards a point of safety. All we see, hear, and feel helps us remain vigilant. We process all that we sense. This arouses our gut feeling and helps us differentiate between those who possess moral principles and care enough to act with integrity and sincerity and those who do not. If we trust cautiously, we can avoid danger and save ourselves from negative situations and experiences.

What we must appreciate is that we, as ordinary citizens, will have doubts about the integrity and trustworthiness of those we happen to meet. In this respect, we are no different from our clients. They will experience the same emotions and feelings and go through the same processes explored here before they feel confident enough to trust us. This is something we should not overlook.

EVERYONE IS ENTITLED TO BE A SCEPTIC

There are perhaps only a few instances when clients would place their trust in us without getting to know us first. Depending on the nature of our business, it can take a long while to gain someone's trust. This is because trust manifests itself through a chain of events, each serving to verify whether we are sufficiently trustworthy. We cannot assume that, just because we think we are trustworthy, our clients and fellow networkers will be of the same opinion. For those new to the business world, this can sometimes come as a shock.

Many of us set up our businesses full of confidence and self-belief. We are personable, dynamic, and well-qualified. What is more, we know our industry inside out. We are full of energy, and there is nothing we cannot do. We come armed with a plentiful supply of bright ideas and offer top-quality services. We even have a state-of-the-art website – what is not to like?

While our authenticity is not something to be dismissed, our trustworthiness is something we cannot personally determine. It is something only others can conclude for themselves. For potential clients, there is much more to consider before they trust us enough to buy our services. Trust is the result of a decision-making process based on several influencing factors. Some of these factors are related to our personal attributes, the consistency of our attitudes, behaviour, and competence. Others relate to our clients' personal characteristics, their past experiences and the situation they now find themselves in. The complex interplay between all these factors determines the extent to which others have complete trust and confidence in us.

The decision to trust does not always start with us. Clients must be willing to trust. The propensity to trust is determined by a person's character. This influences the extent to which trust is extended and the time it takes to build an emotional connection. In order to trust, clients must feel confident in their assessment of our integrity. Personality types vary, and everyone is different. While some people are easy-going and naturally warm to others, some are more reserved and initially wary. Just as some people might look to see the best in us, others are looking to identify the flaws within our character. For every person who is impulsive and willing to take a risk, there is someone quite nervous, preferring to adopt a more cautious approach.

We must also not forget that we live in an age of distrust. All too frequently, we hear of fraud and cybercrime. These have become so prevalent that there are national reporting helplines set up to catch the perpetrators and prevent others from succumbing to these sophisticated scams. In recent years we have witnessed an explosion of misinformation in the form of fake news. Made-up stories are designed to look as if they are produced by official sources and are published only to discredit people and organisations. Through the media, we learn of corporate scandals, false endorsements by celebrities, cases of negligence and malpractice, and of people operating without the appropriate credentials. News bulletins detail unlawful activities of police, politicians and others in authority – the very people we have been encouraged to trust from an early age. Consumer affairs programmes on the radio and television spread awareness of rogue traders. They report stories of unscrupulously dishonest merchants who trick people into parting with their money before mysteriously disappearing. We hear of businesses selling faulty goods, overcharging, or selling products and services people do not need.

Without a doubt, there are plenty of people out there ready to exploit others. Often naïvety allows people to be taken in and taken advantage of. It takes much effort to access the truth and analyse situations. However, this effort is necessary if individuals want to be reliably and accurately informed and avoid falling prey to confidence tricksters, charlatans, and fraudsters. Anyone unfortunate enough to have been the victim of such dishonesty will appreciate the emotional and financial impact. Violations of trust disrupt the sense of security felt, leaving people alert and wary of attack, which influences future behaviour. It can take much time to regain the confidence to trust again. While there are shady characters with dubious ethics in existence, it is only natural for potential clients to be sceptical and on their guard.

TRUST IS A RISKY BUSINESS

To initiate an enquiry, potential clients must themselves be at least willing to extend trust and be ready to rely on us. There are many reasons why people would actively seek our services, but the fact they are seeking them in the first instance indicates they have, in some way, recognised the need to purchase the type of services we offer and are prepared to extend their trust to obtain them.

The purchase of any form of goods or services brings with it personal and financial risk. The level of associated risk determines how easily clients will extend trust and the processes by which they bestow trust. Before they sign up to buy our goods and services, clients will have determined our level of trustworthiness in a very calculated way.

Purchasing goods is relatively low risk compared to buying a service as most purchases are acquired through a relatively simple transaction: an exchange of money for a tangible product or experience. Be it a sandwich, a pot plant, or a fridge, people purchase goods every day. It is part of life. Whether we love or loathe shopping, we are all familiar with it and know what to expect of the seller and the process by which we acquire such goods. Our previous experience enables us to gain a sense of trustworthiness in a short space of time.

Let us imagine for a moment that we wish to purchase a wristwatch. On leaving home, we have a good idea of what we are looking for in terms of functionality and style and know how much we are prepared to spend. We can compare range and price as we browse the windows of the various jewellers along the high street. Before we make our purchase, we have the luxury of seeing the watch, touching it, observing it working, appreciating its quality, and comparing it to other makes and models. There is less opportunity for misrepresentation, and should we change our mind or subsequently discover that it is faulty, we know we can return it. The Consumer Rights Act entitles us to refund, replacement, or repair, mitigating the risk.

Our short interaction with the seller offers little time to establish a deep relationship, but it is usually enough for us to gain an overall impression of honesty. Our decision to trust is determined by the clues we pick up from all we see and hear. We pay attention to the nature of the conversation and scan the environment for evidence of the jeweller's integrity and legitimacy. In these situations, if we perceive that the seller is helpful, conforms to society's social norms and appears to be acting lawfully, we usually have sufficient confidence to trust them enough to make a purchase.

It is the same when we walk into a restaurant. We take note of how we are greeted. We look around and observe the atmosphere, the quality of food, and the cleanliness of the tables before we sit down and commit to ordering. In this case, our senses give us confidence that the food served will be tasty, and the risk of food poisoning will likely be low. By scanning the environment, we monitor if those we are about to trust appear to be doing the right thing. If they are, we buy. If not, we walk away, look elsewhere, and give our custom to those we feel we can trust.

When purchasing goods, we tend to focus more on the product than the seller's direct qualities. The trust we offer is based on our intuition and senses since we know very little about those we have chosen to buy from. By the same token, they perhaps know nothing more of us than our name and credit card number.

When it comes to purchasing services, the tables are turned. From the perspective of our clients, they must trust in the quality of our character, because it is not until much later that they get to evaluate the quality of our service. Buying a service is risky. There is potential for those in business to be all words and promises with no action. When clients sign up for our services, their choice will have, by and large, been made on what they have read, seen, and heard. Unless they have had previous first-hand experience working with us, the outcome is uncertain. New clients particularly must trust in our character and hope that actions will follow. They must remain optimistic that we will do a good job and not just take their money and run. The decision to trust becomes far more complex because the risks and consequences of purchasing a service are much greater.

Fundamentally, when people are looking to purchase a service, they want help in an unfamiliar area. They need to be sure they are getting the right help from the right person, so who we are matters. On the strength of this, clients will want to get a feel for us and learn more about our character and capabilities. Not surprisingly, trust is not given instantly. No one wants to be taken for a ride, so to mitigate personal, financial, and reputational risks, people will naturally want to check us out before forming an opinion as to whether we are credible and trustworthy.

DISASTER LOOMS AROUND EVERY CORNER

Whatever our line of business, clients depend on us to do what they cannot because they lack the skills, are time-pressed, and want things to be done properly. It may be that they need help in achieving a particular goal. Perhaps they want to improve results, progress further quicker, develop their own expertise, correct something that has gone wrong, or be better equipped to cope in some way. In asking us to do what they cannot, clients entrust themselves to us and assign responsibility. In doing so, they place themselves in a position of dependence, which creates vulnerability, depending on their situation.

No doubt, most of us in business will employ the services of an accountant to analyse and interpret our financial records and prepare our tax returns. We do so because tax laws and regulations are complex and ever-changing, and we must comply. For the most part, the intricacies of accounting are beyond our level of understanding, and we need external advice. We lack sufficient expertise and do not have the time to navigate our way through the accountancy maze. Why? Because we are busy leading our lives, running our own businesses, doing what we do best, and being experts in our field. We recognise the limitations of our knowledge and capabilities and fear we will make a big hash of it. The last thing we want is to be accused of false accounting and tax evasion. All things considered, we opt to depend on someone else to do the job for us. How individuals arrive at the decision of whom to select to do the job is something we will explore later in the chapter. The point here is that we trust our accountant more than we trust ourselves to do what is right in this instance because we want to sleep peacefully in our bed at night.

To get the peace of mind we seek, we forfeit elements of control, and it will be no different for our clients. People generally favour self-reliance, preferring to expend their energy and to put faith in their own individual abilities and resources rather than those of others. There is reticence because once people become obliged to rely on others, they are no longer in control. This loss of control brings uncertainty and anxiety. Letting go means giving ourselves over to someone else's capability and judgement, with unpredictable consequences.

In whatever context potential clients seek our services, they expose themselves to risk the moment they engage with us. This is often by virtue of the need to share information about themselves. It would be almost impossible to appreciate, assess and resolve a client's problem without exchanging information. While new clients would recognise this, we must remember that the relationship they are about to enter is not symmetrical. There is no shared history to count on. For potential clients, gaining access to our services requires them to divulge personal information about themselves or their business affairs. They must do so, knowing relatively little about us, making them vulnerable.

In essence, to seek a solution to a problem, a potential client must bare their soul to us, a stranger, to determine if we are the right person to help them. Information sharing carries the risk of exploitation. While potential clients are prepared to extend trust and make us privy to personal information, they do so in the hope that they will be assured of confidentiality and not be preyed upon, taken advantage of, or manipulated in any way.

When buying a service, there is a greater potential for it all to go wrong. The risks are high. Poor decision-making and misplaced trust on the client's part could have personal, financial, and social repercussions. There is a risk to seeking our services, which clients must balance against the risk of not doing so. Looking at it from the perspective of a prospective client, inaction potentially increases the risk, with some probability that their unresolved problem will escalate. Conversely, although acting may diminish this risk, it potentially creates exposure to other risks. It carries a measure of uncertainty, as there are no guarantees as to the nature of the outcome.

Whatever decision is taken, either way, there is the potential for a negative outcome. Trust tends to be extended when the possibility of a positive outcome is greater than a negative one. So, before entering a contract, prospective clients must be confident that nothing bad will happen. They need to be sure of our integrity and motives and that we can be relied upon when they are most vulnerable. When they trust us, they want to feel in control and free from anxiety. Deep down, even though there may be negative consequences, they want to feel secure that, under the circumstances, they have made the right decision and will positively benefit and achieve a favourable outcome.

BE NOTHING IF NOT AUTHENTIC

Whilst the decision to extend trust does not always start with us, it ends with us! Assuming prospective clients have the propensity to trust, are willing to take a risk and be reliant on us, then the rest really is well and truly down to us. If we want to gain clients, secure business, and gain referrals through our network, we need to prove ourselves worthy of trust and work towards deepening and maintaining that trust over time.

The most influential factors that determine trustworthiness relate to our character, our credentials, our behaviour, competence, and past performance, alongside the systems we have in place to safeguard our clients' welfare. Going back to our earlier discussion, no doubt we will have thought about and scrutinised all these factors before we appointed our accountant. None of these factors stands in isolation. Each is inextricably linked. Trust is established by virtue of their unification, as collectively they serve to encourage, confirm, and strengthen trust. It is likely that we will have chosen the accountant who now manages our finances, transactions, and taxes because we were won over by their all-encompassing proof of trustworthiness.

It is hard to trust someone who is incompetent, even if they are charming and honest. The same can be said for someone who acts with kindness and decency but makes poor judgements. The absence of any factor is likely to result in the same outcome: a lack of trust. I say 'likely' because we need to remember that trust is unique, based on personal perceptions. So, depending on the nature of our work and the circumstances in which clients seek our services, some factors will have more prominence. How we measure up to an individual client's expectations determines whether they trust us. There will always be people who do not feel confident enough to trust us, but if we wish to build and secure a positive reputation, we must work to ensure the majority of the people we encounter develop such confidence.

Trust manifests through a sequence of events in which we are evaluated. Remember Rachel's analogy of an onion? Well, this is where the peeling starts. Trust occurs in stages. From the first point of contact, our demeanour, conversations, and actions reveal who we are. Whether we are conscious of it or not, our passions, attitudes, and values transpire in what we say and do not say, what we do or do not do. Throughout this time, potential clients are weighing us up, processing all they see, hear, and feel. If experiences are positive, and people like what they see, if what we say resonates and people feel personally secure in our company and confident of our competence, they will continue to engage and peel away layers. Fail to meet expectations, and clients stop peeling, disengage and withdraw. This ultimately signifies a lack of trust.

In today's digital age, it is easy for people to know things about us before they even meet us. Our website, LinkedIn profile and other social media accounts tell the story of our lives, experiences, values, and aspirations. They are a powerful way to show off our personality, accomplishments, and reputation through the enthusiastic recommendations and glowing testimonies we have received. It is quite a shop window when you think about it: a powerful way to attract interest in ourselves and our services. However, a shop window is just a front. It is easy to portray ourselves positively, all brightly coloured and exceptional. In creating an impression in the minds of others, we are also creating expectations. Those keen to know who we are and what we are about will seek something more tangible. They are looking beyond the glitz, seeking assurance that we are not presenting a façade and spouting hot air. They want to know we are as authentic as we proclaim.

Our authenticity influences and strengthens the connections we make. People want to know we are genuine, with no hidden agendas. They are keen to see the human behind the job title and discover if we are passionate about what we do and true to our mission. They want to see that our actions align with the values we claim to hold. Since we all claim to be unique, people want to establish what sets us apart from others in a similar line of work. To build better connections, we need to be authentic. No one likes a pretender, so hiding behind who we are or professing to be something we are not will do us no favours. If we do not turn out to be all we claim, then people will see this as a form of misrepresentation. In this case, we do nothing more than undermine our own trustworthiness. If we live up to our assertions, there is every chance people will like us, warm to us, and know us in a way that prompts them to do business with us.

THE RIGHT KIT COUNTS

Authenticity extends to the way we dress. People pay a lot of attention within the first few minutes of meeting, and this determines how the rest of the journey pans out. Dress and personal hygiene certainly affect how we are perceived. It would seem people have little time for the unwashed and the untidy, favouring those who look sharp rather than slipshod.

Opinions vary across the different sectors we work in regarding what is and is not acceptable business attire. The nature of our day-to-day activities and the locations where we work will almost certainly influence how we dress. We must remember that what we wear and do not wear sends a message, and that message is open to interpretation by our clients. Our clients and work associates will have some expectations that we need to align with to gain their trust. Casual dress carries an overtone of casual thoughts. Conversely, if we dress as if we are heading out to a film première, we risk coming across as pretentious and inaccessible. Neither of which image characterises professionalism or principles associated with trust. So we need to think carefully about how we retain our uniqueness whilst making a sound choice to be sure we present our true yet professional selves.

Poonam is a funeral director. The solemn nature of her work calls for formal attire. As she says: 'Death is not a casual affair. Clients do not want you to look relaxed. They want you to look serious because it is a significant and emotional time for them.' Regardless of the time of day, Poonam dresses in line with her professional values because, in her case, 'looking scruffy is reputationally damaging. It shows a lack of dignity and compassion and undermines the respect and sensitivity that is needed.' Anneke, a civil engineer, often meets her clients on-site, dressed head to toe in high visibility clothing, a hard hat, safety glasses and cumbersome steel-toe-capped boots. By her own admission, 'it's not a glamorous look,' but it shows safety is a prime consideration and one she takes seriously. Since building sites can be dangerous, Anneke's safety-conscious approach demonstrates that she values her own life. Failing to comply with the requirements of health and safety would suggest otherwise. It is almost fair to say that those prepared to put themselves and others at risk probably should not be trusted.

In these examples, we see that dress says something about our professional standards. Standards inspire confidence and act as a framework by which clients evaluate us and compare us. Before anyone has said 'hello,' judgement will have been passed. If we want others to delve deeper and metaphorically peel back the next layer of the onion, we must find that sartorial sweet spot. If we want to gain someone's trust, we must inspire confidence. This means we must create a positive, authentic self-image that portrays professionalism.

TALKING OPENS DOORS

When it comes to securing trust, conversations are a big influence. They are where the seeds are sown, the magic happens, and business is won. The language and expressions we use, the detail of information we give, and how we respond all give clues as to our competency, intentions, and capacity to perform. To prospective clients and fellow networkers, this is often all they have to go on before deciding to trust us and commit to buying our services or recommending us to others.

If we want to make a great impression, be remembered for all the right reasons, and prove ourselves trustworthy, we must get it right. The expectations are the same whether we communicate over the phone, via email or in person. People want to experience our authentic selves. They want to be sure we love what we do and care about the people we do it for. They want to see and feel our passion and our commitment to solving their problems. They want to know we will do what it takes to meet their needs and, in doing so, act with honourable intentions.

Being pushy and boastful is one sure way to lose credibility because it is not all about us. It is all about the client. Trust is not built solely on who we are. It is built on how we make others feel and relate to the things that matter most to them. When prospective clients engage with us, they seek confirmation that we are decent, fair, and honest individuals. Even if we have been recommended to them by others, they must still independently draw their own conclusions. At the point of 'hello,' they anticipate we are friendly, willing to hear their story and understand things from their perspective. At the point of 'goodbye,' they anticipate leaving informed, with a sense of connection, confident we have their interests at heart and can competently deliver as promised. All along, they anticipate they will hear the truth, that we will be honest and transparent in how we act and communicate. This is something we will explore further in Chapter 4.

The role human factors play in strengthening trust should never be underestimated. The warm welcome we offer, the time we set aside to listen and explain, our openness and transparency, and our readiness to include clients in the decision-making process all matter. They matter because they create a positive experience. They matter because the outcome for our clients depends on our behaviour, understanding of the situation and judgement. They matter because they are the very things that assist in providing reassurance, preventing suspicion, and reducing the weight of uncertainty.

Sincere and encouraging words alone do not create trust. If we spark interest by showing that we can talk the talk, the next stage will be to see if we can walk the walk. False promises and meaningless platitudes are all too common. People need to see us in action to know we are committed to doing what we say we will do. Action is the only way clients can be sure we are reliable and dependable. To our clients, it is like a post-decision check-in to determine if they need to check out, move on and look elsewhere. It is a way of measuring whether the decision to trust and do business with us was justified. Trust relies upon us honouring our commitments, and our reliability says a lot about our ability to keep promises and a sustained interest in our clients. As we will see in Chapter 5, reliability is a truly admirable professional trait. Any unreliability on our part erodes trust and increases the risk to our clients.

RECIPROCATE TO ELEVATE

Trust relies upon strong and stable relationships built over time. This itself depends on continuity and consistency. In business, sales and marketing teams often work on the principle that seven contact points are needed to make a sale. The idea is that familiarity with personnel, product, and brands makes us, our products, and services more appealing, prompting us to purchase. When it comes to developing trust, a similar principle applies. The more times we interact with people, the more we get to know them and the more they get to know us. This, of course, can be a positive or a negative thing, with one of two outcomes: we each find ourselves left wanting more or running for the door!

The quality of the relationship we build with clients depends on mutual trust. We must feel equally connected with our clients, safe and confident that they can fulfil their commitments and conduct themselves in ways we expect. Trust must be reciprocal; we cannot expect clients to trust us if we are unprepared to trust them. A relationship like this starts from a position of weakness because mistrustful thoughts impact both parties' safety, security, and vulnerability.

Over the years, I have chosen not to work with certain people because I did not believe they were principled enough. So too has accountant Emma. She consciously chooses not to take on clients who wish to outwit the tax authorities. When we become involved with those who are duplicitous and morally deceitful, we risk damaging our own reputation. The minute we deviate from our professional values, we undermine our own integrity, and in doing so, we are seen as untrustworthy in the eyes of others. Generally, most of our clients will be decent citizens, and with repeated positive interactions deepening levels of mutual trust will almost certainly follow.

When we first meet people, we tend to focus on making small talk, being careful not to disclose too much personal information until we can be sure of their motives and intentions. Being initially guarded is a natural state of defence. Largely because we do not want to be taken advantage of, but also because we cannot predict how people will respond to what we tell them. It is only with time, as we learn more about others, that we feel more confident to share information about ourselves, our lives, and our opinions with the expectation of privacy. The level of trust, therefore, determines the type of information we share and how much we are prepared to disclose.

A lot of time and energy is required to build relationships, but regular interactions are the very thing that helps to reduce suspicions and uncertainty. Whether we are interacting with potential clients, clients, or those within our business network, each interaction brings an experience. With each email, telephone, or face-to-face conversation comes an insight into us and our organisation in various contexts.

Collectively these experiences are significant because they assist in authenticating our trustworthiness and indicate what is to come. As people come to know us, they can anticipate and predict our accessibility. They have a sense of the type of reception they will receive and the consistency of our thoughts and actions. They recognise the extent to which we understand their needs and commit to delivering in line with our promises. We increase our level of trust when there is consistency and continuity in our characteristics and temperament. We will look at this in more detail in Chapter 5, but for now, it is enough to know that contradictory and erratic behaviour leaves people confused and creates suspicion and a reluctance to trust. If interactions and experiences remain positive, trust will prevail, and people will work co-operatively with us. If not, people look for ways to avoid us.

Recurrent positive experiences not only assist in creating trust in us as individuals but also cultivate trust in the organisations to which we belong. Trust has the capacity to go beyond a direct encounter. The positive experience clients have with us creates perceptions of similar levels of professional behaviour amongst others who work within our field, without any direct encounter. Our pursuit of professionalism extends trust collectively. Through our individual commitment to the values and behaviours expected by clients (and indeed the rest of society), we build greater confidence in our occupational sector, including the establishments we trained at and any associated professional organisations to which we are accredited or belong. We see here that trust in us has a wider and cumulative effect. Of course, this means that any impropriety by others within our field will likely have left people in an untrusting frame of mind. Naturally, this means we will have to work harder to restore public confidence lost through the wrongdoings of others, and to convince people we are indeed different and entirely trustworthy. However, all is not lost. Experience through interaction can easily change people's perceptions about us.

FIRST-HAND EXPERIENCE TRUMPS FIRST IMPRESSIONS

Once, after a lecture, a student said to me: 'Despite what everyone says about you, you really are rather good.' There is a compliment in there somewhere. The student's point was that other students had avoided taking my module because they thought I would work them too hard. However, this student enjoyed the experience and found me supportive. The challenging tasks I had set in the class had stretched their brain, and because of this, they achieved better assessment results than expected. It illustrates that we trust in what we know. A positive personal experience diminishes initial uncertainties and overrides any negative perceptions others may hold about us.

We all know of someone we do not quite trust, yet others seemingly hold them in high regard. The chances are there is nothing particularly sinister about them. It is more likely that we have not had sufficient opportunity to get to know them well or had no cause to experience their work first-hand. This is life. We do not have the time to form deep relationships with everyone we meet. Thus, as professionals, we must reserve our judgement until we have collected evidence.

First-hand experience is one of the strongest measures of whether we are trustworthy. Establishing trust can be challenging, particularly when starting out and new to the business world. It is a catch-22 situation. Clients are needed to build a reputation and vouch for our authenticity and trustworthiness. Without a track record, convincing others that we are reputable is hard. Therefore, credentials are the only things we can rely on. We cannot create a history where there is none, but we can focus on making sure we are credible and thought of as someone who could conceivably be trusted.

Abbi, a bespoke jewellery designer, is a good example of this. She started a business requiring clients to pay upfront for the design and cost of materials and precious metals. To demonstrate her trustworthiness and show how serious she was about the quality and standards of her work and her clients' property, Abbi pursued a course of action that offered clients a tangible assurance of her integrity. She trademarked her company name, protected her designs through copyright, and obtained her own hallmark. In addition to gaining accreditation from the Guild of Jewellery Designers, she took out product and liability insurance covering sales in and outside the UK. Abbi also became an avid networker knowing that part of her reputation would be based on what others said about her, which is quite a big deal. In getting to know people, Abbi could at least gain a few advocates who could spread the word and potentially influence the perceptions of others in a positive way.

If we want to be seen as credible, we must, from the outset, invest time and resources into building our reputation as someone who can be trusted. The more we build trust, the more of an asset it becomes, and one which we stand to gain from time and time again. Trust is like a key that opens the door of possibility. When clients trust us, they return and are willing to refer us. When fellow networkers trust us, they are more helpful and supportive. They will champion us, endorse us, and want to collaborate with us. In either case, it brings new and enriching opportunities.

STAY ON AN EVEN KEEL

If we consistently act ethically and with integrity, remain true to our word, and deliver our services to the high standard we promised, we will undoubtedly continue to secure and strengthen trust. Trust diminishes if we fail to meet expectations, act irresponsibly, or abuse the trust that has been extended to us. It is something that must be continually nurtured because violations of trust shake the very foundations on which the relationship with our clients is built. Distrust creates instability. When we let people down, it undermines their faith in us. This changes the way people feel about us and engage with us. A once strong and stable relationship, along with our credibility and reputation, can soon become tarnished or even ruined.

Violations of trust take many forms and usually arise because of dishonesty, deception, negligence, and omission. They are based on what are perceived to be unacceptable actions. However, because perceptions vary as to what is and what is not acceptable, the enormity of the offence is very much determined by those whose trust we have broken. Although we might not necessarily find ourselves on the wrong side of the law, should we break confidentiality, misinform, waste time and resources, fail to declare a conflict of interest or go against someone's wishes, we might find ourselves on the wrong side of our clients.

The extent to which we are deemed to have violated trust is determined by a combination of things that are linked to the depth of the relationship, the severity of the situation, the number of times it has occurred, the likelihood of further transgressions, and the impact our actions have had for the clients themselves and those around them.

Violations of trust raise emotions. They hurt. Clients are left feeling disappointed, betrayed, and angry. They feel foolish to the point that they regret ever trusting in the first place. Not every client reacts to violations of trust in the same way. However, one thing we can be sure of is that they will trust us far less than they did before and will be rethinking the nature of their relationship with us.

There might not have been any deliberate intent on our part. Nonetheless, as professionals, we must bear the consequences of our actions. We must be prepared to put right our lapses, mistakes and oversights and make concerted efforts to restore that trust if we are to save our reputation. One violation can damage our reputation for a long time if we do not act promptly and appropriately.

A quick response, however, does not mean a prompt end to the matter. Violations of trust can take a while to get over. Righting wrongs is not as straightforward as it seems. The way we reconcile the situation characterises our professionalism and serves to recover the trust that has been lost. Putting it right is challenging when we have acted in unprofessional ways or drifted away from values and principles. We must overcome the temptation to blame others or cover our actions with lies. We must be humble and find it within us to be honest and transparent. This is where the rebuilding starts. At the very least, our clients will expect an apology, a sincere acknowledgement of our failure and words expressing our understanding of our actions' impact. If we account for what happened and articulate the reasons behind our actions, clients can determine if we have just been careless and inattentive rather than wilfully malicious.

If we can right the wrong, we must. If that is not possible, we must compensate clients somehow and offer assurances through our words and actions that we have taken steps to prevent re-occurrence. While our attempts to put things right may gain us forgiveness, it does not mean we regain trust. While some clients might be prepared to give us a second chance, others will not. Some will want to sever connections instantly. Others will continue doing business with us until they no longer have to and then move on. We, too, must move on and recover. This requires some adjustment by reflecting on circumstances that led to the loss of trust in the first instance and seeking to change what we do in the future.

KEEP HEART AND EYES WIDE OPEN

Earlier in the chapter, we explored the idea that mutual trust needs to exist to forge good relationships. We cannot expect clients to trust us if we are unprepared to trust them. In giving our trust, we hope clients will reciprocate and equally value the need to be honest and reliable. None of us likes to think of ourselves as naïve and gullible, but at some point, clients will let us down or fail to keep their end of the bargain. Most of our clients will be honest people who play fair and straight. This lulls us into a false sense of security and makes it harder to identify the untrustworthy in advance.

We may have done all we can to attract the right clients and mitigate against exploitation. Regardless of how honed our instincts, checks, and balances are, or how confident we are that our systems and procedures are up to the mark, we are also vulnerable. At some point, a client will violate the trust we extend to them, and we need to be vigilant.

Commercial insurance broker Colin stresses the importance of honesty and accuracy to his clients. He recognises that clients are not always open with him. They are often anxious about the unknown and mistakenly assume that if they reveal the truth, the outcome will be that they need to pay a higher premium. If Colin thinks clients are not upfront, he probes a little deeper and asks more questions, because it is in his and the client's interests to ensure they have the right level of cover. When it comes to protecting business assets, honesty quite literally is the best policy. Any misrepresentation, non-disclosure or partial disclosure of information can result in invalid or insufficient protection and claims not being paid. Once a policy is agreed upon, based on the information provided, Colin trusts his clients to inform him of any changes. Sometimes, when claims are being made, clients discover they are underinsured. In such cases, there is a tendency for clients to blame the insurer.

Colin recalls one such case several years ago, where it turned out the client did not have the right level of cover for the volume of equipment they possessed. The client claimed they had phoned Colin to tell him they needed to update their policy. Colin had no recollection of this, nor was there any detailed evidence relating to the newly purchased equipment. What followed was an awkward period of one person's word against another, and the company, unable to resolve the matter, went on to honour the claim.

Any insurance claim that is honoured will not damage the company's reputation. Still, it did not stop Colin from feeling that his credibility and reputation were on the line. The incident 'left a mark on his mind for a while.' He chewed over what had happened. It was hard to shake off what seemed like an injustice. It was even harder to shake off the idea that although colleagues were supportive, some might just think Colin was dishonest and unwilling to admit the truth. It illustrates how violations can have a wider impact. It shows how a violation of trust against us not only diminishes our self-confidence but can potentially disrupt the confidence team members, stakeholders, and associates have in us.

Violations do not have to be a major one-off event, which can make them hard to recognise. They can happen slowly: a steady drip-drip of small things over time. It took James, a copywriter, a while to realise that a former client was not as honest and upright as they initially appeared. First, there were delays in payment, then in the commissioning of work, which they continually changed their mind about, followed by an occasion when James agreed to waive the cost for work they claimed not to like. In James's case, he had held out, giving the client the benefit of the doubt for too long. It was not until James discovered the client had gone on to use the work they claimed not to like that he realised he was being cheated.

Any violation of trust has an impact, but we must put it behind us because we cannot approach everyone with suspicion. It is professionally destructive. Being highly suspicious is not good for business. If we are too guarded, we close ourselves off to potential clients, and with this, we close ourselves off to opportunity. By the same token, if we overly trust, we potentially make ourselves vulnerable to exploitation, which can erode our reputation. We are seen as being a soft touch, easily deceived and not careful enough.

There is a fine balance to be found. We need to trust our clients if we are to be trusted by them. We can lose sight of reality if we allow such violations to disturb our inner calm for too long. This leads us to behave in ways that prevent us from building relationships with others. We will forever be on the defensive, anticipate the worst in our clients, or fail to think rationally. Each potentially impairs our level of professionalism because they negatively influence our actions, reactions, and collaborative spirit, which are vital to trust.

We must look to bring closure to the event in a way that does not affect our willingness to trust others or leave us vulnerable. Both Colin and James spent time trying to understand what went wrong. It is an essential part of the process. There is a strong possibility that although we might seek an explanation, we may not get a response. So it is left to us to work it all out. We might not be able to re-establish trust, but we can take steps to ensure it does not happen again. If we are to restore order and harmony, we must look to deal with the root cause of the problem.

At times like this, the frustration and disappointment we might feel within ourselves is not such a bad thing because it empowers us to analyse, reflect and make changes. It might seem like we are shutting the gate after the horse has bolted. We can never undo what has been done, but it is never too late to guard against it happening again. This means strengthening our control of the situation by being committed to operating differently. We might set about improving our personal judgement, polishing up our terms and conditions or altering the processes by which we document and record interactions, for example. Behind all this, we are really showing ourselves and others that our values mean something. We are sending out an indirect message that mutual trust is important. If we allow ourselves to be exploited, we are not being fair to our honest clients, who pay on time and play by the rules. We owe it to ourselves and our current and future clients to preserve that value.

PRINCIPLES, PRACTICE, AND THE POWER OF CONTROL

As professionals, it is important that we both value the notion of trust and respect it. This requires us to see trust as a prominent and distinguished virtue worthy of being upheld through our words and actions. This means regarding trust as something sacrosanct. Trust is not something we are automatically entitled to, so when it is bestowed on us by clients, we know we have earned it. We have every right to feel fortunate and favoured. However, trust comes with responsibilities. There is no place for complacency. Fragile in nature, it is soon destroyed through incongruous actions. We must, therefore, advocate for it and do all we can to preserve it, remaining ever mindful of the damaging consequences that arise when trust is broken.

We have seen in this chapter how reciprocity is a principle of trust. Trust is a shared purpose. It allows us to go about our lives, generates co-operative engagement, and creates wider societal cohesion. We value trust by seeing it as a force for good that makes the world a better place for us and for everyone else. This relies upon us having faith in humanity and recognising that most people are decent citizens, who do the right things in principled ways. That means we must approach everyone we meet optimistically and assume they are well-intentioned until we ascertain otherwise. If we allow ourselves to start from a position of distrust, we break with social norms and limit personal opportunity and future business success.

In business, mutual trust constructively adds value. Here, we have seen how it enhances the quality of interactions, enabling us to deliver a higher service level and achieve better outcomes for our clients. With it comes success in enhancing client satisfaction and strengthening our reputation. Yet we will only acquire these benefits when we earn and sustain trust. To do this, we must uphold trust by respecting it, honouring it, and not infringing it. We cannot simply endorse the principles of mutual trust. We must take them to heart and consciously embed them within our practice. This requires effort on our part because to establish mutual trust, we must actively work to build relationships that continually inspire confidence in our character and capabilities.

Before we can do this, we must appreciate that trust is a complex and multi-layered process. Each decision to trust is taken within a context and driven by our clients' feelings and expectations, considering their personal circumstances and past experiences. There is a strong relationship between trust and being considered trustworthy. We have seen how clients extend their trust following the assessment of our credentials, qualities, and characteristics. If what they see, hear, and come to know of us provides confident reassurance that we are up to the job and not out to exploit them, then clients will look to extend their trust. That, however, does not automatically mean we are trusted or deemed trustworthy. It is only by delivering on our promises and showing ourselves to be reliable and dependable that we come to be trusted, and only then will we be deemed trustworthy.

Many factors influence the strength and nature of the relationship, how it is formed, and the path by which it continues. However honourable we perceive ourselves to be, this is of no consequence to our clients. As we have seen, for them, entry into the relationship is filled with uncertainty, not least because they forfeit control and expose themselves to risk. Trust cannot be attributed to one factor alone: clients must see many aspects of us and gain first-hand experience to feel confident and secure enough to trust us. This is to our advantage because it gives us numerous opportunities to make a positive impression and demonstrate our integrity.

We know that trust is very individual, based on internal feelings and personal expectations, and that we may not always get the reaction and emotional responses we expect. We also know that our character, capabilities, and associations will be heavily scrutinised at each point of contact. We may not have control over another person's decision to extend their trust. However, we have control over how we present ourselves, who we associate with, and the direct and indirect messages we send out. If we adopt a professional approach, we make it easy for people to get to the centre of who we are and gather the evidence they need before they draw their conclusions about whether we can be trusted.

The decision to trust is not made in a vacuum. Trust is reinforced when we remove suspicion, uncertainty, and instability. All of these are within our power when we consider our appearance, equip ourselves with the right credentials, and show ourselves to be authentic in every way. This is even more the case when we look to create personalised experiences in which we show consistency in our approach and deliver on our promises. We show ourselves as advocates of trust when we act honourably and responsibly towards others, right our wrongs, self-regulate our behaviours and interactions, and establish clear boundaries as to whom we are prepared to do business with. All we need to do is make conscious, constructive choices and hold ourselves accountable for the ways we go about establishing and maintaining trust.

When we do this, we remain in control of the situation and how we appear to others. If we align ourselves in ways that work to generate the confidence and security people need to trust, it makes it easier to build and sustain mutual trust. Moreover, each action or behaviour helps validate and reinforce the others. Here we show ourselves to be complete. When there are no gaps, there is nothing to raise suspicion, create uncertainty or incite instability.

By taking personal responsibility, we confirm ourselves to be advocates of trust, a visible sign of integrity. Without self-discipline and self-regulation, there is the potential to get carried away with our self-view or to compromise ourselves in ways that diminish trust. If we fail to hold ourselves accountable such that the principles of trust are not observable through our actions and words, we become a risk that clients will not want to take. If we want success, trust is a virtue we must prioritise.

HOLD THAT THOUGHT

Trust plays a significant part in developing relationships, business success, and reputation. If we expect people to see us as someone they want to do business with, we must exemplify trust and prove ourselves trustworthy. Our level of professionalism, reflected through our choices, creates the emotional connections needed for clients to feel confident and secure that our intentions are honourable. If we can be depended on to do the right thing and, in doing so, adopt certain behaviours with the client's interests in mind, we stand to benefit. With trust comes client loyalty, financial reward, and the enhancement of our reputation. To be deemed trustworthy certainly helps us achieve our aim of building a successful business.

Arguably we cannot be a professional with a self-centred purpose. We must look beyond our own business interests and accept the need to value and respect trust for the benefit of others. Trust gives rise to trust, yet trust cannot flourish without professionalism. If we do not establish personal expectations and hold ourselves accountable for achieving them, our clients are vulnerable, as are we, our occupational sector, and society.

Our professionalism and commitment to developing mutual trust create higher levels of trust. We must not underestimate the scale of our personal influence within that process. When we value and respect trust, we build enduring personal relationships and bring stability to our profession. What is more, as we lead by example, we nurture the values and practices of others, and shape the moral consensus and norms of society. It is a tough job, but someone must do it. The question is, are we fully up to it? To what extent are we committed to adopting practices that advocate and preserve trust? If not, then why not? We must question our lack of professionalism and consider why we are prepared to take the risk when our life, livelihood, reputation and occupational sector depend so much on our co-operative engagement with others.

4

HONESTY AND TRANSPARENCY

TELL THE TRUTH, ACCEPT THE TRUTH AND KEEP IT REAL

If there are two traits that all professionals are expected to have, they are honesty and transparency. Both are the foundation of trust and integrity. Professionalism is based on probity, the idea that we act ethically and have high standards of behaviour. We can never claim to be professional if we are not honest and transparent because these virtues guide us towards the various principled actions that define us as professionals. We are seen to have integrity when we live and breathe our values. Honesty and transparency help us remain true to ourselves and our beliefs. Through these, we resist the temptation to lie, cut corners, deceive, or break the rules. They guide us towards being truthful and accurate. Without either, we are deemed untrustworthy, which, as we know from Chapter 3, is bad for business.

People are more inclined to do business with honest people because honesty inspires confidence in personal character and practices. To sustain our business, we must make honesty and transparency a noticeable part of our business. This relies upon our ability to be truthful in what we say and open about who we are, what we do, and how we do it. If we fail to tell the truth, we are not being honest. If others cannot see the truth for themselves, we are not being transparent. Either way, we will be treated with suspicion. We will only gain trust with their visibility. Trust, honesty, and transparency are intertwined. Honesty and transparency build trust, and trust facilitates honesty and transparency. Not only will being honest and transparent gain us clients, but the trusting relationship that develops allows for open and frank discussions, generating a willingness to expose and accept the truth, and respond to questions and inquiries into our actions.

Upholding the values of honesty and transparency can be personally challenging. As we head into this chapter, we see how our desire to be successful and popular can lead us to act dishonestly and go against what we know to be right. We are often apprehensive about exposing our shortcomings, expressing the truth, and hearing the truth, so we shy away in fear of the consequences. Thus, we will explore the significance of honesty and transparency in empowering our clients, ourselves, and fellow entrepreneurs to make better choices that lead to better outcomes. As we progress through the chapter we learn, through the experience of others, how we can better prepare ourselves to deliver the truth in a supportive way and respond positively to any constructive criticism aimed at us. In the latter part, emphasis is placed on the need to overcome our fears about being honest and transparent and show ourselves to be authentic and human in order to prove our integrity, gain credibility, and visibly promote the values of honesty and transparency.

HONESTY SITS WITHIN US

Honesty is not just about speaking the truth. It is also about accuracy, certainty, and keeping it real. No client wants to be misinformed any more than they want to be deceived. We need to be authentic and be everything we proclaim to be. How accurately we represent ourselves privately and publicly matters. To gain trust, we must be who we say we are and we must have rightfully acquired the qualifications and accreditations we profess to hold. Naturally, we also need to be capable of applying the experience and skills we claim to have. If not, we are fundamentally masquerading as someone else and gaining business by duplicitous means.

The world of business can be notoriously cut-throat. Thousands and thousands of people are out there making a lot of noise, each bidding to show off their talents and authoritative expertise. Everyone is vying to be a go-to thought leader. To compete and be heard, we must shout above the noise. To attract attention, it can be tempting to decorate things up a bit and embellish facts about ourselves, exaggerate our expertise, or commission fake reviews. It is natural to admire other entrepreneurs and to want to be like them. Who does not want to be respected, earn money and be successful? However, mastering the art of self-promotion is much easier and works more in our favour when we present an authentic version of ourselves.

We are often encouraged to fake it until we make it. On the surface, this ego-boosting rhetoric reflects an aspirational intent to be complete and perfect in every way, even though we are not. It gives us the impression that this self-affirming action will bring us all we ever hoped for. However, if we dig deeper, we will see it is encouraging us to misrepresent ourselves by pretending to be better and more accomplished than we are. Such pretence is a form of deception. We are asking clients to believe things about us and make decisions based on details that are not true. Not that we should ever underplay our talents, of course; our aptitude and flair deserve a platform, but we must be cautious about bigging ourselves up too much. For example, claiming to be internationally renowned is all well and good if our business activities mean we are a household name across several continents, but less so if we are basing this claim on a handful of LinkedIn connections with people who happen to live abroad.

We can all embellish something to a point and still be believed. Arguably though, we do ourselves no favours, because clients expect us to carry our credibility. We might be able to convince clients that we know what we are talking about, but they will want to see that translated into action. To them, we are only ever going to be considered any good if we can actually do what we say we can. We might think we can bluff our way into a situation. However, in time, we will find ourselves having to bluff our way out of it. Once we start to fabricate and embroider the facts, we tend to invent and perpetuate inaccuracy and deception to keep up the pretence. We begin to construct a distorted sense of reality and delude ourselves into thinking we are far more capable than we are. In effect, we are lying to ourselves as well as to our clients.

Twisting the facts is by no means an advantage because it creates vulnerability. We risk exposure, and this threatens our business interests. Few are easily fooled. Clients will see through the smokescreen, and when they do, trust is broken. We create a situation whereby people no longer know what to believe, so they simply stop believing.

To be professional, we must be honest with ourselves. Instead of rescripting our story, we should celebrate our uniqueness and learn to love ourselves. This means evaluating and accepting what we are capable of. There is a fine line between making the most of an opportunity that comes our way, and placing ourselves in a situation where we are entirely out of our depth. We misrepresent ourselves when we fail to acknowledge our limitations. When we do not have the relevant professional skills and experience, we are on a risky path heading straight towards failure. As we bumble along, trying to stay one step ahead of the game, the truth of our ineptitude is bound to emerge. Acting as though we know what we are doing when we do not takes time and effort, but it is also stressful and exhausting. What is more, we are wasting our abilities and disconnecting ourselves from our professional identity in the process. We are working so hard at being someone we are not that we forget to be the person we really are.

We often fear that if we are honest and acknowledge our limitations, we undermine people's confidence in us. The opposite is true. By overestimating our ability, we give the impression that we have an inflated sense of self and are prepared to put our interests before our clients'. In this case, we are considered unprofessional and untrustworthy by default. Professionals accept reality and are honest with themselves about their accomplishments and limitations. Candidness creates clarity and empowers us to adjust and make decisions that lead to change. So, rather than simply pretending to be, we take the necessary steps to become all we want to be. From a personal, professional, and business perspective, there is less risk and more reward from achieving and being able to profess the truth than there is by pretending.

NOTHING BUT THE TRUTH

There is no greater form of deception than claiming never to have lied. If there is one truth, it is the fact that we all lie. What is more, we may not even notice we are doing it. At some point, we will have blamed our lateness on the traffic to avoid the embarrassment of admitting we could not bring ourselves to get out of bed. We might even have complimented someone's cooking out of kindness, even though the dish they prepared was inedible. There is often no malicious intent to our lies. However, we tend to lie out of self-interest to either gain or avoid pain. We lie to look good, to avoid hurting someone's feelings, to avoid conflict, or to get out of a sticky situation. It is often much easier to lie than it is to tell the truth.

Moreover, it is often hard for others to prove that they are being lied to, so we get away with it. Sometimes it is not what we say but what we choose to leave out. To prevaricate or omit detail might not be an outright lie, but it is a concealment of the truth. By telling half-truths, we are not portraying the whole picture. Essentially, we are giving rise to false impressions and misleading information.

This might all seem very innocent, but half-truths and lies are like ticking time bombs, primed to explode at any minute. In time, we will get found out and have to face up to the consequences, where we have one of two options: we either come clean and admit it or attempt to cover it up and lie our way out. Taking the latter and less noble path will, of course, only lead to more deception, adding insult to injury to those we have lied to. Regardless, the outcome is diminished trust because dishonesty on any scale is at odds with professionalism. Not only is it disrespectful, but it is also an attack on a person's dignity, and if we are obscuring the truth or lying for material gain, it is a form of abuse.

Recollecting the truth is far easier than remembering a load of lies. Not only does the latter sap our mental energy, but it also creates stress. We tie ourselves in knots, trying to keep the story straight. A contradictory account with inconsistencies, holes, and pieces that do not quite fit together sets alarm bells ringing. If we are prepared to lie about small things, we give the impression that we are capable of greater dishonesty. The risk to our reputation offers reason enough to be straightforward and truthful from the outset.

True honesty takes self-control and requires courage. Professionalism demands that we resist the temptation to tell half-truths and lies or engage in dishonest practices. As Abbi, a bespoke jewellery designer, reminds us, 'we must speak the truth and shame the devil.' There might be good reasons for concealing the truth, but good intentions do not make it the right thing to do. Dishonesty should not prevail. Indeed, clients, associates, and stakeholders will count on our unwavering integrity and moral certitude to be open and honest when the good times roll and when the bad times leave us wanting to roll over.

Clients expect us to stay strong during tough times and not surrender to deception. There is an assumption that, no matter how vulnerable or insecure it makes us feel, or how embarrassing and demanding it is, we will avoid secrecy, remain frank and truthful, and keep people informed. Moreover, should it all go wrong, people anticipate we will apologise sincerely and take steps to put things right. Honesty says a lot about our intentions, but it also says a lot about our character, professional authenticity, and maturity. In being honest, we show that we care and respect others enough to tell the truth, but we also demonstrate that we have sufficient self-respect to be frank and truthful to ourselves by doing what is right.

AVOID MISTIMED SINCERITY

We often fear telling the truth because sometimes the truth is anything but pretty. It can be agonisingly painful to deliver as well as receive. It takes courage and a great deal of effort to tell clients the truth. To be honest, we must be willing to be vulnerable. As Malinka, who provides home care to older people, says: 'Sometimes you have to psych yourself up and put on your battle dress.' Malinka is right. We often approach this with trepidation. There is an awkwardness about telling the truth or bearing bad news that we need to prepare for. We hold on to the idea that we might figuratively get shot as the messenger, and, naturally, we want to protect ourselves. When we speak truthfully, we often tell people things they do not want to hear. What is more, we can never be too sure how they will react. Not only do we risk being disliked, but we also risk creating tension that gives rise to conflict. Taking everything into consideration, it would be easier to avoid telling the truth to keep the peace and protect our self-image.

As professionals, we need to be above such self-serving principles. We must remember that the justifiable truth is valid and needs to be told. In telling the truth, no matter how difficult it is, we empower clients to act, find solutions, and make decisions. Having the courage to be honest protects our clients' interests, reputation, and self-respect, as well as our own. When we speak the truth, we reveal ourselves to be honest professionals. We will be more respected for this than we would ever be if we were found to be hiding the truth.

Although our clients expect to hear the truth, it does not automatically mean they are willing to accept it. In telling the truth, we must show that we are not the enemy. This is where tact and diplomacy come into their own. If we are to earn any respect for being candid, we must make the truth more palatable and make ourselves less contemptible in the process.

Tact and diplomacy require grace and compassion. If we blunder our way through, we risk offending people, making ourselves look foolish, and inflaming the situation. Our credibility is built on the respect we show and the judgements we make. We need to understand people and their circumstances in order to deliver the truth with benevolence. This brings the need to develop our emotional intelligence. The truth needs to be told with natural sincerity. Louise, a virtual assistant, found herself in a position where she felt she could no longer work with one of her clients. Their chaotic approach to business meant they were challenging to work with. For Louise, it was not about finding the right words but delivering them at the right time.

Firing a client is a tough call, but it is an undertaking that is professionally possible when we know our clients and can effectively manage the circumstances in which we begin that conversation. Louise needed to wait and pick the right moment. This meant a time when she knew her client would be less distracted and more receptive to what she had to say. We often feel a conflict between our desire to tell the truth and the need to spare our clients' feelings. It is possible to manage this inner battle. By waiting for the right time, Louise took the pressure off herself and her client. With this, she optimised her chances of being able to explain and convey her message in its entirety and provide her client with an opportunity to listen with the intention of understanding.

The truth deserves respect. Blurting it out under the wrong circumstances shows a lack of concern for our clients. Whatever the situation, we must continue to value our clients as individuals. We must invest enough time to tell them the truth in the right way. Being honest relies upon an empathetic understanding. This depends upon us being able to see things from our clients' perspectives and understand the emotions the news or information they are about to receive will evoke. If we are capable of this, we can preserve the dignity of our clients as well as our own.

HAVE NO FEAR

As an insurance broker, Colin sometimes has the job of telling clients that insurers will not honour their claims. On hearing this, Colin's clients are often frustrated and angry. Something unpleasant has already happened to them, and now they stand to lose a lot of money. For Malinka, there invariably comes a time when the service she delivers no longer meets the care needs of the individuals she supports. As people become older and more frail, they often need greater assistance and more specialised medical care. This sees her initiating conversations with clients or their family members, many of whom are in denial about their relative's health and often conflicted at the thought of putting those they love into a residential or nursing care home.

The fact is, if we can pre-empt what people might be feeling, we start from a better position. With calmness and sincerity, we can be better prepared to tell the truth. It enables us to listen and respond in ways that prevent hostility and alleviate the discomfort the truth may cause.

Both Colin and Malinka adopt a very similar approach. They emphasise the need to gather facts and stick to the facts. We can assert the truth without feeling compelled to lie when we adhere to the facts. It helps us remain impartial. It removes the need for self-justification, which prevents us from getting emotionally pulled in. We are less likely to be drawn into saying what people want to hear rather than what they need to hear. For Colin, the facts help him demonstrate why the insurers have come to the decision they have. For Malinka, the facts help demonstrate events that have occurred and why the conversation needs to be had now.

There is no doubt it can be awkward; it is not unreasonable for clients to feel angry, frustrated, or tearful. This is a natural response when people are in situations they cannot change. However, Colin and Malinka believe that if we listen and explore what lies behind the emotion, we are less likely to respond negatively and insensitively. By controlling our own emotions, we retain control of the situation and progress towards helping clients resolve or navigate the issue. As Colin says: 'People will always appreciate the truth over lies and exaggerations, but they will appreciate how you dealt with it even more.'

Our clients might not like what we have to say, but they will like us even less if we mishandle things. We are responsible for telling the truth, but the truth has a nasty habit of changing relationships. We can tell the truth out of respect for our clients, only to lose their respect. To maintain the mutual respect we once shared, we must approach our clients with a feeling of partnership. We cannot simply present the truth and walk away. This traumatises clients even more. If we can help clients see a way forward, there is every chance of retaining their respect and strengthening the existing relationship. For Colin, this means advising clients on how to best protect their future assets. At the same time, Malinka works to connect families with various agencies so that they can discuss and explore alternative care options.

In offering support, we help clients become more accepting of the truth they did not want to hear. We allow clients to see things for how they are rather than how they would like them to be. Malinka sums it up quite nicely as she says, 'we always have to remember that our courage in telling the truth gives others the courage to make decisions.' For Malinka, it is about seeing the bigger picture. Our apprehensions about telling the truth will always be short-lived. Moreover, they will always translate into something more heartening and longer lasting. The truth alongside the facts allows clients to own the outcome and work towards finding the best possible solution. In time, clients will value hearing the truth. The details of the conversation will be long forgotten. It will be the changes that the truth brings, the memories of our kindness, and the support we offered during those difficult times that will be remembered and earn us respect.

BE SURE TO PERSONALISE IT

To build trust, we must be consistently honest in the way we communicate and in the way we acquire business and foster honesty throughout our working practices. The level of consistency and the standards by which we conduct our activities reflect our integrity and commitment to honesty and transparency. We build honesty and prevent dishonesty when we communicate effectively and create systems and practices that promote transparency and raise our level of accountability.

Honesty and transparency are characterised by their visibility. This means operating in a way that makes it easy for people to access and understand information. If we want to be seen as trustworthy, we must be willing to provide answers and openly share information about ourselves, the services we provide, and how we do business. We often fear sharing too much information in case we play directly into the hands of the competition. However, we must remember that whatever we broadcast and publish about our business is the very thing that stimulates people to engage with us in the first place. The information we give through websites, social media platforms, leaflets, seminars, etc, builds public perception. The details we provide about things like pricing, sourcing of products, the client journey, reviews, environmental sustainability, and social responsibility are essential facts – facts that draw in potential clients and help them decide whether our services are right for them and whether they want to enter a relationship and do business with us.

By being upfront about our activities and making it easy for people to access us directly, we show we are committed to attending to our obligations and already assume open channels of communication. Holding our cards too close to our chest creates mystery and ambiguity, which casts suspicion. We stand to gain more by putting it out there than we do by hiding it. The decision to wrap ourselves in a veil of secrecy might alleviate anxieties about our competitors but it potentially stalls business and collaborative opportunities. People will only engage with us once they get to know us and know what we are all about. It is through information that we become readily understood. An insight into what lies behind who we are and how we operate allows people to do their own governance and due diligence in earnest. In providing information, we respect individuals' rights to check us out beforehand.

If we are sincere about this, we must be amenable to answering questions, be prepared to share something of ourselves and create opportunities for participation. All these things make us approachable. When clients feel vulnerable, it makes a difference to how we are perceived and the value we add to their journey. Being approachable makes it easy for people to seek further guidance and ask questions. Of course, we do not always end up winning the client. But, as Colin sees it: 'We can at least pride ourselves on an honest job well done.' Colin believes that helping people decide what is right for them and guiding them towards services that suit them better is a sacrifice worth making. It is better to be remembered for being honest than for having mis-sold something that was not right or was unnecessary. When we have the self-respect to stand up for honesty and fairness, we will always be trusted and respected.

The strongest professional relationships are built when we level it up and allow clients a window into our world. In revealing our personal side, we show our authenticity. It is another way to keep it real and provide evidence of our well-meaning intentions. For Colin, an insurance broker, Emma, an accountant, and Diana, a financial advisor, this is an important part of doing business. The sectors they work in have historically acquired a reputation for underhand and dishonest practices. This is no longer the case thanks to tighter regulations and inspections, but all three of them feel they carry the burden of their earlier colleagues' unprofessional behaviours. But, in Colin's words, 'not everyone's a crook,' so how we work to differentiate ourselves from the less scrupulous amongst us is critical to reassuring clients of our integrity and credibility.

When Emma meets potential clients, she uses this as an opportunity to set the record straight and show sympathy for any lack of confidence her clients might have. She shares her own family's negative experiences of employing an accountant before she became one herself. Describing her experiences in the real world helps remove clients' doubts and fears. Having personally fallen foul of unprincipled practices and harmful guidance, the last thing Emma wants is for her clients to go through what she went through. To Emma, sharing is caring. It shows she is on her clients' side and equally devoted to a precise and law-abiding approach.

We cannot sustain relationships without an open exchange of information, so revealing something of ourselves is one of the first steps to creating an environment conducive to sharing information without judgement. It adds a personal touch that humanises us and makes us seem more approachable. Not that we should necessarily bare our souls or share the most intimate details of our life, but small self-disclosures connect us for the better. Sharing insight into our lives and experiences builds trust because it helps to break down preconceptions, makes clients feel less vulnerable, and fosters a willingness to mirror our actions.

SHARE THOUGHTS FREELY AND MATTER-OF-FACTLY

When we openly give something of ourselves to a relationship, we tend to get something back. What comes back allows us to communicate more honestly and better serve our clients' interests. We find that the window into our world becomes the window through which we see the world of others. As we learn more about each other's personalities, lives, experiences, and aspirations, we understand each other better and appreciate each other's perspectives. If we create an environment where it feels safe to be open and direct, we have a platform to educate each other. This enables us to share thoughts and feelings without judgement, display empathy, show compassion, and allow honesty to flow both ways. This paves the way for frank discussions and admissions of error and makes it easier for everyone to do what is difficult: to tell the truth in ways that do not hurt or offend.

Frank and open conversations aside, if we want to build and maintain trusting relationships, there must be transparency. Transparency is how we show our honesty to be true and unquestionable. The clients who invest in our services and the stakeholders who have an interest in our business will want to know what we are doing, how we are doing it, and what we have achieved as a result. They want proof that, behind closed doors, we are as upright as we claim to be.

As professionals, we must hold ourselves accountable and be answerable for our actions and decisions. To do this, we need to document and present information in ways that are accessible and understandable. If we are to be transparent, nothing should remain hidden. We must openly share what clients and stakeholders need to know. This is not to suggest we break confidentiality, reveal sensitive information, or disrespect people's right to privacy, but that we openly share what we legally can with those who need to know. We can develop and promote transparency within our policies and practices and reflect our commitment to honesty and openness in many ways. If we want to show that we take our responsibilities seriously, we must be proactive. When clients and stakeholders ask us to make what they need to know visible, then we need to ask ourselves if we are doing all we can to show we value honesty and transparency and are acting according to these professional virtues.

To provide reassurance of commitment to her responsibilities, Diana uses a clients' charter – a document that sets out a series of promises and outlines shared expectations alongside a clear plan that includes timelines. All clients are unique, so if financial markets, products, or tax allowances change, Diana makes an effort to personally keep clients informed of such changes in relation to their circumstances. Iain, an electrician, provides detailed itemised quotes so clients know exactly what they are spending their money on, and, for larger projects, delivers regular updates in relation to progress. Colin and Emma meet clients face-to-face to explain and interpret documents and answer questions. In doing so, they can be sure clients understand the terminology, various figures, and content, and fully appreciate what it is they are signing. Ranjit, an IT support engineer, uses his monthly newsletter to regularly inform clients of forthcoming service changes and update them on the software developers he is currently working with.

These might seem like small things, but we should consider their significance in providing clarity, keeping people informed, and maintaining trust. While these are just a few examples, they illustrate how we can advocate and make known our commitment to honesty and transparency at each stage of the client's journey, from initial points of contact to the completion of services and beyond, particularly when we want repeat business.

To be noticeably transparent, we must adopt an all-embracing approach that uses various ways and means to validate our openness and accountability. Clients will only be reassured if there is consistency within our processes, procedures, and actions. Variability and inaction are like red flags. They portray unreliability and unpredictability, which personify the inconsiderate and untrustworthy. If we leave clients in the dark about their affairs or have them second-guessing how our actions align with their interests, we immediately create suspicion. Our integrity is doubted. We are seen to be dishonest by virtue of the fact that we are not transparent. Transparency conveys our willingness to hold ourselves accountable and afford clients the consideration they deserve. By being transparent, we show we care and are careful enough to ensure we do not mislead anyone at any point.

LEARN TO VALUE CRITICISM

To be admired for our transparency, we must know what our clients and stakeholders need to know. Without this, we cannot remain ahead of the game and offer what is required. One way to do this is to create opportunities for shared deliberations and ongoing feedback. At the end of each face-to-face meeting, Diana puts time aside to reflect with her clients and gather feedback on her performance and activity. Since much of Diana's work arises through recommendations, she wants to be sure she is doing a good job and meeting her new clients' expectations. By exploring her success in achieving what her clients set out to achieve, or by gaining opinions on the nature of the decisions taken and the comprehensiveness of supporting information, Diana has the capacity to respond immediately and, if necessary, follow this up with action. We learn from this that by creating the right environment and adopting such an approach, Diana empowers her clients to engage and share their thoughts and feelings candidly. People feel valued when they are allowed to be heard. By listening, we can face issues head-on and deal with them more effectively.

If we are to build our reputation as someone who values and upholds honesty and transparency, we need to show that we are open to, and willing to accept, constructive criticism and act on it. If we are to be accountable, then we need to be answerable. This means we must come to terms with evaluation, inspections, and examination of our activities from clients and various stakeholders.

We know that, as professionals, we need to be honest. But, as much as we fear being honest, we also fear the honesty of others. We often erroneously assume that people will focus on the negative. We imagine that they will be all geared up to trip us up or drag us down at the first opportunity. On top of this, we rely on external assurances to feel good, so it is no surprise that we want to avoid anything likely to dent our self-confidence. The last thing we want to feel is inadequate: that somehow, after all our hard work and effort, we do not measure up to people's expectations.

We can never anticipate how others interpret our opinions, intentions, and actions. In our attempt to justify our activities and rationalise our decisions, we fear how we will be perceived and how the information we provide will be used. In laying our cards on the table, we make ourselves vulnerable. Rather than physically hide, embellish the facts, disguise, or withhold information, we should simply tell it as it is. If we report the facts in a straightforward manner, are open about our actions, and describe what we believe is the truth, we have less to fear. By doing this we are, in fact, treating our audience with the respect they deserve, and the chances are that this will be reciprocated. When we open ourselves up to evaluation by others, we must trust that they too are sufficiently professional to be honest, transparent, constructive, and considerate in their approach and response.

There is no doubt that we will, at some point, face negative criticism. However, if we want to achieve success and maintain healthy relationships with those who have a vested interest in our business, we must embrace it. There is an art to giving negative feedback. Whilst we hope critics have the skills and grace to deliver this with kindness, tact and diplomacy are not everyone's forte. Some are bound to approach it like a raging bull, leaving us wounded. From experience, it is not that our clients, business associates, or stakeholders are necessarily out to attack us. It just seems like it. It is easy to be on the defensive and close our ears to what they say. Let us not forget how awkward telling the truth really is. It takes as much courage to offer personal opinions and perspectives as it does to tell the truth. Unless those offering such criticism have nerves of steel and have honed their skills, there is every chance the words will come out wrong. The message they are trying to convey will, in all probability, be a criticism of our actions, not us as individuals. Our critics will not be saying we are no good. It is more likely that they will be saying there is scope for improvement and a need to approach things differently. Rather than react defensively, we must respond more positively and reframe the criticism as an opportunity to be a better professional and be better at what we do.

ACCEPT CRITICS AS FRIENDS

If we are to handle negative criticism in a professional way, we must do so with grace and gratitude. This means focusing on the message being conveyed. Even if it is unsolicited information that we would rather not hear, there will be something meaningful and enlightening within it. To clarify the underlying message, we must separate it from the person and how it is said. No one really likes giving criticism. Few would ever criticise us for the sheer enjoyment of it. The critical views people express are often driven by their own experiences. They see in us that which they have seen in themselves and others. They have been there, done that, got the T-shirt, and do not want to see anyone else fall into the same trap. Hard as it is to believe, they are rooting for us, wanting us to learn, grow and succeed more quickly.

Our critics are not the enemy. If we think they are, we immediately create an atmosphere of hostility and distrust. Moreover, any knee-jerk reactions to their comments undermine their goodwill and leave us short on respect. In fact, our critics are friendly allies. We need to be gracious in accepting their opinions because what they are really doing is helping us appraise our situation.

In providing feedback, critics offer us the opportunity to reflect and process our decisions and actions by drawing on the wisdom they have acquired through hindsight. This often comes with ideas and suggestions, which, by its very nature, makes for constructive criticism. This allows us to learn and make positive changes. Without constructive criticism, we may never know of our need to improve or how we could do things so much better. Constructive criticism is often described as feedback. Yet it is not so much feedback as it is feedforward. The opinions of our critics will make no difference to what has been and gone. Instead, their value lies in boosting our future chances of success.

When we accept constructive criticism, we learn more and improve personally and professionally, but only if we remain humble. Our humility allows us to be receptive to thoughts and ideas from the lived experiences of others. Through this, we open our minds to alternative perspectives, fresh ideas, and the exploration of our practices, attitudes, and behaviours. This allows us to make better decisions, take ownership of our development, and navigate our way forward much more effectively.

Those prepared to offer us constructive criticism are usually well-meaning in their intention. They offer advice and opinion in the spirit of collaboration, and for that, we need to be thankful. However, thankfulness does not gain us any admiration, nor does being weak-minded. If we want to secure any long-term support and encouragement, we need to reflect on the ideas and opinions of others and follow them up.

When we consider alternative viewpoints, seek solutions, and revise our understanding of the issues raised with those who have raised them, we reveal our mindset for growth and personal development. Our desire to improve boosts people's trust and belief in us. This changes the nature of the relationship and deepens the bond formed. Potentially we move on from having a one-off critic to having a lifelong critical friend. In following up, we acknowledge that we value the very people who can be trusted enough to tell us the truth. In showing that we are prepared to respond, we reveal ourselves to be equally open and honest. This is a solid basis for building a relationship that offers us longer-term support and encouragement.

If we can secure ourselves a critical friend, we are onto a winner. We have someone we can trust to listen, provide feedback, challenge our thought processes, share their experiences, and offer us an alternative perspective – all because they want the same things as we want for ourselves. When we have a critical friend, we have someone who champions our success. Phil, who runs a cleaning company, likens it to a charitable offering in which we survive through the generosity of those willing to volunteer their ideas, help, and support.

Candid conversations with others bring so many benefits, not least because they help us remain accountable and achieve the standards expected. We are prompted to rationalise our actions, evaluate the quality of our work, set goals, make better decisions, and accept responsibility for managing and fulfilling our obligations. Critical friends assist us to live and breathe the values of honesty and transparency. Phil talks of the cyclical nature of honest feedback. The benefits of frank and open conversations with people he trusted helped him shake off his fears about being honest. Over time he found himself more willing to share information about himself and his business decisions in the interest of his success. As relationships strengthened, Phil became open and receptive to the feedback given. Through the open-hearted response he got from his critical friends, he, too, was encouraged to speak freely. With this, he felt at ease in offering others constructive feedback without fear of reprisal. Having a series of approachable critical friends to whom he could turn fuelled Phil's desire to help others see what they cannot always see for themselves. As Phil says: 'To be accountable, we often need a second pair of eyes. Sometimes it is the outspoken insight of others that points the way.'

Indeed, the directness of others is often what directs us. Phil's cyclical view shows us that the story ends where it begins, but the bits in between change us for the better. What is clear is that if we are willing to receive constructive criticism offered with benevolent intent, we are likely to give constructive criticism with a similar commitment. Moreover, when we do both, we show in all sincerity that we value honesty.

TAKE PRIDE IN FAILURE

I like to share in the success of others. Seeing people set out on a course of action that leads them to achieve their goals and ambitions is always inspiring. But the journey to success has its challenges: it takes a great deal of physical and mental effort to get where we want to be and navigate the various obstacles that stand in our way. So, when success comes calling, I am the first to clap and celebrate people's resilience and accomplishments.

One thing that always strikes me is how soon those challenges are forgotten. Whether we are setting up in business for the first time or embarking on new business ventures, there is never an easy way. No matter how experienced we are, there will be times when we make mistakes, do something we regret, or mess up big time. Yet few in business ever talk about these experiences. It is as if failure is a dirty word. No one wants to expose how they wandered around clueless because they had no plan A or plan B. They do not share how they overestimated their skill set, nosedived because they misread the market, or lost huge profits because they took bad advice. Instead, people mask their ineffectiveness by giving the impression that they have sharp business acumen, are nigh on perfect, and are fast becoming living legends. Of course, it is all in their mind's eye, but faced with such swagger, it is easy to get sucked into believing that the luck everyone else seems to have has somehow passed us by.

The truth is that everyone has their fair share of disappointment and misfortune. Blunders and oversights are all part and parcel of being in business. It is just that some people prefer to sweep them under the carpet and keep up the pretence rather than admit their struggles. It is easy to see why people do this. Aside from the pressure to prove themselves capable, no one wants to feel as if they are washing their dirty laundry in public. The stigma associated with dereliction and defeat leads us to think that if word gets out that we have made mistakes, we damage the faith people have in us and in our reputation. This is a flawed way of thinking because people value authenticity. We get greater respect when we show ourselves to be human like everyone else than we do pretending to be perfect, because no one is perfect and pretending arouses suspicion.

We might occasionally get it wrong, but if we are still in business, we are still here to tell the tale. It is all a matter of perspective. We have not totally failed; we just happen to have been unsuccessful and subsequently managed to put things right. We have shown ourselves to be professional. To straighten things out, we will have understood where we went wrong. We will have picked ourselves up, dusted ourselves down, reflected, and re-evaluated our actions. As we started again, we took advice, sought guidance, adopted a different approach, and steered ourselves on a course of action that brought success. Behind all this, what we have really done is show our willingness to learn from our mistakes and demonstrate our capacity to take it on the chin and not give up. We have proved that we have a growth mindset and are responsible and resilient enough to see our way out of a sticky situation. In all respects, we have acted with professionalism. We have not one but two stories worth telling. Not only did we slip up, but we also weathered the harsh conditions, turned things around, moved on, and came out the other side better and stronger. It is incredibly admirable, and if we can be proud of it, others will be too.

Here lies a message about how failure is often the start of success. Each setback is a lesson through which we learn and move closer to success. It is a powerful message that needs to be shared. This is not to suggest we offer a warts-and-all, blow-by-blow account. If we want to make an impact, we had best stick to the edited highlights. Nonetheless, by sharing our personal experiences of the challenges we have overcome, we promote open discussion amongst the business community. Through this, we allow others to learn vicariously through our experiences and endorse the value of honesty and transparency.

Many of us are where we are today because of the wisdom and support people gave us along the way. Being open and transparent is a way of giving back to the community that supported us through the good times and the bad. By sharing, we help fellow business owners, particularly those just starting out, to achieve success and feel less alone. We often overlook the fact that others have similar experiences and can potentially fall into the same traps as we did. Through hindsight, we can guide others away from making the same mistakes. Moreover, we can reassuringly show that our misjudgements are not as ill-fated and damaging as they might initially seem. Because, as we have discovered, there is a professional way out of it all that allows us to proudly emerge with our dignity and reputation intact.

By offering candid insight into our shortcomings, we show ourselves to be responsible and accountable and make our personal honesty and transparency more visible. Through this, we can inspire others to share their experiences too. Our stories are a powerful narrative that can change how failure is perceived and help shape a culture that values authenticity, bringing honesty and transparency to the forefront of professional behaviour.

FORGET BEING PERFECT, JUST BE HONEST

In being open and candid, and by remaining true to ourselves, we acquire the confidence and trust of others and inspire professionalism in those around us. We all want to be the best, but our desire to prove it and stand out above our competitors can see us falling into the trap of wanting to appear perfect. The fear of being unsuccessful and unpopular can entice us to lie, deceive, hold back information, and misrepresent ourselves. As this chapter shows us, we do not gain from this. We are mistaken in thinking that these falsehoods will enhance our credibility, because they only enhance our vulnerability. When we lie, we are unbelievable, and when we act as if we are perfect, we are unconvincing. Both create suspicion, and neither wins us the support of clients or fellow entrepreneurs.

Being honest and transparent is challenging, for lying and pretending are often easier than being truthful. The examples we have seen illustrate how we must often fight with our conscience to do what is right. We fear that by telling the truth, we will damage our reputation, hurt people's feelings, and play into the hands of our competitors. To navigate our way through, we see how we must overcome our internal struggles, assume responsibility for speaking the truth, and avoid deception, out of respect for ourselves and others.

What is apparent within the chapter is how honesty changes our relationships with ourselves as individuals and with others. When we are honest with ourselves, we develop greater self-respect. Our positive self-image enables us to celebrate our uniqueness, accept who we are, and appreciate what we are capable of. As a result, we know our worth; because of this, we have sufficient belief in ourselves to successfully address our shortcomings. Rather than lie, distort, or put on an act, we present ourselves along with our existing strengths and put genuine effort into developing ourselves into the professionals we aspire to be. This makes us more credible and authentic and helps us keep it real.

When we are, in all sincerity, truthful, we empower people to make decisions. Our openness and candour strengthen rather than weaken the relationships we form with others. We have seen how, with the right approach, we can help others be more accepting of the truth. With an empathetic understanding, we generate feelings of a collaborative partnership that prompts clients and the business community to be equally frank and truthful with us. By having the courage to be honest, we can work more effectively in generating solutions to other people's problems as well as our own.

Our honesty will only change our relationships with others if we make the truth accessible and hold ourselves accountable. We must eliminate any mystique and uncertainty by being approachable, transparent, and willing to share information about ourselves and to justify our activities. As the examples in the chapter demonstrate, the onus is on us to adopt systems, policies, and practices that make our honesty and transparency self-evident and create the right environment for people to get to know us more personally. For when we give something of ourselves and show ourselves to be human, we get something back in return. We get to build strong, trusting relationships, in which all parties can directly share information and tell the truth comfortably without fear of the consequences. We get to be respected as professionals who consistently tell the truth because we have created conditions that remove personal insecurities and the discomfort of being forthright and honest.

Throughout this chapter, it is evident that creating these conditions demands a lot of us. No matter what situation or circumstances we find ourselves in, we need to resist the temptation to lie or mislead, and find the courage to speak the truth. With this, we must stay strong and deal with the inner turmoil and pain that comes with it. As professionals, we need to look beyond ourselves and appreciate the significance of truth in enabling our clients to make better choices. We cannot ignore the truth, even when others would prefer it if we did. To remain committed to being open and honest, we must develop our emotional intelligence and invest in relationships. Through our insight and personal development, we place ourselves in a better position to deliver the truth with empathy and help clients deal with the reality and the emotional discomfort it causes. To control the situation, we must learn to control our emotions in the process.

In addition to all this, we must be ready and willing to expose the real us, justify our actions, rationalise our decisions and hold ourselves accountable. We must overcome our fear of being judged when we are honest or admit our limitations and fallibilities. This requires us to accept scrutiny and evaluation by others and respond positively to constructive criticism received by acting on it.

It really is a tall order. What is evident from the discussion and examples within this chapter is that when we are self-respecting enough to uphold the values of honesty and transparency, we gain immeasurably. We must remember that if we focus on portraying ourselves as perfect, we misrepresent ourselves, we are led to act in unprofessional ways, and thus we lose all credibility. If we focus on being honest and transparent, we get to be trusted and respected by our clients and, with this, we can build our reputation. With our openness and willingness to accept criticism, we gain feedback and the support of our clients and others in business. We learn how to visibly be more honest and transparent and reconcile our dilemmas. Through this, we enhance the quality of our character and our business practices. We act with greater authenticity and genuine integrity, and that makes us trustworthy and credible. The more honest and transparent we are, the more honest and transparent we become. If we can tell the truth, accept the truth, and keep it real, we will never need to lie or deceive to succeed.

HOLD THAT THOUGHT

Being honest and transparent requires grit and determination. Without this strength of character, it is easy to deceive, with little thought of the impact on personal relationships or its consequences on our business. If we are to be authentic professionals, we must avoid self-deception. For if we lie to ourselves, we also lie to others. It is a form of self-sabotage, because when we allow dishonesty to creep in, we destroy the success we are working hard to build.

Honesty comes from within, and for it to be visibly apparent on the outside, we need to build a positive relationship with ourselves on the inside. Professionalism requires us to have self-respect. We must be proud of who we are, what we have achieved, and what it has taken to get here. When we are clear on our principles and values, we act appropriately and with the best intentions. With self-respect, we build and retain our authenticity because we do not feel a need to falsify information to obtain the validation of others.

If we struggle to tell the truth, accept the truth, and keep it real, we must ask ourselves why. The answer probably has little to do with an innate intention to deceive. Nor is it likely to stem from something we deliberately wish to hide from others. More likely, it is something that we are hiding from out of anxiety or a lack of confidence. So, what is it we fear about being honest and transparent? Because whatever it is, it is stopping us from being responsible and authentic professionals who are frank and caring, open, and receptive to the ideas and opinions of others. What is more, it is sapping us of the courage needed to take the more demanding route that allows us to uphold the values of honesty and transparency and grow and develop simultaneously. We will never be perfect, but that does not stop us from having authenticity, integrity, or credibility. Whatever we fear, it can be overcome. We just have to be honest enough to admit it. Only then can we change it.

5

RELIABILITY AND CONSISTENCY

FROM START TO FINISH AND BEYOND

Trusted professionals do what they say they will do and deliver what they promise to deliver time and time again. Both reliability and consistency are building blocks of trust. Reliability is important because it is the point at which our words turn into actions and validate the trust that has been extended to us. Reliability is all about following through. Every promise made needs to translate into positive action. This is the first 'big test,' and clients will be looking to see if we are on our mettle, paying close attention to how we return the trust they have extended. By being reliable, we reinforce the idea that we are not only right for the job but also trustworthy. On the other hand, if we cannot be relied upon to be honest, arrive on time, and do an excellent job, we lose trust and credibility. With this, we weaken relationships and jeopardise the chances of future work, which hampers business success.

Anyone can deliver great service once. If we want to keep our clients satisfied and deliver our services effectively and profitably, we need to prove we can do this on every occasion, to set ourselves apart and earn our reputation as someone who is both reliable and consistent. It is through consistency that we demonstrate our ability to replicate our performance. Establishing a track record for quality and commitment to every client, every time, will go a long way to enhancing our professional reputation.

This chapter examines why reliability and consistency are profoundly valued and make us distinctive. Here we get to explore the issue from our clients' perspective and see why such characteristics make us highly sought-after professionals. So, too, we get to see the damaging effects of their absence and the many ways unreliability and inconsistency affect ourselves and our clients. There is no doubt we start out with every good intention, but the best intentions do not always make for the best outcome. This leads us to explore the circumstances in which we can inadvertently make ourselves unreliable and how we need to hold ourselves accountable to take back control and limit our inconcistency.

Furthermore, we see that acting conscientiously, using effective systems, and adopting good habits lessen the opportunity for unreliability and inconsistency. Finally, we consider how we retain the momentum to remain reliable and dependable through self-discipline, reassuring ourselves and our current and future clients that we can, from start to finish, and beyond the here and now, deliver on our promises.

BREAK A PROMISE, SHATTER CONFIDENCE

When we have secured a client, one of the first things we do is set up some form of contract and seek an agreement to our terms and conditions. Typically, we present our overview of costs: what we will do, by when, and how we will keep clients informed throughout the process. To our clients, the promises we make are an assurance that something will happen. Unfortunately, when nothing does, the outcome for them is frustration and disappointment.

Not everyone proves themselves to be reliable, which makes it a valued trait. We all have a tale or two to share on how others have proved themselves inconsistent and unreliable. Unreliability presents itself in many ways. Take, for example, Mohammed, a fitness coach who was promised a website in six weeks, only for it to take 18, or Jonty, a property developer whose solicitor never responded to emails or returned calls. Christine, the owner of a printing company, outsourced her human resources management and regularly found herself chasing up documents and contracts purported to be 'on their way.' Not to mention Alison, a network marketer, who sat in all day waiting for a builder who never arrived.

What we see within these examples is the failure to follow through on the promises made. Naturally, there may be legitimate reasons for such delays or lack of response. After all, we do not work in isolation, and there are often processes to follow and things that need to be done in a systematic way. Sometimes, before we can progress, we may find ourselves waiting on a delivery from suppliers or awaiting information from other agencies and our clients themselves. Plenty goes on behind the scenes, and there is always more to our work than is visible on the surface. The journey we take in getting to the desired outcome is different from the one our clients will see or fully appreciate, and how they perceive the experience of doing business with us will differ from our perceptions. To clients, it matters not how the job is done. To them, what matters more is if what we say we will do actually gets done at all. The issues in the examples are one and the same. To be deemed reliable, we must manage our obligations and commitments to avoid disappointing our clients and tarnishing our reputation.

To clients like Mohammed, Jonty, Christine, and Alison, broken promises bring disappointment with wide-ranging ramifications. False impressions, lack of punctuality, missed appointments, and delays in project completion might seem like minor transgressions but, for the client, there can be consequences of varying magnitude. The knock-on effects of unreliability are hold-ups, inefficiency, and personal and financial inconvenience, not to mention unfulfilled hopes and dreams.

Behind any act of unreliability lies a multitude of messages that can be interpreted negatively. Clients regard it as a reflection of how they are perceived and valued. Being unreliable implies that we do not care and are not emotionally invested in our work or committed to resolving our clients' problems or serving their interests. It evokes feelings that we are disorganised, lack diligence, and are easily side-tracked. It gives the impression that we are without a sense of moral obligation, that we are self-centred and unappreciative of the impact our actions or inactions have. These represent characteristics that would define someone as unprofessional. We need to be conscious that unreliability, in any way, shape, or form, leaves us falling short of the mark by a long way. It does not take much for clients to lose faith in our ability and level of professionalism.

However, all is not lost. There is a point of redemption through communication. We are viewed more negatively when we fail to communicate the reasons and circumstances that led to our unreliability. People are more forgiving and willing to give us a second chance when there is prompt, honest, and direct communication, and an acknowledgement that we have lapsed somewhat. To some extent, most people will tolerate the odd slip-up and bout of forgetfulness. Life is unpredictable. Various crises and unforeseen events occur now and again. People appreciate that untoward incidents happen and they are ready to empathise when circumstances are beyond our control. If we are falling behind on schedules, it is always best to be upfront and keep clients informed because, by taking a timely and proactive approach, we grant clients some control over the situation. Together with the client, it is possible to agree on a revised way forward to sustain their confidence and protect our reputation. By adopting this approach, we deal with the issue head-on, making it less of an issue overall in the longer term.

BE AWARE! CONSEQUENCES STING

Communication is a basic expectation, and without advance notification, an explanation, or an apology, we increase the level of disappointment clients feel. A lack of communication exacerbates the situation, and we will indeed find ourselves losing clients, goodwill, and profits. Take, for example, Alison. Remember how she sat in all day waiting for a builder who did not turn up to provide a quote for some much-needed house maintenance? His no-show left Alison doubly disappointed. Alison's friend had recommended him based on his reliability. However, not only had the builder failed to turn up, but he had failed to live up to the endorsement of Alison's friend. The fact that the builder had not communicated furthered Alison's disappointment and raised her suspicions even more. In Alison's own words: 'If they are not capable of picking up the phone, what else are they not capable of?' Being unreliable early on in a relationship creates the anticipation of future disappointments. Not wanting to take that risk, Alison looked for another builder. The overall impact for Alison was one of wasted time. She could have been doing something more constructive with her day. Instead, she was left having to find the time to check out and contact other builders.

For Ellen, an independent author, other people's mistakes cost her financially and potentially damaged her reputation. What is more, they inconvenienced many people other than Ellen herself.

Ellen had sought the services of a book-formatting company to professionally prepare the manuscript of her first novel and upload this onto Amazon, the e-commerce site. She was extremely impressed; the process was smooth and efficient, and she had regular communication and support from a pleasant and efficient employee within the company. So naturally, Ellen used the same company for her next novel. This time her experience was hugely different. The efficient employee had left. The person she was assigned to was, in Ellen's words, 'not a people person' and turned out to be someone who made too many assumptions about what Ellen would be happy with. When the proof copy arrived, there were many inaccuracies, and it contained sections of material from someone else's book. Consequently, it took a long time to arrive at a version Ellen was happy to approve. A few days later, to Ellen's horror, she discovered the version on Amazon was not the one she had approved.

Despite the evidence, Ellen had a battle on her hands in correcting the mistake: the company refused to admit the blunder and adopted what Ellen describes as 'aggressive tactics' to criticise her rather than accept responsibility. It took the threat of non-payment of her outstanding balance to get the book removed from the Amazon platform and the correct version uploaded. In the interim several people had purchased the poorly formatted book, potentially affecting Ellen's reputation and the prospect of future sales. She had to delay and reschedule her marketing campaigns and book launch. Naturally, this inconvenienced her guests, the venue, and the event organisers. This one error had a significant impact. Ellen regrets using the company's services for a second time because the company fell short of meeting the high standards she previously experienced. Having extended her loyalty and entered a contract that had brought the company repeat business, Ellen no longer felt valued as a client.

A track record for repeated reliability is exceptional and a very appealing feature. Clients relish the thought of finding someone dependable. To them, it is like hitting the jackpot because where there is consistency, there is predictability. This generates positive feelings and reduces uncertainty. Clients know where they stand, what to expect, and the course of action we are likely to take on their behalf. This reinforces our level of professionalism. They see us as an efficient and productive individual rather than as someone who constantly flies by the seat of their pants. To this end, as far as business is concerned, our ability to remain reliable helps us build relationships and attract and retain loyal clients, and affords us longevity.

DEVELOP A CONSCIENCE

Ellen's story demonstrates how reliability depends on the capacity to be consistent. To be seen as professionals, we need to constantly deliver the same level of high-quality service time and time again. Clients expect a good job as standard at each point of contact and even more so with each return visit. History acts as a precedent for future expectations. Through inconsistency, we fail our clients and fail ourselves. To our clients, variable interactions, attitudes, systems, processes, and quality are profoundly troubling and tedious. All of this makes us less pleasurable to work with, and we become a burden to the very people who are paying for the privilege of our help and support. In being unreliable and inconsistent, we dash clients' hopes and we also confound their problems. They feel short-changed because they have received less of a service than expected and have been treated with contempt in the process. This makes us disreputable.

Alison's and Ellen's stories highlight that to be reliable and consistent, we need to have a conscience: one that guides us towards doing the right thing and leads us to take our obligations seriously. Having a conscience will likely keep us in business because it connects us emotionally with our work and makes us more invested in social relationships. It is our conscience that gives us a greater sense of duty. It provides us with the motivation to achieve a positive outcome for clients. On top of this, it makes us much more self-aware of our actions and their impact on others. Having a conscience prompts us to care about doing an excellent job at every stage and care for how we do it and the clients we are doing it for. Our conscience generates care and compassion and incites us to be mindful of the promises we make and the assurances we give.

The more conscientious we are, the more likely we are to deliver on such promises because being conscientious helps us to be better professionals by introducing deliberation. Our thoughts and attention to our obligations and our clients' needs allow us to be in control, so that we resist the urge to promise the earth without assessing what is realistically achievable. When we are conscientious, we avoid doing things that are likely to damage our reputation. This allows us to be disciplined, behave responsibly, be more thorough, and do a good job in an organised way. It makes us diligent. We pay attention to detail and invest in ways to achieve our goals and deliver on our promises.

In business, it is all too easy to overpromise and underdeliver. It is natural to want to please potential new clients and tell them what they want to hear to secure their business. After all, who wants work going to a competitor? Survival in business requires a can-do attitude and high levels of self-confidence. Yet these positive traits could be our downfall, particularly if we are keen to portray that nothing is too much trouble. In the eagerness and excitement, we can soon fall foul of making an unrealistic commitment. Promising clients the moon on a stick and that which is unachievable only serves to build false expectations. When we overpromise, we are really setting ourselves up to be unreliable.

As Tom, who provides clean air systems, says: 'No good turn goes unpunished.' In our hearts, we might believe that anything is possible. However, whilst we set out with every good intention, things can go wrong and backfire on us. For example, if we agree to work within a short time scale when we cannot commit and deliver on our promises, people will think we are no good and we will soon lose credibility. To clients, overpromising is a form of deception. When we fail to do what we say, clients feel as if they have been conned. Consequently, they become disgruntled.

Confident professionals with an optimistic outlook are not the sort of people to say 'no,' but neither are they people who indiscriminately say 'yes.' To be sure we can commit, we must first assess the situation. We must be sure the promises we are about to make to our clients are realistic in the circumstances. This requires us to be honest with ourselves and with our clients.

We often overestimate what we can achieve within a given time frame. Taking on too much work is counterproductive as it diminishes our effectiveness. We believe we can multitask. Yet, in reality, it is not easy to perform tasks simultaneously or give equal and full attention to a series of competing priorities. We start the day thinking we have it so well planned out. We forget the potential to run into problems or the times when we might need to react to unexpected clients' needs. Without some flexibility in our day, we risk not being able to complete all the things we need or have promised to do.

If I had one superpower, it would be the power to say no. Invariably, I find myself overloaded with work. True, I like to be busy and not waste time. Yet there are times when I allow people to take advantage of that because I cannot say no without feeling guilty about disappointing people and letting them down. As I have developed and honed my self-assertion skills, I have realised that saying no is perfectly acceptable, primarily because saying no helps me protect existing priorities and set boundaries that permit a better work-life balance. By saying yes all the time, we are simply preventing the achievement of both our business and personal goals and ambitions. The word 'no' does not have to be the final word of a sentence. We can still help people as best we can and boost our reputation in the process. We might not have time to do the work, but we will have some time to listen and advise. This allows us to acknowledge the satisfaction we feel in being approached. Moreover, it provides an opportunity to point people who seek our services in the right direction. If we can make the proper referral to someone we know and trust, then we show ourselves to be someone who can be relied upon. For that, we will be admired, albeit in a small way.

The fact is that we cannot do everything because our time and energy are not infinite resources. We can only attend to so much at any one point in time. If we spread ourselves too thinly, we arrive at a state where we are overloaded with work and can no longer work at a steady pace. Having promised too much to too many people, we become stressed, distracted, and less productive, and burnout ensues. It leads us to take our eye off the ball. In doing so, we become less meticulous, and the quality of our work suffers. We neglect our responsibilities, and things slip down our to-do list or completely fall off the radar. In professional terms, we become a walking disaster, bearing the hallmarks of someone who cannot be relied upon.

BE IN CONTROL; LEAVE NOTHING TO CHANCE

We need to be organised to be fair to ourselves and to our clients, taking the time to plan and consider things carefully before we make promises. As Tom neatly points out: 'To act now would only mean apologising later.' Before we take on new clients or additional work, we need to see them in the context of a much bigger picture. Taking the time to accurately understand what we are already committed to, and are about to promise, is an investment in our professional reputation.

Considering clients' problems, and what it would take to meet their needs, enables us to view potential obstacles and bottlenecks alongside the time and resources needed to complete all the composite tasks. If we are mindful of all this, we are more likely to be upfront and less likely to overcommit and make false promises. Our reputation for reliability is largely under our control. Being reliable is very much something of our own making and is a delicately balanced practice. For each client, there is a tipping point at which our actions or inactions change how we are perceived. This moves us from being deemed someone who is reliable to being someone who is not.

To be reliable, we need to take control. If we do not, our reputation for reliability is left to chance. On the other hand, if we can resist being impulsive and plan before making promises to clients, we can build and protect our reputation for reliability. To replicate our performance, we must bring order to how we plan, operate, communicate, and function. This requires us to have systems in place to keep ourselves on course. Since we all work in different ways, it matters not what type of system we adopt, so long as it enables us to navigate and keep track of our progress to deliver on our promises.

For some of us, this takes the form of a to-do list in a diary or on a whiteboard. The list reminds us of what is important and focuses our minds on things that require our attention now. Both Yvonne, a network marketer, and Diana, a financial advisor, keep a diary and activity journal. They note the nature of their conversations with clients and the outcomes agreed upon. This helps to plan future actions and follow-up conversations and ensures clients receive the correct information at the right time. Others, like Sarah, a virtual assistant, use an electronic planner and task management system to set reminders, prioritise activities, and block out time. This helps her focus her efforts within a specified time frame to meet her deadlines. In addition, Sarah has introduced standardisation into her practices. By creating templates for letters and emails, she reduces the potential for errors and ensures essential tasks are not overlooked.

For recruitment consultants Steve and Georgina, the series of policies and procedures their staff members follow ensures that everyone takes a logical and systematic approach. These are designed to ensure everything gets documented correctly and nothing gets missed. The introduction of an automated communication and tracking system allows Steve and Georgina to measure and monitor activity. The data generated by these systems enable them to ascertain how effectively the system works at the client interface and provides them with information that assists in sustaining a reliable and consistent service. They have access to a wealth of information, allowing them to pre-empt and stave off any issues that might slow or delay processes. With this, they can deal with matters promptly and meet service-level agreements more effectively.

Our use of pen and paper, electronic apps, and automated systems helps us structure our day and manage our time, resources, and communications efficiently. It brings order and frees up time, so we can effectively get on and achieve other things. Through this, we create the capacity to act on what we say we will do and do things the way they are meant to be done, and to the standards expected, not just once, but every time for every client. Of course, none of this happens without a commitment to set up such systems and the discipline to use them continually. It would be no good setting up strategies and techniques to help us function better if we only used them intermittently when we could be bothered. This defeats the purpose and creates the type of inconsistency and unreliability such systems are designed to overcome.

It stands to reason that the more disciplined we are, the more consistent and reliable we will be. Being organised, systematic, and productive requires practice. We need to develop good habits and routines and learn to use our chosen systems effectively to be effective. If we are to adopt and implement a particular system, we need to hold ourselves accountable for making the best use of it. This often means prioritising our self-development, expanding our skill sets, and training those we might employ. The systems we choose to adopt will only ever be as effective as we are. As Neil, a graphic designer, points out: 'It's OK to develop ourselves and believe in the model and practices we set up, but we should not be so arrogant as to believe there are no better ways of doing things.' We can learn a lot by exploring what others do. Not only is it essential to have suitable systems in place, but we also need to be assured of their effectiveness in helping us stay on track, and replicate our performance, particularly as our business grows.

BE BOTH EQUITABLE AND EQUIPPED

Nothing impresses people more than an efficient delivery of a promise, but we must be able to maintain the momentum. It is easy to remain in control and on top of things when we have only a few clients, but as client numbers grow, we need to be able to stay true to our word and deliver the same great level of service. If we are to retain our credibility and reputation, our track record for reliability and consistency must be sustained. Clients not only want a great experience at each stage of their journey, but they also want to be confident they are getting the same great experience as all our other clients. When we generate consistency in our approach to different clients, we demonstrate our capacity to provide a fair and equitable experience.

People are easily offended if they think they are receiving a lower level of service. They take it personally and see it as a form of discrimination. Being equitable makes us more trustworthy and reinforces our professionalism, and there is no room for complacency. We must work to establish ways of being reliable and consistent that make our clients feel like individuals whilst at the same time ensuring fair and unbiased treatment.

Signing up a new client is always worthy of a celebration. However, the party will soon end unless we monitor our ability to deliver in line with the promises we make. The systems we adopt need to be fit for purpose and enable us to sustain our capacity for reliability and consistency. After all, this is what reinforces professionalism and sets us apart. Without monitoring our performance or gaining client feedback, we cannot measure our success or know where to improve. Fulfilling our promises and meeting expectations is a continual process.

Our ability to meet the needs of different clients at every stage of their journey, and replicate standards and behaviour, day in and day out, defines us. If we are neither reliable nor consistent, we are ineffective, which is reputationally damaging. If we find ourselves unable to deliver on the promises we make, then we need to reconsider our personal attitudes, values, and behaviours. As well as the systems we use, and the methods by which we hold ourselves accountable, we should also review our business growth strategy.

As our business grows, there will be a point at which we have too much work to handle. At this time, we need to consider either adjusting the volume of clients, buying in business support, outsourcing, subcontracting, or expanding our team. Whichever choice we make, we need to act fast to resolve the issue in order to avoid any discontinuity of service. Our capacity to remain reliable and consistent in times of growth speaks volumes about our sense of diligence and the extent to which we have the interests of our clients at heart.

It is great when we become a product of our own success and see our business go from strength to strength. It is a fantastic feeling to know that we are popular and in demand, not so much for the personal glory but for what it represents in terms of external professional admiration. There will come a time when we reach total capacity. For recruitment consultants Steve and Georgina, that day came when they realised they had no spare time and their working days were getting longer. They either had to forgo taking on new clients or, as Steve says, 'risk hitting the wall,' becoming exhausted and worn out from the sheer volume of work. Either way, they were going to hinder their success. They knew that with more clients, they risked damaging their reputation.

Without additional resources, they would be unlikely to fulfil their promises to existing clients or be able to provide a complete service to new clients.

Steve and Georgina took the time to plan their expansion strategy. They outsourced their CV database searching activities and recruited and trained new staff members before they took on any new clients. In adopting this approach, Steve and Georgina could sustain the quality of service for existing clients. Moreover, they could prevent any discontinuity in service and be confident that growth would not affect their productivity, reliability, and consistency, nor would it compromise the parity and quality of their service as they welcomed new clients.

By prioritising existing clients, we can protect our reputation. We must always remember that current clients have the potential to be loyal clients, but not if we alienate them by becoming tardy and unreliable. It is no good trying to retain the goodwill of existing clients as we start to expand if, at the end of that process, we undermine it. Existing clients will have come to value our dependability. With familiarity they expect similarity, and there should be no visible interruptions when it comes to providing a fair, equitable, reliable, and consistent service.

Business growth can be a time of excitement. With this, we tend to focus on expanding our client base and the profits that come with it. However, we learn from Steve and Georgina that, as we go through the expansion process, we must have one eye on the future and the other on the here and now. Our professionalism is not just reflected in the service we provide. It is reflected in the proactive way we ensure the continuity of our service. If we value customer loyalty, we must do everything possible to grow seamlessly. If we succeed with this, we also succeed in ensuring the seamless integration of new and existing clients, all receiving the same great level of service. This allows us to further our reputation for being reliable and consistent right through our client base.

COLLABORATE WITH CARE

Alongside the growth of our business, the very nature of our business may see us working in conjunction with others. It makes good business sense to broaden our appeal by offering a range of services. To do this, there is often a need to seek the support of other businesses with the resources and complementary skills that will enable us to provide a personalised and complete service.

Any form of joint working puts us at risk. Interdependency makes us vulnerable as we are at the mercy of the consistent and reliable behaviour of others. The people we collaborate with become part of a chain of activity and are often critical to completing an activity or project. This shared endeavour enables us to fulfil our promise to our clients – the very same clients who have placed their trust in us in the belief that we are steadfastly dependable. Anyone we contractually delegate aspects of a project to must be equally as competent, reliable, and trustworthy as we are.

To our clients, getting the right outcome in a timely manner is the only outcome. We will be remembered for the result more than we will be remembered for the process. Not only this, but if things go wrong, and the work of our collaborators falls short of meeting expected standards or requirements, we will be the ones deemed unreliable, because we were the ones who initially made promises and provided assurances of timeliness and quality. When things go off course, we cannot blame others as if we were not accountable. The fact of the matter is that we are very much part of the situation by virtue of our misjudgement of someone else's dependability. To avoid correcting other people's mistakes and ineffectiveness and preserve our reputation, we must take ownership of the situation and mitigate the risks.

Finding those who not only offer the services we require but are as conscientious and attentive as we are can be a challenge. There is a lot of groundwork to be done to be sure those we work with are not only reputable but hold the same values and work to the same standards as we do.

Abbi, a bespoke jewellery designer, produces unique individual pieces, often for special occasions. With this comes the pressure of producing something flawless within a specific time frame. To create the final product from her 3-D designs, Abbi must collaborate with companies with the expertise and technology to cast, assemble, and polish the items. It took Abbi a while to find the right people for the job. Before embarking on the process, she made personal connections with various companies and reviewed client testimonials. She did much research into the companies themselves, exploring their history and their suppliers, testing their honesty about meeting deadlines and the quality of their casting production. In addition, Abbi had developed her own criteria for the type of professional she was willing to work with. She needed to be sure she could trust them, knowing they were equally as committed as she is to working ethically and providing excellent quality and customer service.

Recruitment consultants Steve and Georgina outsource services to various companies that offer CV database searching services. For them, it works well. They can use these companies interchangeably: if one company cannot accommodate their needs at a particular time, Steve and Georgina approach another that can. If at any time a company falls short of meeting Steve's and Georgina's expectations, they can step away and cease working with them, and draw on other companies' services without significantly damaging their reputation. Before outsourcing their services, Steve and Georgina, like Abbi, do their research. However, Steve and Georgina initially test a company's performance with a small piece of work. If the company has found candidates matching their brief, it gets more contracts. If not, it gets paid for its work, and Steve and Georgina look elsewhere. It is a bit of a gamble, but in Steve's opinion: 'It's better to discover a lack of initiative and unreliability early on than when you have a significant amount of work from an esteemed client.'

Neil, a graphic designer, works in a similar way. He uses a variety of printing companies. Should he find himself using a company he has not worked with before, he asks for samples of materials they have previously printed and requests to be present at the first print run. As a sole trader, he is very conscious that he cannot afford for a client to be disappointed, nor can he personally afford to meet the expense of an extra print run. This approach reassures Neil that the printing company can deliver to the standards he and his clients expect. Moreover, if there is a problem, he can immediately intervene, saving his reputation and that of the company he is collaborating with.

Collaboration is something we should take our time over. We should only enter a collaboration when we have gone through a due diligence process to mitigate the risk of being let down by others. Abbi, Neil, Steve, and Georgina took ownership of their situations by gathering intelligence on which they could make informed decisions. When we evaluate and verify things for ourselves, we collect evidence that all we read and hear matches what we see. It is a form of quality control. To protect our reputation, we must feel confident that whomever we collaborate with can be relied upon. By having that confidence, we free ourselves of worry, which frees us up to do other things.

It is not just about finding the right person or company to collaborate with. It is also about being the right collaborator ourselves. When we collaborate, we rarely work independently of each other. Our collaborators will be expecting things from us to be able to do their job effectively. Abbi wanted to feel she could trust others to work well in her desired ways. Getting to that point meant she had to establish mutual trust. Abbi sets about getting to know people and engaging with them in ways that create a shared understanding of the intricacies of the work they each do. This helps generate respect for each other's expertise. It also brings about an appreciation of the responsibilities each has to the other so they can jointly get to the desired outcome. Abbi has a clear idea of how thorough, reliable, and consistent she needs to be for her collaborators to do their part of the job. Unless we model the standards of reliability and consistency, we cannot expect others to behave similarly. We risk being let down by virtue of our contrary behaviour, and with this, we risk our reputation.

CONTINUE TO LIVE THAT FIRST IMPRESSION

Professionalism demands that we always present the best version of ourselves. Those we meet will be expecting to see the same version of our best selves time and time again. As well as consistency in how we carry out tasks, perform and operate as a business, clients anticipate that we will, as a person, show emotional consistency. Regardless of the circumstances we find ourselves in, clients will expect us to remain respectful to them and to treat everyone we meet the same. Our attitudes towards clients and our temperament need to be affirmative and harmoniously aligned with our values. Any variation in our mood, manner, and conduct will negatively affect client relationships and levels of trust.

If we have successfully secured business, then the chances are we will have created a good impression. There is nothing like the prospect of a new client to motivate us to adopt good habits and behave professionally. We will have dressed well and greeted our client with a smile. We might even have prepared in advance. Maybe we tidied up or conducted some preliminary research. We will undoubtedly have been polite and respectful and chosen our words carefully. We will probably have been attentive and taken the time to understand our client's needs. We will have expressed great empathy and maybe lightened the mood with a bit of humour here and there. Without a doubt, we will have made bold statements about our attitude and values that provided reassurance of how much we love what we do, how principled we are, and how delighted we are to help. Finally, we will have put their mind at rest by telling them nothing will ever be too much trouble and they should not hesitate to pick up the phone and contact us.

With this, our clients leave feeling special. They believe they have found the very person who can help them because it appears we genuinely understand their situation. In their mind's eye, they feel lucky that someone so lovely and kind is there to guide them, support them, and solve their problem. They feel in safe hands because the gestures played out and the story we have portrayed demonstrate authenticity and reliability.

However, that great first impression must endure if we value customer loyalty and wish to preserve our credibility and reputation. The positive image we created to secure a client sets the precedent. Clients leave believing that the level of interpersonal engagement, humanistic values, and emotional behaviours that we show truly reflect who we are.

Outside our working environment, we are not the same person as we are within it. As we live our lives, different aspects of our personality can be observed through our interactions. Only the closest to us see what we are truly like as people. For the most part, clients only get to see a small aspect of who we really are. To them, we tend to present our public-facing persona. Nonetheless, clients will expect consistency in the way we conduct ourselves.

Life always has its stresses, whether related to work or home. At some point, some unexpected situation will preoccupy us or create an inner tension that destabilises our otherwise happy mood. Our emotions affect how we think, how we work alongside others, and how we interact with them. Any negative feelings generate the potential for us to react and respond to clients in ways that deviate from the professional conduct they have come to experience and expect. In such cases, our actions are often unintentional and manifest in subtle ways. We are probably unaware that we are showing ourselves in a very different light. If we are curt, less engaged, unsympathetic, or suddenly indifferent, when we were once courteous, attentive, compassionate, and falling over ourselves to help, there is a change within us that exemplifies a shift from being professional to being unprofessional.

MIXED SIGNALS LEAD TO SECOND THOUGHTS

However momentary our transgression may be to our clients, it represents an inconsistency that mirrors a scene from Robert Louis Stevenson's book, *Strange case of Dr Jekyll and Mr Hyde*. To clients, it looks as if we have suddenly acquired a dual personality. They thought we were akin to the kind and considerate Dr Jekyll, but our actions now suggest that, like Mr Hyde, we have a more selfish and menacing side. This leaves clients questioning which one of the two characters we are, and which one is likely to turn up at the next meeting.

Our contradictory attitudes and emotional responses are probably more reflective of what else is going on in our business or lives at the time than they are to do with any of our clients. Yet clients will see it differently. To them, it is personal and generates a great deal of anxiety and uncertainty. Our unexpected actions and reactions leave clients doubting themselves and us at the same time. Whilst wondering what they might have done to provoke such a response, they are also examining why they no longer have a sense of who we really are and what we stand for. A lack of emotional consistency creates doubt in the minds of our clients because we are different from the person they originally believed us to be. With an unpredictable nature and emotional inconsistency, we send mixed messages about our personality, values, and commitment to serving our clients' interests. We appear false if we fail to replicate the attitudes and personal traits we initially displayed. This leads clients to question our personal qualities, and wherever there is doubt, there is distrust.

To clients, emotional extremes become an obstacle they must navigate their way around. Any variability in how we engage and interact makes clients feel tense because the onus is on them to guess how we are feeling. No one likes to feel they are constantly having to walk on eggshells. This introduces an element of fear and resentment and we become more trouble than we are worth. When clients find themselves having to make more of an effort to feel valued, they will soon take their business elsewhere.

There is no escaping the fact that we, as individuals, are steered by our emotions. It comes as no surprise that emotional consistency takes effort. However, consistency creates predictability. For clients, this brings an element of comfort because they know what to expect, which makes us someone they can depend on. Since clients expect the best of us with each interaction, improving our self-awareness and developing our emotional intelligence becomes even more pertinent. By recognising and managing our emotions positively, we stand a better chance of presenting our best professional selves when life and work present us with challenges or unexpected problems. Reliability and consistency strengthen our integrity and help to secure stable client relationships that lead to loyalty. When we blow hot and then blow cold, we show ambivalence. This shakes the foundation of the relationship our clients have worked equally hard to build.

EVERY CLIENT'S JOURNEY HAS A START, MIDDLE, AND END

Throughout this chapter, we have seen how reliability and consistency are highly sought-after characteristics. By putting words into action, we show a commitment to acting responsibly and doing the right thing in the interest of our clients. This makes us trustworthy. The reward for the confidence, happiness, and satisfaction our clients feel as we deliver an excellent service, time and time again, is loyalty. Everyone is a winner. Yet it is far easier to make a promise than deliver on it. When we show ourselves to be unreliable and inconsistent, frustration and disappointment ensue, and suspicions are raised. Everyone loses out. Our clients are left inconvenienced, cleaning up the mess we created as we stand there kicking ourselves because we missed the mark and let things slip.

In business, every client is a business-sustaining opportunity. To benefit financially and enhance our credibility and reputation, every promise must be followed up with planned and executed actions. To achieve this, we must be in control of the situation and act conscientiously. This brings us back once again to the issue of accountability. Not only must we make promises we know we can fulfil, but we must also, having made those promises, be sure to fulfil them. Professionalism comes when we take our obligations seriously, seize control and live up to the positive impressions we have created.

To avoid letting ourselves and our clients down, we must organise ourselves. From the outset, we must be equipped and well-prepared. To stay on top of our existing workload, commit to new clients, and deliver the same high-quality service time and time again, we must lessen the opportunity for unreliability and inconsistency to arise. This requires us to be honest and selective, and to put quality ahead of quantity. We have seen how it is counterproductive to overpromise or indiscriminately say yes to everything without first considering what is involved and required. Moreover, if we do not have effective systems to manage our time, resources, and communications effectively, or we do not seek to collaborate with those who share our work ethics, we potentially make ourselves unreliable.

Even if we are well prepared and confident that we can deliver on our promises to the expected standards, we need to reach the endpoint. We need to know we can rely on ourselves to keep up the momentum and enhance client confidence by being unvaryingly attentive, fair, and equitable in the process. However, things are always easier said than done. As we stride into action, we enter a danger zone. It is at the point in the middle that we are most likely to take our eye off the ball and see it all fall apart.

This happens when our days are full of competing priorities, and we find ourselves dealing with the unexpected. It is here that we often get side-tracked. We lose sight of our priorities and miss deadlines; we neglect to communicate or record and systematically document things; we become tempted to cut corners or compromise on standards. As our stress levels rise, our emotions change. Before we know it, we have gone back on our word, broken rules, destabilised relationships, and undermined our integrity.

In this chapter, we have seen how developing a conscience fuels a sense of duty, something that is needed in the middle phase of our client's journey more than at any other point in time. In the hectic world of business, our conscience gives us the strength and ability to value clients in more considerate ways. Amidst the hustle and bustle of the working day, being conscientious helps us to proactively sustain our commitment to clients, knowing our actions and inaction affect their lives and our reputation.

The outcome is determined by how mindful we are of our actions, in line with the initial impressions we created and the assurances we gave. Of course, the ultimate endpoint should be happy ever after for all, where we see one satisfied, loyal client after another and a business that is booming. But, as we have seen, it takes self-discipline, emotional intelligence, skill development, and new habits to cross the finish line with our heads held high.

As we conclude our work with one client, we start working with another, so the cycle continues. With each client, we are building a track record that we need to monitor to ensure we can improve or sustain our performance, not least because reliability and consistency are highly valued by clients and profoundly associated with trust and loyalty. If we show ourselves to be reliable and consistent, people will want to share their happiness and satisfaction. This helps us build a positive reputation, but it comes with a permanent expectation that, regardless of circumstances, growth, and success, we will forever remain reliable and dependable. If we prove ourselves unreliable and inconsistent, clients will call us out to avoid others having to go through the same disappointments, frustrations, and inconveniences. These things are not inconsequential. It makes it harder to prove to potential clients that we are anything but third-rate when it comes to commitment.

As professionals, we need to look beyond the outcome. The endpoint for our client is different from the endpoint for us. We must keep going. Whether we have proved ourselves reliable or unreliable, we have only one real course of action: to go forward. If we want to show how much we value clients, we must show integrity. This means we will always need to diligently invest in ways to keep our word and not allow our commitment to fade. It is only by holding ourselves to account that we get the inner confidence to know that when we make a promise, we can rely on ourselves to fulfil it in a conscientious, reliable, and consistent way.

HOLD THAT THOUGHT

Reliability and consistency are desirable professional characteristics that win the hearts and minds of clients. Yet these are not inherent traits. Instead, they derive from the conscious choices we make and the actions we take. Reliability and consistency are no more than an accumulation of good habits that engage us with the task at hand. They are, however, critical habits because our integrity, trustworthiness, reputation, and overall success depend on them.

The difference between those who have mastered the art of being reliable and consistent and those who have yet to do so is simply a matter of priority and self-discipline. Fundamentally, we all have an equal chance of success if we prioritise our clients, standards, and self-image. When we do, we are inclined to invest our time, energy, and resources to discover how reliable and consistent we are and to commit to addressing our shortcomings.

The answer to becoming reliable rests in recognising and breaking bad habits and developing and applying good ones. Reliability comes when we engage in effective routines and activities that help us meet clients' expectations. To achieve consistency in the longer term we need to ask ourselves this: when it comes to developing good habits and implementing routines, how self-disciplined are we in ensuring that they become second nature and an automatic part of our everyday practice?

Professionalism demands proficiency and the willpower and determination to build and improve our performance. It requires that we train ourselves to be the best we can be. We can only take control and live up to the positive impressions we create when we prioritise our self-development, avoid variability and stay the course. Our actions act as a prototype, a model for the future. From start to finish, we must be self-disciplined enough to establish and perpetuate reliable and consistent practices to deliver the reliable and consistent service our clients truly value.

6

DIGNITY AND RESPECT

MAKE IT WORK BOTH WAYS

How we behave towards others speaks volumes about the values we hold. There is an expectation that, as individual members of society, we will appreciate people for who they are and treat them as we would wish to be treated. By affording others dignity and respect, we help to build trusting relationships, which transcend our business activity to create a more secure, happier, and harmonious society.

Respect can be appreciated in two ways: it can be something we earn and something we give. The two are not exclusive, in so far as to earn it, we must be prepared to continually demonstrate it through our words and actions. In doing so, we create an impression that leads us to be admired and held in high regard by others. This furthers the potential for business and allows us to garner goodwill and support and to inspire others to follow our lead. Quite simply, life gets better for us and everyone else when we incorporate and model the values of dignity and respect.

However, modelling these values requires us to pursue endeavours beyond direct interactions in the here and now. As professionals, we must create an atmosphere of dignity and respect in which these values are directly observable at all times throughout our lines of communication, standards of practice, and business operations.

Respect centres around the concept of unconditional human kindness. It comes with the expectation that we will unselfishly act in courteous and considerate ways. Dignity is founded on the notion of individuality. It is an extended form of respect. It relies upon our capacity to acknowledge people's distinct characteristics and differences and accommodate their personal needs to avoid showing disrespect. In business, if we are to exude dignity and respect, we must protect our clients and ourselves from being shown a lack of respect. The absence of dignity and respect destabilises our endeavours to secure vital, trusting relationships and continued business. Hence, as professionals, not only must we value others without discrimination, but we must also value ourselves enough to ensure dignity and respect work both ways.

This chapter starts by exploring how our respect for others influences the extent to which we forge relationships and come to be admired. The need to acknowledge individuality means that we cannot assume one size fits all. With this in mind, we consider the significance of getting to know clients personally and developing our emotional intelligence to respond sensitively and respectfully. Dignity and respect manifest in direct and subtle ways. As we progress, we see how we can create an atmosphere of care and respect by enhancing the quality of our interactions, establishing boundaries, and attending to our surroundings. Not surprisingly, all of this sits alongside a discussion that focuses on avoiding and managing disrespect. In this discussion, we consider the importance of self-respect and self-possession as means of acknowledging how we also wish to be treated, and how they influence our ability to remain professional and uphold these values in challenging circumstances.

ASPIRE TO INSPIRE, IN ORDER TO BE ADMIRED

Only when we sincerely invest in relationships, establish our credibility, act with professionalism, and prove ourselves trustworthy, do we earn the respect of others. This respect is born out of admiration for our personal characteristics, values, committed actions, and personal success. To earn the respect of others, be they clients, business associates, or fellow networkers, we must exemplify professionalism through our work. For this to happen, we must not only meet their exacting standards but exceed them. Over a long period, we need to create such a good impression that others are willing to hold us in high regard.

People do not admire everyone on the same level. We must make an effort to demonstrate dignity and respect if we want to be admired and respected beyond the norm. We cannot command people's respect, but we can, through our professional actions, influence the impressions we make.

When we enter business or join a new group, some part of us naïvely thinks that by telling others what we do and what we have achieved, we will suddenly be admired and respected. Without a doubt, we will currently have clients, business associates and fellow networkers who admire us. However, the chances are these people have come to know us exceptionally well. This is a crucial issue because people will only afford us this type of respect when they deem us credible and trustworthy, which, as we know from Chapter 3, takes time.

We will not earn the respect of everyone we meet or forge relationships with. This is because admiration is based on individual preference and is linked to personal emotions. The admiration people have for us stems from how they feel about us. This is based on our distinctive characteristics and talents: we come to be admired because something about us stands out compared to others, be it our charm, strength of character, zest for life, proficiency, or accomplishments.

Admiration represents a seal of approval and a form of appreciation. It is an expression of gratitude in response to the satisfying feelings people experience when in the company of others. People like to be associated with those who share similar values and ideals. This is mainly because seeing such ideals and virtues being played out by others, and experiencing what happens as a result, promotes feelings of contentment. People are touched by pride when they experience, share, and believe in the merits of those they know and are associated with.

We acquire admiration when people identify with us or want to be like us and to make all that we are, and all that we have achieved, part of their own identity. To those who admire us, we symbolise a desired state of being; we are someone they aspire to emulate. We might not be conscious of it, but our distinctiveness can inspire people to be a better version of themselves. When we inspire people, they are inspired to act. In a heightened motivational state, they feel confident, happy, energised, and eager to progress with their personal goals.

People will look up to us and want to follow in our footsteps when we have positively inspired or influenced them and changed or transformed an outcome. We stand out when we are perceived in some way to have made a difference, either to their world, their lives or those of others. If we are fortunate enough to have gained someone's respect this way, we are in a very privileged position indeed. We only get this type of respect when others judge us to be worthy of it.

WHAT MATTERS IS THAT EVERYONE MATTERS

Being admired certainly makes us more attractive to work with and gives us leverage to maximise business opportunities. Existing clients return out of loyalty; new clients or other businesses are keen to work and collaborate with us, and we get to generate business through referrals, recommendations, and partnerships. However, this is only an advantage if we continue to act in the ways that led to us earning that respect in the first place. To have earned respect from our clients, associates, and the communities we are part of, we must have treated them – and everyone else we meet, for that matter – with respect.

The need for respect is instilled in us from a young age. We are brought up to respect and honour people around us for no other reason than the fact that they are human. Therefore, great importance is placed on manners. Our teachers, and those who care for us, guide us to act in considerate ways and treat others as we would want to be treated. We are reminded to say please and thank you and not to interrupt. We are encouraged to tell the truth, not to say or do hurtful things, to share, and include others in our activities. This is because respect is a form of social glue. It keeps society together. There is a shared expectation that regardless of age, gender, sexuality, race, ethnicity, or ability, everyone is entitled to receive the respect of others. Respect is, therefore, an affirming act and in showing it, we value the very existence of others within our world, no matter who they are or how we come to meet and know them.

When respect is shown to us as individuals, we feel loved, appreciated, and secure. It heightens our sense of belonging and self-worth and motivates us to reciprocate that respect. Without respect, the world would be very hostile and unfriendly. It is a powerful force, essential to building trust, creating harmony, and preventing harm.

We cannot convey respect without treating others with dignity. The two are linked. Dignity propels respect from a simple, courteous interaction to one that recognises individuality and acknowledges personal identity and the right to independence. To treat people with dignity, we must behave ethically in ways that do not dehumanise individuals or undermine their autonomy. Our clients will approach us with the expectation that we will value and respect their wishes, privacy, ideas, and opinions. Moreover, they anticipate being included and informed, having the right to choose, and being in control of their decisions.

The act of showing respect and dignity makes people feel safe and secure, which consequently reduces stress levels. Furthermore, by treating everyone with kindness and dignity, we encourage trust and cultivate situations that allow greater freedom of expression, co-operative engagement, equality, and a positive sense of well-being for all.

GIVE IT TO GET IT

When it comes to respecting others, what goes around comes around. If we show respect to others, they will almost certainly return it. If we fail to show respect, we can expect to receive little, if any, in return. Respect is both reciprocal and infectious because positive affirmations lead to positive responses. Respect creates personal contentment and leaves us with a sense of gratification. Through our happiness, we elect to pay it forward, which has a cascading effect. We invariably respond to the respect we receive by being respectful to anyone we happen to meet. In turn, these people are likely to show similar kindness to others. In this regard, there is a cyclical aspect to it.

Everything we say or do signifies the value we place on others. Our words and actions are like a litmus test. People will use these as a baseline reference point to establish what we are like. If those we interact with do not feel respected, or if they see us being disrespectful towards others, they are unlikely to admire us, no matter how talented we are in other ways. Only when we are constantly respectful do we earn greater respect from others. People will only hold us in high regard when we primarily act in ways that build trust, create a sense of well-being, and promote respectful values.

To that end, we as individuals have a role in creating and supporting a culture of dignity and respect where everyone is valued, regardless of their personal qualities and physical and mental attributes. As professionals, we must promote and model respectful values and behaviours with sincerity. We must respect others even if we do not feel they have earned it. Without a doubt, it is far easier to respect people we like and those we have things in common with than those we do not. But to be considered professional, we must respect everyone in equal measure. We cannot pick and choose to whom we show respect. We must treat everyone fairly and equitably and not discriminate.

This does not mean we have to admire everyone we meet. What it does mean, however, is that we must continually adopt a respectful attitude. We must put aside our prejudices and biases and suspend our judgement, even when there are aspects of someone's character that we do not like, or when they display attitudes, values, and behaviours that we do not agree with. This can be hard, uncomfortable, and frustrating. Thus, it requires us to draw on our better qualities and have the presence of mind to act with restraint.

RESPECT DIFFERENCES AND RADIATE SINCERITY

Everyone wants respect. Our clients want respect, and so do our business associates and fellow networkers. Yet there is a combination of expectations. Everyone wants the same thing, but at the same time, everyone wants different things. Our clients arrive expecting a warm welcome that leaves them feeling happy, safe, and valued. At the same time, they want a personalised service that aligns with their individual needs. They anticipate the personal touch on two levels. First, clients expect to be given respectful attention. They count on being shown courtesy and kindness and envisage that we will treat them equitably and fairly. Second, they hope we will make them feel special by respecting their differences.

It is within us all to act in such ways, but it is not always within us to do it with sincerity. We can all pretend to be friendly and suck up to people to get their business. However, clients will soon see through this pretence; in the longer term, this will not serve us or our business well. The respect we show must be genuine and naturally come from the heart. To be professional, there must be sincerity behind our words and actions and an appreciation of what it is like to stand in our clients' shoes. This means we must understand the type of service they expect to receive and be ready to deliver it. Clients are confidently reassured when we have a passion for what we do, a strong desire to help, and a genuine interest in them, over and above ourselves or our profits. If clients are to trust us, they must believe we are acting with feeling. What we express on the outside must match what we feel on the inside if we are to be considered authentic.

We can only give attention and make clients feel special when we genuinely appreciate them for who they are and are concerned with meeting their individual needs. To show respect with sincerity, we must get to know our clients personally. As professionals, we must do this with an open mind and suspend our assumptions about our clients' expectations. This is important because, to others, the world is not as we see it. It is wrong to assume that our behaviour is universally accepted as the right way to conduct oneself.

Only when we get to know our clients on a much deeper level do we begin to increase our understanding of their situation, feelings, and frame of mind. With this comes insight into their values and the extent to which we have personal or cultural similarities and differences. Consequently, we begin to see our clients as individuals, and to acknowledge and accept them as such. The insight we gain increases our ability to understand our clients and recognise their customs and values. Only when we begin to see things through the eyes of others can we respond with sensitivity and respect and be more aware of what actions are appropriate and those which are likely to offend.

Iain, an electrician, lives and works in a multicultural area, so understanding ethnic and cultural diversity is critical to his business. He feels he works harder than most of his contemporaries to mitigate his prejudice and biases. Iain believes cultural differences should not serve as barriers to being respectful. Keen to broaden his perspectives, Iain made it his business to get to know people from different ethnic and cultural backgrounds. He asked them questions and took an interest in learning more about their faith. He wanted to feel confident serving his clients well by adhering to their cultural and religious traditions as he entered their homes. For Iain, this has a positive impact: he gets regular work and referrals. In his words: 'They respect me more because I showed a genuine interest, cared to listen and act when others simply could not care less.'

We see here that the personal discoveries we make through our interactions are significant and serve as an extension of our knowledge and expertise. In seeking to understand, we improve our ability to interact, relate to our clients, and flexibly adapt to their needs. This lessens the chances of any misunderstanding and helps us be more respectful towards our clients, which in turn enhances their respect for us.

SMALL ACTIONS, BIG IMPACT

Conversations are, therefore, central to building mutual respect. The extent to which we are willing to invest in building a relationship with our clients is a mark of our respect. It is, however, the quality of the interaction that humanises and dignifies the exchange and affirms our sincerity. Creating an atmosphere of respect is more than just a matter of taking time to engage with clients. Respect transpires through what we say, how we say it, how well we listen, and how appropriately we respond. This requires us to have good verbal and non-verbal communication skills. It is not the intention here to give a lesson on how to communicate, but to emphasise that respect is reflected in how we approach and engage with our clients.

What is evident is that we do not have to go all out with whistles and bells to show we value our clients. The small things often make the most significant difference when building mutual respect. We make the biggest impact when we display the type of respect that clients value the most, and what matters most often comes down to basics.

This can be anything from pronouncing our clients' names correctly to minimising distractions or avoiding technical jargon. Respect is reflected in how we show discretion, secure data, protect privacy, and ensure confidentiality. It is marked by the patience we show in holding back from giving our opinion until we have heard our client's point of view. It is evident in how we ask focused questions and listen attentively, as well as through the amount of time and space we give clients to think through the options before deciding.

The personal touch certainly goes a long way towards forging respectful relationships. Collectively, these small actions help develop mutual respect, creating harmonious working relationships and better outcomes for our clients and ourselves. In doing these things for every client, we signal how much we value and appreciate them.

Adam, who owns a computer repair company, checks in with clients several times after he has repaired their laptops and workstations and before he issues an invoice. He does so to put their minds at ease and take the fear out of contacting him should problems persist. From a cash flow and administrative perspective, it would make better sense to collect payment on completion of service. Yet Adam waits because, in his words: 'I want to know I have done a good job and the only way of knowing that is to care about how the equipment and applications function according to my clients' needs.' It is a good point, highlighting that respect encapsulates our ability to see into clients' everyday lives and appreciate what lies beyond the direct interactions and the service we provide in the here and now.

Iain holds a similar view. After completing a job, he takes time to clean up and dispose of any rubbish. He feels strongly about the need to respect people's property but also appreciates how disruptive renovations and repairs to the home can be. Untidiness has a negative impact on people's emotions. To Iain, relieving clients of this stress is a vital part of service. Cleaning up means he finishes the job properly and restores some order and normality to the homes of his clients. We learn from Adam and Iain that the level of respect we show needs to emanate from a much broader personal regard for clients' feelings and the day-to-day reality of their lives.

SURPRISE, SURPRISE!

When we show due regard to clients' circumstances, emotions, lifestyles, needs, and viewpoints, we build a personal and unique experience. This makes clients feel special, and even more so when we can add an element of surprise. Neil, a graphic designer, wishes to leave his clients on a confident high as projects end. For Neil, the design process often develops through digital interactions. At the end of a project, it would be easy to package up the printed materials, send them by courier, and then email his clients to thank them. Instead, Neil personally delivers the final printed artwork, flyers, and brochures. It is a gesture that, for his clients, is a pleasant surprise. Yet one which serves as an opportunity for Neil to have an additional conversation in which he can earnestly convey his appreciation for their patronage. As Neil says: 'Sometimes, to stand out from our competitors, we must think outside the box and go beyond our clients' expectations.'

A thank you is a respectful acknowledgement of gratitude for supporting our business – one that is frequently overlooked. Having completed the work, our brains often move on as we think about our next client. Sometimes, we believe that people should be thanking us. After all, we did the work and solved their problems. Nonetheless, business is not a state of entitlement. On the contrary, in a competitive world where others would envy our success, we should feel privileged to have our clients' support since they ultimately keep us in business. This makes a show of our appreciation even more critical.

Just as we need to make a positive first impression, so do we need to make a positive concluding one. Our clients anticipate courteous respect throughout their journey, from beginning to end. No matter how proficient we have been, a lack of good manners in the closing stages of business quashes previous beliefs in our character. Ungracious behaviour and thoughtlessness on our part lead people to think we are inconsiderate and uncaring. Without consciously taking the time to say thank you, we discredit ourselves and lose the trust and respect of the clients we worked hard to secure.

Saying thank you might reflect and define the end of a project, but it does not signify the end of a relationship. We sometimes think of a thank you in terms of a goodbye, when really it is a 'goodbye for now' because expressions of gratitude act as a springboard for future business. Failing to voice our thanks is a missed opportunity to strengthen personal connections and create an opening for future interactions. It is both the gratitude we express and the way we communicate it that make us memorable. By adopting a personalised and distinctive approach, we enhance our clients' overall experience. This reinforces the value we place on our clients, and with this comes an assurance that we do not just value the work; we value those we work with. The respect we have for our clients generates positive energy, the kind which motivates them to offer us their repeat custom, which grants our business longevity.

OFFER THE GIFT OF TIME

The respect we have for others is not always portrayed through interpersonal communication. We show respect in less tangible and subtler ways, often without direct interaction. It is not necessarily what we say that makes us respectful. What we do and how we behave also reveal the extent to which we value others. We do not have to be in the presence of someone to be discourteous. How we act behind the scenes can also be very telling of just how sincere we are.

There is no doubt that running a business is time-consuming. Our dedication and commitment to success often see us working long and unusual hours. Time is precious; naturally, we are keen to use it effectively. With so much to do and so few people to do it for us, we get annoyed and frustrated if our time could be better spent. It is exasperating when our well-planned schedule goes awry, particularly if those we arranged to meet arrive late or entirely unprepared. The same is true when people seem unmindful that they are talking too much and outstaying their welcome. With an ever-expanding to-do list, we can easily slip into thinking that our time is more valuable than that of others. If we are to respect clients, we need to believe that their time is just as valuable as our own.

We must remember that when clients have booked an appointment, they have put time aside to see us. We convey respect when we hold ourselves accountable by being realistic about what we can achieve in any given time frame and by honouring the commitments we have made.

If there is one sure way to irritate clients, it is to arrive late or not devote the amount of time their circumstances warrant. We often espouse the principle of 'better late than never.' However, when we apply this notion, we assume that our clients are not restricted by time. If we arrive later than agreed, we risk an unsatisfactory outcome and a meeting cut short because either we or our clients must leave to be elsewhere. Clients feel insulted, short-changed, and undervalued. Late arrival and early departure on our part suggest that we are inconsiderate and full of self-importance. We should consider this when we agree to squeeze clients into our busy schedules, as such honourable intentions become a great disservice when, after only ten minutes, we find ourselves ushering people out of the door because we have many more things to do.

There are limits to our time and that of our clients. The time clients have available is not ours to determine. They, too, have duties, responsibilities, and commitments that demand their attention. Respect comes through how we consider this when we arrange our appointments and engagements. Our ability to adhere to agreed times and grant sufficient time to tend to our clients' needs shows how much we value their time as equal to our own. At the end of the day, clients are paying for our time. The very least we can do is give them some.

Electrician Iain makes an interesting point about the need to respect our clients' time by not trespassing on their time. Much of Iain's work is conducted in family homes between 9am and 5pm, between Monday and Friday. Over the weekend, Iain often catches up with paperwork, quotes, and invoicing. He says: 'Rather than ping emails out at all hours, I schedule them to go out on weekdays before 5pm. People work hard like me. They want to unwind and spend time with their families rather than fret about the bill that has just landed in their inbox. I like to be efficient, but it is unfair to badger them.' Iain's point is that it is easy to become absorbed in our own world and to carry on without due regard for our client's free time. Sometimes, to show our respect, we need to step back and establish client-friendly boundaries, to avoid being thoughtless and selfish.

No one likes their time or money to be wasted. Seeing clients at the agreed time is one thing. Using the time we have set aside to do the work effectively is another. The extent to which we arrive prepared is a measure of how we value the need to be familiar with our client's situation. The effort we have put into planning and our ability to keep discussions focused on the needs of our clients indicate the level of respect we have for their priorities and needs. How we lay the groundwork, set up, and prepare shows how much we value our clients' time, happiness, safety, and welfare.

Our clients look for assurances that we have the time, energy, and inclination to prioritise their needs. We will gain their respect more readily if we manage our time effectively. Clients will want to feel that progress is being made. When we are tardy and fritter away time, we arouse suspicion. Clients think we are either grabbing the opportunity to raise their bill or are not disciplined enough to achieve their goals. Either way, it will lead them to question the service they are getting and how much they are genuinely valued and respected as a client.

SOPHISTICATED SUBTLETY MAKES A BOLD STATEMENT

The respect we show others is noticeable through physical communication and interactions. The words we choose, the tone of our voice, our emotional response combined with our level of eye contact, and other non-verbal gestures signify our regard for others. Yet the environment we create, the resources we use, the services we provide, and the provisions we make also create an atmosphere of respect. These intangible aspects are influential in the way respectful relationships are built. The aesthetics and cleanliness of an environment often characterise the extent to which those who pass through are regarded. What clients experience, and feel, creates an impression. This is often unrelated to what they hear and directly observe. Clients will detect through their senses the degree to which we seek to uphold the values of dignity and respect.

Take, for example, my visit to a firm of solicitors. On arrival, the courteous receptionist took my jacket before hanging it neatly on the coat stand. Then, after offering me a drink, she showed me to a quiet area with clean, comfy chairs. Here I waited, admiring the artwork and reading through some well-presented documents in a neat-looking folder. As I sat, I felt important, in safe hands, and honoured to receive such special attention.

To be asked to sit in an unclean or unstimulating environment would have robbed me of my dignity and self-worth. But, on the other hand, being seated in lavish opulence would almost certainly have left me questioning the motives behind such pretentious richness and splendour. Was it me being appreciated or my money that was being prized? Indeed, there is a balance to be struck between the needs and comfort of our clients and the needs and sustainability of our business. If we get the ambience right, we convey authenticity, avoid alienating people and ensure everyone feels welcome and respected for all the right reasons.

We might not all be able to afford stylish premises or indeed need them. For many of us, the nature of our work often dictates where we meet our clients and where we conduct our business; the location and venue choices are not always ours to make. However, we can take pride in whatever surroundings we find ourselves in and value the space as if it were our own. For example, as a trainer, I would arrive at various centres and organisations armed with a box of cleaning products and accessories. I was fully equipped to wipe down dusty tables and chairs and remove rubbish from previous events. Not only did I care about any mess that would reflect on me, but I always cared about the impact on those attending. An unclean environment is certainly not conducive to learning. Sitting through a session with dirt on my clothes would be beneath my dignity, so I cannot expect this of others.

We can make choices that reflect the standards of respect and dignity we hope for ourselves. Simone, a social media communications manager, sometimes meets her clients in hotels but is selective about which hotel she suggests. Her choices are based on the venue's character, atmosphere, and ability to inspire creative thoughts. However, she also factors in the availability of free parking, the area's safety, the level of privacy, the quality of service, the friendliness of staff, and overall standards of cleanliness. Simone always tells clients the reasons behind her choice because she wants them to know she is safeguarding their interests from the beginning. Therefore, Simone looks for places that reflect her values. 'If it has a good vibe, a good reputation, and everyone's respectful, I can relax, and so can my clients,' she says.

We should not underestimate the importance of such small touches in building respect and maintaining our clients' dignity. The extra thought we put into looking after our clients' welfare and belongings helps generate better engagement and construct a culture of mutual respect. We cannot honestly claim to respect our clients unless respectful conversations are matched with respectful actions. The value we place on our clients' property and welfare reflects our value for them as individuals. No matter how kind or polite we are, we create disparity if we do not show consideration in other physical ways. Such incongruence weakens our clients' sense of security and diminishes their trust. We will only be respected when we prove ourselves guardians of people's feelings, welfare, and belongings.

MAKE PEOPLE FEEL WELCOME, NOT UNWANTED

It is easy to be disrespectful and indifferent towards others, so if we want to live up to our professional ideals, we must work hard at being respectful. Disrespect embodies a broad spectrum of behaviours, some more overtly noticeable than others. We find physical and verbal threats and abuse, bullying, humiliation, and incivility in the mix, alongside demeaning actions, negative attitudes, and unco-operative behaviours, all of which stall co-operative engagement and make people feel insignificant. While we might not actively condone abusive and intimidating behaviour, we will all have crossed a line ourselves at some point. Few of us could wholeheartedly say we have not been guilty of gossiping, acting condescendingly or deliberately ignoring someone.

We might not intentionally set out to be disrespectful, but a simple omission or a lapse in manners can subtly undermine our endeavours to create an atmosphere of respect. We can soon get consumed by what we are doing and forget to make the effort. Frustrating and challenging situations prompt us to be momentarily curt or self-absorbed. When preoccupied with our thoughts and feelings, we are far less likely to be empathetic towards our clients. If we cannot tune in to what others are feeling and experiencing, we are seen as insensitive, inattentive, and ill-mannered.

Many of us would consider aggressive and intimidating behaviour an out-and-out show of disrespect. However, there are lesser degrees of behaviours that divide opinion because respect and disrespect are all very subjective. To some people, arriving late is considered disrespectful. To others, it represents a personal trait or a cultural difference they are prepared to accept. People have different levels of sensitivity to actions and omissions based on the expectations they have, the values they hold, and the importance they place on specific behaviours. Therefore, ideas about what constitutes respect or disrespect differ. Depending on the level of personal significance, other people's unmannerly actions may go unnoticed. Just because something does not offend us, does not mean it will not offend other people.

Feelings are very personal, and we can never predict how others will feel or what the impact will be. Our own experiences should tell us that disrespect is not something that can be easily brushed off. It is unpleasant and uncomfortable, and it hurts to be on the receiving end. Whether this is a disregard for our uniqueness, our feelings, dignity, or welfare, disrespect cultivates negative emotions and affects relationships. The subjective nature of disrespect is often why inappropriate behaviours are tolerated and not called out. It is hard to determine how the perpetrators of disrespectful behaviours have genuinely made others feel. People need to consciously know this for a fact to be confident about intervening. The most professional thing to do would be to confront the toxic behaviour of others. This is awkward and difficult, and sometimes we cannot find it within us to challenge such behaviour. Instead, we often overcompensate and hope the kindness we display rights the wrongs of others.

Respect makes people feel wanted, so it is no surprise that a sharp rebuff or blatant act of disrespect has the opposite effect. Disrespectful behaviour creates feelings of anger and crushes the soul. It is a form of rejection that deflates the inner spirit, undermines self-worth, and diminishes self-esteem. In being disrespectful to our clients, we send only one message: quite simply that they do not matter to us. Not only does this leave them feeling unimportant and emotionally violated, but it also leaves them with self-doubt.

Our clients are often drawn to us because they believe our values align with theirs. Therefore, a respectful attitude will undoubtedly be seen as an essential requirement. Since respect is fundamental to building rapport and developing trust, showing disrespect is a sure way to damage relationships.

Our feelings of self-worth grow from how well we relate to others and how well others relate to us. Disrespect tips the balance. It strikes at the heart of our very being. To be denied personal validation feels like a personal attack. Not only will our clients question their judgement of our character, but they will also question the worthiness of their existence. This creates fear and uncertainty and increases stress. It leads people to feel they are somehow inferior or a nuisance. They lose confidence in themselves and in us to the point that they are no longer willing to extend their trust. When trust is lost, so, too, is the feeling of security. A natural reaction is to behave defensively or pull away. Disrespectful actions lead to irate clients giving as good as they get, or clients that become disengaged because we no longer appear to have the same corresponding regard.

RESPECT YOURSELF FIRST AND FOREMOST

It is important to remember that respect is very much a two-way street. As individuals, we all have different personalities and mindsets. We will inevitably meet people we might not get on so well with. To work well with clients, we must match together in some way or be comfortable with the differences we share when their views and values run contrary to our own. If our intuition tells us we might struggle to form a relationship or show our clients respect from the outset, the most professional thing we can do is decline the work and look for clients we feel we can work alongside and be respectful towards.

Unquestionably there will be challenging clients and disagreements at times. We will not always see things from the same perspective or hold the same opinions. Dealing with clients means dealing with their emotions and differences. That does not mean we must accept acts of disrespect and abuse shown to us by clients. Part of being a professional is learning how to deal appropriately with these emotions and differences in ways that do not compromise our capacity to respect our right to receive respect.

Showing respect comes more naturally to some than to others. Our capacity to be respectful originates from our personality, experiences, and values. To build mutual respect, avoid offending people and prevent mistreatment of ourselves and others, we must recognise boundaries and effectively read the situation. To do this, we need to possess self-respect and emotional intelligence.

Before we can begin to respect others, we need to respect ourselves. Self-respect helps us acknowledge our worth as individuals in society and assert the standards by which we expect ourselves and others to be treated. A high level of self-respect prompts us to love ourselves for who we are and rightly judge ourselves to be worthy of respect from others. If we can accept that we are bursting with good qualities and that our lives and work are equally as significant as anyone else's in society, we are more inclined to preserve our dignity and that of others.

A big part of self-respect is self-care. The more self-respect we have, the more likely we are to take responsibility for our well-being. Much of our well-being relies upon the existence of positive relationships. To build and sustain such relationships, we must be sure we connect and work with those who will treat us well. Self-respect allows us to develop our own standards and determine what we will and will not accept. In setting such boundaries, we define what we believe in and what we are prepared to tolerate. A lack of self-respect puts us at risk of being treated unkindly and without the dignity we deserve. It becomes a vicious circle that continually erodes what self-respect we do have.

The boundaries we set and the values we hold will not necessarily protect us from being disrespected by others. However, they help us frame our perspective, allowing us to take care of ourselves and others. Firm boundaries help us retain our sense of what is important and shape our actions. This will enable us to openly acknowledge and express our feelings when disrespect is shown to ourselves or others. Establishing boundaries helps us maintain our integrity and regard for others, such that we treat others as we wish to be treated by acting in fair and kind-hearted ways. Boundaries help us make better choices when determining who we should associate and collaborate with. They prompt us to avoid the ignorant and toxic and drift towards the kind and considerate. Without developing a strong sense of self-respect, we risk being on the receiving end of undignified and disrespectful treatment, as do our clients.

Our boundaries keep us within the realms of professionalism, even when those around us falter. Rachel, who runs a legal marketing company, does her best to discourage gossip. Not only because it wastes time and stifles productivity but because she knows people would be hurt to learn what others were saying about them behind their backs. 'When you hear gossip, the kindest thing you can do is ignore it and not repeat it,' she says. It is a good point because gossip is an indirect form of disrespect. Such casual conversations often lead to untruths and the disclosure of what is otherwise private information. In gossiping, we feed idle thoughts and create breaches of confidentiality.

Just because people do not hear the derogatory comments made about them does not mean these comments are acceptable. In situations like this, as Rachel says: 'We must advocate for others to protect their dignity and self-respect, as well as our own. The people we meet deserve respect whether in our presence or not.' Rachel's message is that respect needs to come from the heart, go beyond direct interactions, and be present in all our words and deeds.

If we expect loyalty from our clients, we must also show our faithfulness by not tarnishing their reputations. The act of treating clients with contempt also serves to tarnish our reputation. Few would wish to collaborate with those whose actions did not cultivate mutual respect. If we cannot be consistently respectful, we are not acting sincerely and lack professional authenticity.

BUILD EMOTIONAL INTELLIGENCE

Our ability to relate to others is central to developing trust and our business success. To develop respectful relationships, not only do we need to be effective in our communication, but we also need to be emotionally intelligent. Behind every message we give or receive, there is an underlying emotion. When dealing with clients, we must handle a range of emotions, not just theirs but our own. The possession of emotional intelligence allows us to identify, understand, and manage these emotions, as well as improving our ability to interact with greater respect and sensitivity. As professionals, we must invest in strengthening our emotional intelligence to build relationships and meet our clients' expectations from the outset.

Regardless of the type of work we do, the emotions our clients convey will vary. It is an emotional response that prompts clients to seek our services in the first place. For Louise, a virtual assistant, new clients fall into three categories. Some are overjoyed that their business is growing and relieved to have the additional support to take it to the next level. Then there are those who feel disappointed at the service they have previously received from similar companies. Lastly, some feel overwhelmed yet apprehensive about delegating tasks. As Louise says: 'Initially, it can be quite a job to act in response to their enquiries, particularly if they are emotionally roused in some way.'

Clients come to us with the expectation that we will take the time to understand and appreciate their situation. However, listening to what people say and hearing what is being said are two different things. Like Louise, we have to determine the underlying cause of the emotions and establish the facts of the message before we can appropriately respond to clients' priorities and needs. If we possess a high degree of emotional intelligence, then we are more likely to be able to interpret what is being communicated.

As we journey along with our clients, their emotions will undoubtedly fluctuate. For whatever reason, joy can soon turn into sorrow, confidence turns to doubt, and even the seemingly unperturbed can grow agitated. How we respond to their words and emotions matters; it makes us professional. Our clients come to us with real-world issues and expect that, regardless of whether we can solve their problem, we will at least be prepared to show genuine concern and behave empathetically. We are regarded as ignorant and insensitive if we cannot respond in such ways.

A higher level of emotional intelligence gives us the flexibility to respond in line with the emotions expressed. Not only this, but it also raises awareness of how our actions and words affect others and how they influence the relationships we forge. This allows us to judge the right way to respond so that we can demonstrate respect with sincerity. Of course, we are not always going to get it right, but if we work on developing our emotional intelligence, we have some hope of responding in ways that meet our clients' expectations.

PUT OUT THE FIRE

Not only do we have to deal with our clients' emotions, we also must learn to manage our own. During our daily activities, there will be at least one interaction that raises our blood pressure and leaves us feeling frustrated. How we respond says a lot about us as a professional because it is through our actions that we portray our values. Being respectful can be challenging when situations exasperate us and people annoy us. We need to possess the quality of self-possession. As professionals, we must respect ourselves by controlling negative emotions, maintaining composure under stress, and not letting the actions of others influence our own.

Andreas, a freelance journalist, reflects on his younger self and the times when he would, in his words, 'try to even the score.' Looking back, he notes how it only inflamed the situation and led to more aggravation and stress, which he could have done without. Andreas admits he probably lost business because of his strong-minded approach. Now older and wiser, Andreas feels less need to react and be 'all out to win.' More confident in his expertise, he knows that there are times when he will be correct, but he no longer feels the compulsion to prove it. His key message is: 'At the end of the day, no one gets hurt if you hold your tongue.'

Andreas shows us that it is hard not to feel negative emotions when things go wrong, or when we come up against contemptuous individuals. The temptation to retaliate and return like for like is counterproductive, and angry responses are futile. We have nothing to gain from this; it only increases the tension and makes the situation worse. We risk saying and doing things we later regret, jeopardising relationships, our happiness, and our business.

We can never control the actions of others, but we can control ourselves and take responsibility for how we respond. Those who express themselves with serenity, remain calm in a crisis and accept criticism without being over-sensitive have learned to master their emotions. Staying respectful when emotions are high is certainly a quality to be admired. What matters is how we deal with the situation and treat others with respect in the process. To maintain professionalism, we must suppress the urge to strike back. We must act maturely and uphold our professional ideals to avoid making poor judgements that defile our reputation.

Most of our clients and those we work alongside are polite and caring. Occasionally, though, we stumble across those who are not. Funeral director Poonam knows only too well how grief can bring out the worst in people. The death of a loved one is naturally an emotional time; people can act unexpectedly and find it difficult to express kindness. Poonam accepts it as part of the grieving process and believes these emotions are only temporary. As she says: 'Underneath, there will be a nice person. It is just that, at this moment in time, their usual pleasantness gets overpowered by other feelings. I try not to judge them because experience tells me I will see their kindness in time. I always do.' Poonam's view is that we should maintain a human perspective and see expressions of anger and frustration within a context. Poonam feels she has a duty to care for the well-being of her grieving clients. To her, they are vulnerable, and because of this, she has no option but to restore peace and calm respectfully and courteously.

It is the same for Niamh, a human resources manager. Employees often consider they are being treated unfairly, and in her words, 'like to express themselves in colourful ways.' Niamh explains that employees often misunderstand the role of human resources and think she is 'going to stir things up, rather than be of help and support.' Niamh's view is that, although we might not agree with the opinion of others or like the way it is expressed, as professionals, we have a responsibility to manage the relationships we have with others. Niamh's thoughts are that if we do not do the right thing and act respectfully, we fail to set an example of what is acceptable. This, as she says, 'means you just end up laying the ground for a toxic relationship to grow.'

Poonam and Niamh show us that it is easier to remain respectful when we have some appreciation of what lies behind people's behaviour. This is something we touched on in Chapter 4, where we explored how pre-empting clients' feelings helps us be better prepared to tell the truth in different ways and navigate our way around difficult situations. The same principles apply when it comes to dealing with disrespect. With the right approach, we get the right outcome. We cannot, of course, ignore forms of disrespect as if nothing happened. We must address them. When boundaries are crossed, this needs to be articulated. In Niamh's words: 'The only way to put out a fire is to smother it or pour water on it.' Her point is that where acts of disrespect are concerned, a lack of response or an inappropriate one allows the disrespect to continue.

If we can control our emotions, pick the right moment, maintain our standards, and convey our thoughts tactfully and diplomatically, we stand a better chance of resolving things fairly and turning the situation around. But, of course, this demands well-developed emotional intelligence and we need to have mastered the art of self-possession, not to mention the ability to simultaneously combine positive communication, serenity, empathy, and assertiveness. The bottom line is that, if we want to be respected and restore the level of respect shown to us by clients, we must rise above it and connect with them in ways that align with the type of respect we want back from them.

LEARN TO TAKE A DEEP BREATH

If we are to model respectful behaviours in challenging times, we need to adopt personal strategies that allow us to act rationally and remain composed and courteous. Before we can address our clients' rudeness, anger, and frustrations, we must first bring our own emotions under control. Here we require self-possession, which gives us the strength to control our emotional state and show kindness. Whether we are on the receiving end of a curt email, an uncivil comment, or an abrupt manner, the chances are it will provoke some internal negative emotion. If we respond when our emotions are riled, we risk acting impulsively and inappropriately. We stand a better chance of controlling our words and actions when we step back, redirect our anger, and restore our inner calm.

So, when Yvonne, a network marketer, is subjected to disrespectful comments, she stops, takes a deep breath, and counts slowly from 5 to 1 before saying something positive. Yvonne's theory is that: 'Once you say something positive, it is hard to follow this with anything negative.' Interpersonal therapist Yasmina chooses 'to have a moan then pick up the phone.' Having a private grumble allows her to get it out of her system before making personal contact rather than sending an email. Her view is that we can never know how clients feel, and emails can be easily misinterpreted. By phoning, Yasmina can explore the issue sensitively, empathetically, and with an open mind. As a result, she can defuse the situation and resolve the matter quickly.

On the other hand, Jake, a business development manager, opts to take himself away from his desk for a while and goes for a walk. Working in an office alongside others, he understands how negative emotions can affect the whole team. For Jake, it is essential to keep work stress levels to a minimum and avoid being a bad example to others. Time out allows Jake to reflect on the situation and how he should handle it. With that, he develops a plan to make everything better before sounding out his ideas with colleagues. Jake puts a positive spin on it and sees it as an opportunity to learn from the alternative perspectives and advice his colleagues offer on how to best approach the situation.

Yvonne, Yasmina, and Jake each have their own personal strategy. Although different, these strategies effectively all do the same thing: they help put the brakes on and prompt conscious thought. They help us step back long enough to be able to deal with our negative emotions. Moreover, they buy us time to put things into perspective, devise a rational solution, and choose our words carefully. In essence, such strategies help us remain respectful and manage relationships professionally. When we do this, we turn things to our advantage.

If we can remain respectful in the face of disrespect, we create opportunities to show how authentic, consistent, sincere, and genuine we are. By exhibiting self-possession in this way, we make our standards known. We show that we do not hold a grudge and are prepared to build better relationships. It helps retain the self-respect needed to treat others with kindness and courtesy. Ultimately, taking a deep breath puts us back in control and reinforces how much we value respect and dignity.

MAINTAIN AN EQUILIBRIUM

Without a doubt, we all wish to be admired and held in high regard. However, we must see any form of social recognition as icing on the cake, because it only comes when we extensively invest in building personal relationships. To be held in high regard, we must prove ourselves in other ways first.

The underlying message within this chapter is that unless we demonstrate dignity and respect for others, we are unlikely to receive it. Even then, it is not an inevitable outcome. Not everyone will return the same level of respect or treat us as fairly and equitably as we have treated them. Nonetheless, we must remain optimistic and committed to upholding these values to nurture mutual respect.

Mutual respect relies on positive dynamics. The respect we show others must be matched with the respect they show us. Any imbalance makes it harder for both parties to remain respectful. Our efforts to build and maintain an atmosphere of dignity and respect should not be confined to giving but also receiving. We must make it work both ways. When there is mutual respect, the energy changes and strengthens. Relationships progress because dignity and respect influence how people perceive and respond to each other.

The illustrative examples throughout the chapter highlight the many ways in which we can show respect. These fall into three broad categories, all functioning in parallel. First, there is that of individualism. We show respect when we provide a personal touch and treat people as distinctive individuals. This manifests through how we act without prejudice, acknowledge differences, and appreciate similarities. It arises through the practices we adopt that take account of the day-to-day realities of the lives of our clients. Second, respect becomes apparent through courteous interaction. It is reflected in what we say, how we say it and how we respond to what we hear. It is visible in the way we display sensitivity and empathy and in our approach to expressing gratitude and establishing client-friendly boundaries. Third, it shows through in our regard for creating an atmosphere of respect. It develops when we give due consideration to people's personal welfare and belongings and the physical environment in which interactions occur. When we look at it like this, it becomes glaringly apparent that many dynamics come into play.

Whether it is our behaviour, the systems and the procedures we have in place, or the standards we set, the combination of all these factors validates the existence of others. The small things we do have a cumulative effect. They provide emotional and visible confirmation of our endeavours and commitment to upholding the values of dignity and respect. However, to make an impact, all three aspects must work in a synchronised way. Each element is critical to building mutual respect. This is under threat if we do not get the balance right. The absence of one part can create perceptions of disrespect.

To be able to show respect, we must avoid showing contempt. To get the balance right, we must ensure respect comes our way. We cannot function as professionals in an atmosphere that lacks dignity and respect. It is demoralising and raises harmful internal emotions that potentially prompt us to act inappropriately. Being respectful relies upon us having the self-respect to protect and advocate respect for ourselves and others. Therefore, we must use our emotional intelligence to stand up against disrespect and appropriately respond to the negative emotions we feel. As we have seen, this relies upon us withholding judgement, expressing an opinion, and setting a positive example, in addition to making conscious choices about whom we work and associate with. This can be furthered by defining standards and boundaries of acceptability and having strategies to deal with our emotions.

We see here that an emotional equilibrium encourages presence of mind. Through self-possession, we empower ourselves by being in control of our feelings. This stability allows us to be composed under stress, so that we think, act, and resolve issues appropriately and respectfully.

The respect we show others relies upon us being respected. The two are closely connected, so we must create conditions that promote an equal exchange. When all the varying dynamics associated with dignity and respect come together in the right proportions, relationships strengthen and change. This cascading effect cultivates a culture of dignity and respect amongst individuals in society. To be professional, we must always think and act in line with a broader vision. To function harmoniously as a society, people need to respect one another. How we behave can shape society and make the world a kinder place. The onus is on us, even in the most challenging times, to foster the development of mutual respect in the interest of the co-operative engagement and well-being of our clients, ourselves, and others. If we can make dignity and respect work two ways, then we can make it work three ways. We create harmony within society when dignity and respect are exemplified in all that we do.

HOLD THAT THOUGHT

When it comes to matters of dignity and respect, we will, as professionals, be judged on our selfless acceptance of others and how exceptional and consistent we are in portraying these values. To be all these things, we must make clear choices about the standards we wish for ourselves and others. Moreover, we must go out of our way to convey the dignity and respect we wish to see in others.

Professionalism demands that we sit up, pay attention, and invest time, energy, and effort in creating a culture of dignity and respect that is evident from the outset. Forging strong, mutually beneficial relationships requires a deeper level of regard and some forward thinking to avoid causing offence, acting without sincerity, or enduring disrespect.

In business, success only attracts attention if we have respectfully paid attention to others in the process of getting there. With this in mind, we must question our ability to model the expected professional behaviours confidently and consistently. We are unlikely to demonstrate anything more than basic common courtesy if we lack the personal skills and internal drive to embrace these professional ideals. Professionalism demands more than good manners. The question is: do we hold positive affirmations of self and a deep-rooted devotion to nurturing a culture of dignity and respect? Are we the person others wish to emulate? Because we will only be admired and respected for our professionalism if we lead by example.

7

MAKING DECISIONS

ASK QUESTIONS TO GET ANSWERS!

Every day, from the moment we wake up to the moment we go to bed, we make decisions. But if you are anything like me first thing in the morning, you will put off making any decisions until a strong cup of coffee has been consumed. In fact, if you really are like me, you will be so fatigued by the decision as to what to wear that a second cup of coffee will be needed before any further decisions are made.

If only the biggest decision we had to make each day was what to wear. Sadly, it is not. Unless, of course, you happen to be a catwalk model or fashion influencer. If not, then there will be more significant decisions to make. Whether business decisions are strategic or operational, we must be prepared to make decisions and act on them. If not, we leave it all to chance and gamble with our fortune and reputation.

How we make those decisions is critical to the success of our business and the extent to which we are considered professional. In serving the interests of our clients, we will be judged on whether our proposals and actions turn out to be the most appropriate and sensible thing to do. Clients come to us with real-life problems and issues they want a practical solution to. They are looking for a level of guidance that empowers them to make the best decisions according to their aspirations and circumstances. Our decision-making competence has consequences for their future. Where we fail to be judicious in our approach, we risk acting in unprincipled ways and potentially compromise the quality of the service we offer and the outcomes achieved. Leave clients dealing with the fallout of our incompetence, and we are viewed as untrustworthy amateurs who are unreliable and unfit to be in business.

Decision-making is not for the faint-hearted. There are many practical, emotional, moral, and ethical issues and dilemmas to contemplate. As we progress through this chapter, we discover why courage, commitment, and resolve are imperative to the process. To avoid acting on impulse, we explore how we can prepare ourselves for a deeper level of conscious thought, and devote time to the process of deliberation to better serve the interest of our business and that of our clients. Within this debate we examine how, by adopting an investigative, systematic, and analytical approach, the consistency and validity of our ideas and the quality of outcomes are enhanced. As the professional significance of applying good-practice principles becomes evident, we discover how these extend our capacity to empower others to be equally confident autonomous decision-makers.

During the chapter, it becomes evident that professional decision-making hinges on diligent curiosity. We discover various ways to make decision-making practices more effective. Through this, we learn that if we have the right mental resources to ask the right questions and do the proper research, we maximise our opportunity to arrive at an answer that allows us to make principled decisions responsibly and professionally.

ADOPT GOOD HABITS

In essence, decision-making starts when we analyse a problem, and concludes when we pinpoint a course of action that provides a solution. Arguably there are no right or wrong decisions, just different and potential courses of action, some of which favour our interests better than others under the circumstances. So, no matter what problems we need to overcome or what goals we wish to achieve, it makes sense to be making sound, logical judgements.

At some point in life, we will all have chosen a course of action we thought was in our best interests, only to discover later down the line that it was a big mistake. For example, Dominic, a chef, went to an international trade fair and bought a £1,000 food processor, only to discover it was not designed for the European market and incompatible with the UK electricity supply. Even with adaptors, it was forever overheating, and after a short time, the motor burnt out. In his defence, Dominic claims he was, back then, 'young and impressionable.' While he laughs about it now, at the time he was 'kicking himself for being so naïve' and focusing on its look rather than its functionality.

It was the same for interpersonal therapist Yasmina, who thought she had found the perfect consultancy room. Not wanting to miss out, she agreed to lease it there and then. Only when she moved in did she discover the floor above was used as a dance studio. The noise levels affected her and her clients' ability to focus. She had no choice but to relocate her practice, forcing her to pay two lots of rent for a while. Throughout this time, Yasmina directed her anger back at herself. As she puts it, she could not believe she had 'been so brainless and not asked enough questions or thought it through.' It was a long time before she could forgive herself, mentally move on, and let it go.

Jamil, a photographer, shares his embarrassment about how he was persuaded to let the friend of a friend design and build his website. Jamil's gut feeling was to say no, but in Jamil's own words: 'The guy needed a break, and in the few times I had met him, he seemed OK and fun to be around.' In time Jamil did get his website, but, although it looked great, it did not function as it should. The problems seemed endless, and with each new issue, the friend of the friend got harder to get hold of, and so did Jamil's friend. At the time, it seemed like the right thing to do, but on reflection Jamil realises that, through misguided loyalty, he allowed himself to walk into a situation that cost him time, money, and friendship.

Dominic, Yasmina, and Jamil are the first to admit that they momentarily allowed their heart to rule their head. Most decisions start on an emotional level; however, from this point on, facts and logic must guide us. If we are overcome by a false sense of urgency, or caught off guard, our impulsive actions will leave us with nothing but remorse. The decisions we make should be such that they ease the burden, not hamper our progress or increase our anxiety. By acting on a whim, we can set ourselves back and create situations that give us more to agonise over.

The positive from all of this is that as we live, we learn. No one likes the idea of making the same mistake twice. The anger, guilt, and shame we feel often sharpen our wits. Loss of money and threats to our reputation motivate us to tread more sensibly. We will never get it right all of the time. As Dominic says: 'When we mess up, the best thing to do is own it, fix it, learn from it, and move on.' This is a good point because if we spend time worrying about the past, we fail to progress. We impede our ability to take the next steps that ensure we live in the present and develop our future.

If we are looking to define what differentiates an appropriate decision from an inappropriate one, these candid examples leave us in no doubt that it depends on how clearly we think things through. A good decision is one that brings positive benefits, solves a problem, progresses us towards our goals, and leaves us free of worry. If we are in the habit of adopting good practices when it comes to decision-making, we reduce the negative consequences we have to deal with. By taking a more considered approach, we limit the risk, spare our feelings, and avoid extra work or a tarnished reputation.

As professionals, we must assume responsibility and manage the decision-making process. We must be prepared to take responsibility for our actions and deal with the consequences. We cannot blame others for our lapse of judgement. The decisions we make do not stand in isolation. Every decision comes with risks and can have a wide-ranging impact on ourselves and those around us, potentially affecting livelihoods, relationships, health, well-being, and future decisions.

The decisions we make need to be ethical. Whatever course of action we take, we must do so with fairness and integrity, showing respect for others, avoiding emotional and physical harm, and honouring the trust that has been extended to us. So not only do we have to assume responsibility, but we also have to think responsibly. We must understand the bigger picture and consider how decisions will affect ourselves and others. That way, we avoid doing anything we might later come to regret.

TAKE TIME TO DECIDE

There is never a right time to make decisions, but decisions must be made. If we bury our heads in the sand out of fear, or sit around waiting for the perfect moment to arrive, we will wait forever and achieve nothing. On the other hand, if we fail to decide, we starve ourselves of opportunities and of the chance to control the outcome.

We can never predict the outcome of any decision we make, partly because of the dynamic world we live in. Nor can we eliminate the uncertainty or possibility of making a wrong decision. We can, however, steer ourselves towards a more appropriate course of action and stop ourselves from repeatedly making bad decisions.

Professionally we place ourselves in a better position when we are confident that we are making our decision for all the right reasons. Good judgement is not about luck. It is about standards. It is no good crossing our fingers and hoping for the best; we need to take a considered approach and adopt habits of mind and patterns of behaviour that remove some of the guesswork.

If we want to be regarded as a professional who can be depended on to make sound judgements, we must openly show this as one of our key strengths. Otherwise, no one will trust us. To provide ourselves and others with an assurance of our capacity to make good decisions, we must commit to educating ourselves to effectively synthesise and monitor our thoughts, actions, and outcomes. As a professional, the quality of our judgement is reflected in how we reach our decisions, how we execute them, and what results as a consequence. We gain credibility as a professional when we are conscientious, do things well, and respond appropriately no matter how challenging the circumstances. To be effective and competent decision-makers, we need to repress our impulses and put time aside to think and follow a process of conscious deliberation. In doing so, we create a system by which we can quality-assure our thought processes.

In finding the time to take a considered approach, we come to think and act in a distinctively different way. In that interval, we gain clarity and generate more insight that helps us confidently articulate and rationalise our decision. The deeper our level of understanding, the more informed we are, and the sounder our judgements will be. If we opt to take a less conventional path, provide an innovative or experimental solution, or even resolve a crisis, we can at least rationalise what we are doing, why we are doing it, and whether it is good, fair, and by all measures the right thing to do.

Decision-making is not something to be rushed. We need to give ourselves sufficient time to be confident that what we plan to do is right. Herein sits a dilemma of how much time we should take before we reach a firm decision and act. The less time we give to the decision-making process, the less favourable the outcome. In contrast, the more time we give ourselves, the less likely anything will get done as the tendency to overthink or dither can be equally paralysing. The more time we have to think, the more time we have to sit and doubt ourselves. As a result, opportunities can soon pass us by, and we risk never achieving what we set out to accomplish. Either that, or the world around us decides for us, such that the decision is no longer ours to make.

Over the years, James, a copywriter, has come to appreciate the value of knowing when to make a quick decision and when there is a need to take his time. Many of our day-to-day decisions are inconsequential, so sometimes there is scope to act swiftly. If we need to make a swift decision, James's advice is to stop briefly and, at the very least, ask ourselves: how would this look if it was reported in tomorrow's newspapers? James's point is that, even if speed is of the essence, there is always time to register and process the idea in our minds before we proceed with our intended action.

Unless the clock is ticking and a deadline is fast approaching, we can allow ourselves to take our time. In the grand scheme of things, there is no harm in sitting on our ideas for a few days or even a few weeks. Adam, who repairs computers, thinks something should be said for 'sleeping on it for a while.' For him, the gap between decision and action creates a space where the subconscious comes into play. In that time, ideas mature, and new ones can surface. Adam notes how it assists in managing the stress of the process and helps him compartmentalise his thoughts. Having decided what to do, he uses the headspace to think and revisit his motives and intended course of action. He likens it to an aeroplane cross-check procedure, confirming with himself that it is 'safe to boost the engines and take off.'

Recruitment consultant Steve uses this time to gain clarity by reading opinion pieces and exploring his ideas with others. In Steve's view: 'When all things are considered, if it still seems a good idea, then it probably is a good idea.' Steve notes that what emerges through our exploration can lead us to change our minds. After some thought, our great idea might not seem such a great one after all. Yet it can be challenging and deflating to let go. As professionals, we must learn to accept that decision-making is a process of determining if our intended course of action is the right one to be taking. If it is not, it is OK to park it for now or entirely dismiss the idea.

As Steve points out: 'It is better to have second thoughts and reject the idea, because it is harder to reverse a wrong decision.' Of course, this might mean we return to the drawing board, but as Steve says: 'With elimination, there is still progress.' Time has allowed us to show discernment. We have to see this as something to our advantage. Sometimes to judge what is achievable and appropriate, it is necessary to discover what is unachievable and inappropriate. As we rethink our ideas, we acquire a more realistic and focused insight. Whether the outcome of our deliberations leads us to act or not, we have enhanced our capacity to be rational decision-makers.

NO SECRET RECIPE, ONLY VITAL INGREDIENTS

There are no scientific methods or hard and fast rules to follow when making decisions. However, we stand a better chance of making appropriate decisions if we adopt an objective, analytical, and systematic approach. This demands a lot of us, for we need to possess a curious and open mind, think critically, step back from our feelings, have patience, and eliminate all things likely to distort our judgement. It is a skilful process that requires specific personal strengths to process our thoughts and emotions with conviction.

We cannot always rely upon the wisdom of our past to help us determine future courses of action. One thing about life is that it is never static. Numerous challenges and problems present themselves, some of which we will have no prior experience of dealing with. As our business develops, we can only really achieve our goals and aspirations when we actively seek to guide ourselves towards them. The path to success will test us; circumstances change, and things beyond our control will invariably arise. We must therefore be ready to adapt, to consistently do what is essential and necessary in the most appropriate way. Our unfaltering steadfastness, coupled with the quality of our approach, will lead us to act with professionalism.

Sadly, there is no magic formula to help us get it right every time. The best decisions do not automatically result in the best outcome. Indeed, it is possible to make the poorest of judgements and still emerge from the situation smelling of roses. It would be foolish to accept this as something that happens, over which we have no control. We are unlikely to get what we aim for with such a happy-go-lucky approach. We will only be seen as competent decision-makers when we are getting it right more times than we are getting it wrong. This requires strength of mind and character on our part.

The time and effort we put into making decisions will inevitably work in our favour if we embrace a system that helps us to make better decisions consistently and reduces the risk of unfavourable outcomes. If we want to get things done and done right, we must be prepared to give decision-making the energy it deserves in order to secure our credibility and ability to compete alongside others. To be professional, we must be responsible decision-makers and hold ourselves accountable for how we make decisions and for the outcomes resulting from that process. This requires self-discipline, critical thought, and a quality-focused approach.

No one ever said that decision-making was easy. Thinking is hard, and it makes your brain ache. What is more, any decisions we make are likely to require action. Getting where we want to be can leave us emotionally conflicted, with compromises and sacrifices to be made. We are often pushed outside our comfort zone, challenged to try new things, learn new skills, and overcome anxious thoughts and self-doubt. There are times when we could be forgiven for labelling decision-making an unpleasant chore.

However, seeing it as something burdensome will only hold us back because as we resist, procrastinate, and put in less mental effort, we limit our potential. It is best to see it the way Steve does. For Steve, there is something exciting about decision-making. As he says: 'When you find yourself making big decisions, you are changing your future. It is an opportunity that drives progress.' Decision-making provides clarity and generates innovative solutions, which opens us up to new possibilities and the potential for growth. If we can see the bigger picture, we are steps closer to developing our ideas and achieving our ambitions. If we can make it less of a chore, then it is even better, because we feel good throughout the decision-making process and more confident about the decisions we make. Having fun is one of the easiest ways to change our attitude. Introducing creativity into the process makes thinking seem far less challenging.

Anna and Ray, owners of a communications company, take themselves out of the office on what they describe as a 'mini-retreat in a creative space.' Away from distractions in a place that inspires imagination, they arm themselves with paper, pens, and Post-It Notes and get busy creating and conceptualising ideas by generating spider diagrams, concept maps, and timelines.

For Iain, an electrician, the thought of going self-employed after accepting redundancy was a big step. It was a time of mixed emotions and a decision he needed to consider carefully. As an art lover, Iain decided to draw his thoughts about potential options, representing them in a series of pictures. Iain noticed that as he was drawing he was also processing his thoughts. It helped him weigh up the advantages and disadvantages and the impact on his family. As he explored each scenario, he discovered he connected with his feelings. In doing so, he realised which option he felt most comfortable about and could live with.

It is a technique I, too, use from time to time. Since I have no talent for drawing, I opt to create a vision board. The inner child in me likes to cut and paste pictures from magazines onto paper. For me, it is a form of mindfulness that connects me to the present. In crafting, I become curious about my ideas and as I talk myself in and out of things, my mindset shifts. Through this I appreciate the direction I need to be heading in. At the same time, I find I am building up the motivation and confidence to act.

What works for one person will not necessarily work for another. We each have to experiment and find an approach we feel comfortable with that fits the situation and the types of decisions we need to make. Creativity makes the process more enjoyable, but it is no good if the outcomes do not amount to much. The approach we take not only needs to be pleasant, but it also needs to be effective. To achieve this, the process must promote deep critical thought, leading to pragmatic solutions.

MENTALLY AND PHYSICALLY PREPARE

When it comes to decision-making, it is not enough to bracket off time within our diary. We have to bracket off our emotions and biases too. Both time pressure and our feelings can affect the quality of the decision-making process and the outcomes that arise. We are more likely to make better decisions when we are in the right frame of mind. Emotions, whether happy or sad, can distort our judgement, shift our focus, and affect our attention span. So, before we sit down and actively engage in the decision-making process, we need to leave our emotions at the door and approach the task with a clear and open mind. If we feel overwhelmed, insecure, or paranoid about getting it wrong, we should reschedule to a time when we are free of emotional baggage. To focus, we need to feel inwardly calm, outwardly composed, and ready to think creatively.

Interpersonal therapist Yasmina and Jonathan, who runs a business network, set aside specific days throughout the year to make strategic decisions. Jonathan schedules this after a holiday. Revived in himself, he feels ready to refresh his ideas. For Yasmina, the night before is almost as important as the day itself. In preparation, she clears her workspace, collates all the materials she feels she will need, and is sure to get a good night's sleep. Then, she starts the day exercising, eating a healthy breakfast, and engaging in a short period of mindful meditation. To Yasmina, there is more to preparation than getting ourselves into the right headspace: first, we have to feel good. This involves feeling invigorated and limiting the surrounding negative energy by creating a tidy physical environment that allows us to work unhindered and uninterrupted.

Being focused, emotionally calm, and in a place with a cheerful ambience is only part of it. We are a central part of our business and integral to the decision-making process. We are never going to be truly independent of the decisions we make. Unfortunately, being close to something often narrows our vision of what is possible. We all have our opinions, likes, and dislikes and we know what we prefer or are comfortable with. Thus, we tend to lean towards our preferences rather than consider reasonable alternatives. Our individual biases limit what we can see in our mind's eye. So, unless we can find a way to detach ourselves, we risk overlooking various aspects and options. While we can never really separate ourselves from the process, we can work to isolate our subjective thoughts. To avoid being swayed by our personal feelings and beliefs, our existing assumptions and prejudices, we must explore ideas and assess all options objectively. Hence, part of the preparation is setting ourselves up to view things through a broad objective lens. This requires us to adopt a robust process that raises our consciousness to a range of possibilities and allows us to view the situation as if we were looking at it through the eyes of others.

If we want to be confident that the big decisions we need to make are logical and rational, we need to be methodical in our approach. This requires us to develop a framework that prompts us to engage in deep thought and analysis. This framework should stop us from overlooking essential factors without constraining our ideas or limiting our potential, and enable us to examine the basis for our judgements. In using a framework, we have a point of reference that allows us to make decisions in the context of our business activity.

We will explore what this might look like in the next section; for now, let us stick with the fact that such a framework serves as a powerful tool of accountability and governance that reduces risk and limits bias. In addition, it introduces an element of self-regulation and helps us establish boundaries, live by our values, and achieve high standards. With regular use, we create the consistency and efficiency needed to increase the chances of us making appropriate and timely decisions over and over again. With this, we become more confident that the outcomes generated through the process are the best solutions.

If we want to prepare well, we must be conscious of what must be considered and build this into the process. Collectively the various things we need to consider act as filters that distil our thoughts and sharpen our focus, ensuring our decisions are consistent with our values and priorities, are morally and ethically right, and within the law. In this, at least, we exemplify professionalism in the decision-making process. But the story does not end there: we must remember that professionalism requires implementing our ideas and solutions in the same principled ways.

DEVELOP A FRAMEWORK THAT WORKS

Fundamentally, decision-making is about analysing a problem or determining our aspirational goal. We set about developing an action plan through the critical exploration of information and ideas. We can only begin the process of analysis if we clearly define the nature and complexity of this issue. Few of us would think of getting on a bus unless we knew where it was going. A magical mystery tour is less fun than it sounds. Senseless choices are costly. We risk losing time, money, and our sense of pride when our journey leads us to a place far from where we expected to be.

It would be unwise to make any decision without first doing some research. By gathering facts and information, we become better informed, more confident, and less anxious and conflicted about the direction we should be heading. What is more, we get an idea of how realistically achievable our goals are.

Thanks to the internet, we can gain information quickly. The amount available to us is almost infinite. The more we search, the more we come to know, and with this comes the discovery of all the things we do not know. As Alannah, a make-up artist, neatly puts it: 'It is easy to end up down a rabbit hole, transported to the world of information overload.' To be productive and efficient, we need to get the balance right. Without sufficient up-to-date information, we are unlikely to understand the complexities and intricacies of the problems and challenges we are trying to address. On the other hand, too much information overwhelms us, creates confusion, induces stress, and eventually prompts a loss of interest.

There is no answer as to what constitutes a desirable amount of information. Quantity does not always equate to quality. Naturally, we need to be selective in where we choose to look and what we choose to read. However, many unknowns will exist even with access to the best resources. We might not find all we seek or get an all-inclusive insight. The bigger picture can still be hidden from view. So, no matter whether we have too much or too little information, we may find ourselves in a situation with the potential to overlook important factors, constrain our ideas, and limit our potential. That said, whatever information we find serves as a point of reference, even though we will always need to be resourceful in our approach to obtaining the most current angle or filling in the gaps before we figure it all out and reach a conclusion.

We make better decisions when reading and digesting information with a critical eye, which we will explore in the next section. Right now, let us consider that as a professional, we are not only judged on the outcomes of our deliberations and whether they make good sense; our professionalism is also embodied in the approach we take to reach our decisions. It is qualities like diligence and pragmatism that lead to quality judgements. Therefore, the onus is on us to introduce accountability into the thinking process to ensure we make logical, rational, and informed decisions that we can explicitly articulate. If we work on the principle that professionalism is driven by standards and our ability to operate according to those standards, we can maximise our chances of success by setting standards and boundaries as we make decisions.

In building these into our decision-making framework, we lay the foundation for quality and transparency throughout the process and create uniformity in how we objectively evaluate the decisions we are about to make. Following a systematic approach might seem very formal, but it means we are not left second-guessing the outcome of our actions. As a result, we reduce the risk of taking a decision we later regret. To be effective we need to consider a variety of factors and explore our problems and aspirations from multiple standpoints to obtain a balanced perspective.

Before Alannah makes any plans, she returns to the starting point. She reminds herself of why she is here, sitting and thinking. Whether the reason is positive or negative, it gives her a starting point for reflection. In recent months Alannah has considered branching out into make-up training. Knowing if the initial driver stemmed from personal needs or that of her clients helped Alannah focus on addressing the most significant perspective. Jonathan, who runs a business network, considers the risk to profits and reputation. Alongside this, he considers the benefits any change will bring to himself and those who share in his journey, since he is keen to retain the ethos of building a supportive business community.

For Dominic, core values and cost-effectiveness are both significant factors. Whatever the outcome of his critical ponderings, unless it is evident it will broaden his capacity to showcase his creativity, improve the quality of the dining experience, or create responsibly-sourced dishes, Dominic is prepared to rule it out. He is keen to present at cookery exhibitions, but, although this aligns with his overall ethos, he appreciates the need to consider whether the potential benefits are worth it or whether his money would be better spent elsewhere.

In finding himself with more work than he can handle and bigger projects in the pipeline, Cameron, a heating engineer, has been exploring his options for hiring other engineers. His initial idea was to employ someone permanently. However, having researched, he discovered several alternative ways to proceed, many of which he had never considered. As Cameron explored the advantages and disadvantages of each potential scenario in terms of performance and overall business growth, he also weighed the positive or negative consequences for himself, his clients, and those he might hire. In addition, Cameron considered the short- and long-term impact on his business and the overall effect on his work-life balance. As he cross-referenced his ideas with industry standards and regulations, Cameron noted that there was another category for consideration, another filter to add if you like. This was the notion of whether or not he was compliant with expectations and thus capable of responding to his strategic vision and adapting to new responsibilities. This has now become a standard part of his decision-making criteria.

From the few examples here, it is clear that whatever decision we make, there will be many things to explore before we implement our plans. No final decision will ever be clear-cut. There will always be trade-offs between what we desire and what seems sensible. There might well be some concessions to be made, but a framework makes these all apparent. With visibility comes transparency. With this, we see what lies behind our thoughts and actions. Through our discernment here, we present ourselves as accountable and responsible professionals.

BE CRITICAL AND BE CONFIDENT

If we are to solve problems, formulate ideas, and make decisions, we must be able to evaluate and analyse information. Furthermore, if we are looking for support or want investors and stakeholders to buy into our plans, we must be able to articulate this information confidently, whether in person or on paper. We cannot do any of this without first being critical thinkers.

To understand the value of critical thinking, we first need to appreciate that it is not about negative criticism. We are not seeking to find fault or expose flaws and mistakes. Instead, we are looking to delve deeper and, in doing so, to question and investigate before we decide. To be critical thinkers, we must be active in the process of thinking, which means thinking about how we think while we are thinking. It is a skill that takes time to develop, but the more actively engaged we are in thinking, the more proficient we become.

In life and business, nothing is ever black and white. There are lots of grey areas that make situations hard to assess. Every day, whatever we read or hear needs to be objectively processed and balanced. Not everything will be an accurate or valid opinion, but we cannot afford to be lazy in our approach to thinking because that leaves us incapable of discernment and without the acuity to make sound and autonomous decisions. Critical thinking starts when we stop taking things at face value and are ready to examine a range of perspectives, including our own, in detail.

This requires us to be curious, open-minded, and willing to learn. So, unless we are driven to develop a deeper understanding and question everything, we limit our capacity to create new ideas and arrive at a suitable decision.

If we can develop a decision-making framework that makes us more critical, we become more objective and evaluative in our approach and can confidently use all we discover to inform our ideas. For Cameron, critical thinking is central to justifying what he is doing and why he is doing it. He observes that, by introducing critical thought into the process, he can assess the pros and cons, the options, and the consequences. In addition, it helps to validate his thoughts and feelings. Assured that his ideas, proposals, and decisions are well-reasoned, he is confident to express them and act on them.

Effective decision-making not only requires us to think rationally but also requires us to trust our judgement. This means being comfortable with the decision-making process we adopt and seeing it through. We need to keep going until we are in no doubt that we have arrived at the best decision and one we would be happy to act on.

We cannot afford to be left wondering if better choices exist because doubt holds us back. Nor can we be in a position where we have too many options, because we will be tempted to keep changing our minds, achieving very little as a result. We have to narrow down our options. This means we must be prepared to choose, even if that means more critical deliberation. When faced with two viable choices, Steve always plumps for the option that will fit the future best. Jonathan shares a similar view, noting that what might serve us well in the here and now may not make for a profitable and successful business in the longer term.

We must remember that the most appropriate decisions are not always the simplest. Taking the easy option is not necessarily the wisest option. We must be prepared to put into action what is right in the circumstances, even if that is difficult. If not, people will see us as casual and doubt our ability to perform.

Decision-making takes courage. Sometimes, we have to do what we feel is right, even when others think we are wrong. Many years ago, Cathryn decided to start a public relations consultancy business when she was eight months pregnant. Although to others it seemed a crazy idea, to her, having thought it through, it was a perfectly rational judgement. Cathryn's progress and achievements since that time show that her decision was spot-on.

Once we have made our choice, we have to be confident that we have made the right decision. Confidence and optimism motivate us to stay the course and not bail out too soon. But, of course, we will only know if our decision is correct once we implement it. As Jonathan reminds us: 'We live in a space where we never know the outcome until it is tried and tested.' Consequently, in implementing our plans, we must monitor the outcome, be prepared to reflect, and confidently respond to any uncertainty. In reality, there is no end to the decision-making process. We will always have to deal with the effects and consequences.

Several years ago, Kriss, who owns a sustainable travel company, offered individual travellers the option of a group tour. He partnered with a company that shared the same ethos. Ecologically it fitted the bill and offered a mode of operation that was affordable and seemed very practical. However, it soon became clear to Kriss that the company's booking model was not working out for him or for his clients. The process was challenging to manage, and the places were difficult to fill. Having lost several nights' sleep,

Kriss decided to pull out of the deal and minimise the pressure he was placing on himself. Looking back, Kriss notes: 'It was the right thing to do but at the wrong time.' It was too soon to be in the game. Over the last few years, several sustainable tour operators have evolved with different booking models, which means Kriss now has more workable opportunities to extend his group tour services to individual travellers.

What we learn from this is that just because our idea does not translate well into the real world, it does not mean we have the wrong idea. Here we have another example of how timing is everything. It is OK to shelve ideas until the right opportunity presents itself. The critical point here is that if the outcomes are not in line with what we anticipated, we need to have the same confidence and employ the same level of analysis we took in making our decision to review or suspend our decision. In applying the same process, we can retain our decision-making confidence, knowing that we are making the right choice at the right moment for the right reasons. In doing so, we can confidently move on and eliminate nagging doubts that start with 'if only...' and 'what if...?'

INVOLVE OTHERS!

It is natural to be fearful of making wrong decisions. Yet we do not have to make decisions all on our own. We can often make better decisions when we involve others in the process. Taking the opportunity to run our ideas past others before acting makes perfect sense. It is a way of gaining alternative perspectives. By seeking the opinions of others, we get to access a view that is not ours from someone who is not compromised by an emotional connection. We actually get to see how our ideas look to those on the outside looking in, because people who are not involved in our day-to-day activities often have a clearer vision.

Jonathan, Steve, and Steve's business partner Georgina all use critical friends – people whom they know and trust to give them an honest opinion. Jonathan seeks advice from those likely to appreciate the stage his business is at and those who have lived through a similar experience. Steve and Georgina explore their ideas with their business coach and those within their network. Jonathan, Steve, and Georgina believe no one understands small business owners better than other small business owners. Therefore, a business network can be a rich resource for assessing and validating our ideas and examining the logic behind our decisions.

Critical friends help us to think critically because they ask us thought-provoking questions that warrant explanations. The more we have to account for our intentions, the more we learn about our line of reasoning. Alannah notes how more experienced critical friends have helped her venture into new territory, get the balance right and gain clarity as to the significance of her intended actions. With their encouraging insight, Alannah has pursued promising opportunities, noting that many of her ideas 'would probably still be sat on the back burner' were it not for their critical observations. At the same time, she feels her critical friends have moderated her fear of missing out on deals and arrangements that seemed too good to be true by highlighting fatal flaws so that Alannah could 'see the catch,' allowing her to 'confidently withdraw from a situation rather than chance it.'

When we start to share ideas, we soon find that we are not alone in the challenges we face. Good critical friends make it easier for us to make decisions and navigate our way around issues that might otherwise have stopped us in our tracks or put us into a tailspin. Critical friends do not necessarily need a wealth of knowledge and experience; even the naïve amongst us can offer illuminating insight.

Several years ago, I was asked to give my opinion on an educational strategy developed by a charitable foundation. Primary and secondary education was not an area I was particularly familiar with, yet this was an advantage. I asked many fundamental questions on matters everyone else had taken for granted and overlooked. I saw things others had inadvertently discounted, things that mattered if learning was to be improved. Arguably the only attribute a critical friend needs to possess is a critical mindset, coupled with a willingness to help us process all that we understand differently.

Jonathan is fortunate in that he can test out some of his ideas with clients before he goes heavy on the planning and makes a firm commitment to roll out to his business network across the UK. Business networking is forever evolving. It is a world of constant innovation, which means Jonathan always has to have one eye on what other groups are doing so he, too, can meet the demand and gain a competitive edge. In addition, Jonathan's networkers are resourceful people with a large part to play in his business success. Jonathan is thus not without a plentiful supply of seasoned networkers and critical thinkers, ready to engage in his pilot schemes and judge the overall experience compared to others. Jonathan's view is that feedback allows him to experiment and quality-control his ideas, enabling him to continue providing rich and varied networking opportunities.

Steve and Georgina involve their employees in the decision-making processes. They strongly believe that business growth can be attributed to the growth of the individuals within it. Steve and Georgina's view is that their employees have a great deal of potential, including the ability to make sound decisions. Team decision-making has proved beneficial in gaining different opinions and insight into the practicalities of what is being proposed. It has also helped staff understand the business and take ownership of the decisions made, so that they can act with knowledge and insight and are ready to align themselves with the future mission.

There is no doubt that involving others in the process makes it a win-win for everyone. Not only do we get to see and explore the feasibility of our ideas, but new insights also emerge. Through the process, and with each new challenge, everyone gets to think differently and enhance their capacity to be critical thinkers and autonomous decision-makers.

EMPOWER OTHERS!

As professionals, we need to be able to empower clients to make decisions that are appropriate and right for them. Indeed, we would be doing clients a great disservice if we allowed them to make a poor decision. Our professionalism in helping clients reach a decision is reflected in our competence to make our own decisions. We can never hope to help clients make critical decisions unless all that we do is done with sound judgement. Any irrational thoughts, groundless actions, and ill-considered ideas on our part present a risk to clients.

Clients often come to us because they do not know what to do or cannot decide what to do. It is not for us to tell them what to do. We can, however, take time to define their problem and present several solutions. Getting from one point to the other requires open communication and a great deal of mental effort on our part. Essentially clients commission us to think on their behalf, which is why we need to be skilled in the art of critical thinking.

A problem is a problem, regardless of whether it is ours or our client's. Therefore, the same level of energy and commitment we put into making personal decisions must be evident in how we work to overcome our clients' challenges. That means applying the same principles we adopt when making our own decisions. The onus is on us to create a calm environment that supports autonomous decision-making. This relies upon our capacity to empathise with clients, promote active participation in the process, and present information that allows clients to own the solution through the choices they make.

We must remember that clients are similar to us when it comes to making decisions. They will experience the same emotional uncertainty and confusion and be equally keen not to rush into anything or fall into traps. If we can mitigate this, we add value to the experience. Everything about the process needs to feel comfortable. If we can ease the stress throughout the process and leave clients feeling respected and in charge of their decisions, we create the potential for a better outcome.

To ensure an outcome, we need to consistently work in partnership with clients. For business advisor Clayton, this starts by appreciating that although we are experts in our field, our clients are experts in their own lives. Getting to know what clients understand and feel about the issue and the impact it is having is imperative. If we show optimism and interest, and devote sufficient time to engaging in an exploratory conversation, we discover the root of the problem and gain clarity on priorities and expectations. By listening and questioning, clients feel assured that we have the knowledge and means to help them find the right solution.

We only have the means to help when we have worked out what needs to be done. As we analyse the situation and develop our creative ideas, we must remember to act in the interest of our clients and not ourselves. As Malinka, who provides home care to older people, says: 'Sometimes it can be hard to steer your mind away from what you would want for yourself if you were in the same situation.' It is a pertinent point. There is a skill to be had in standing back and being able to view things through the lens of our clients and come up with a solution that fits their long-term vision and not our own. Above all, we must not let money sway our course of action, or forget to take account of governance. The ethical, legal, and moral aspects of our proposal cannot be overlooked. If they are, we risk directing clients towards decisions that we would never care to make. That, in itself, is a dereliction of duty.

To empower clients to make decisions, we must give accurate information and educate them on the options. We have to take time to inform clients of our deliberations and present unambiguous and easy-to-understand information. In providing information, there is a difference between talking and communicating and we cannot assume our clients will understand. We must be prepared to demystify the language and go through it more than once. If we are to be sure clients have taken it all in, we need to be alert for signs of bewilderment, correct any confusion, and iron out any misunderstandings. Conscious that clients are not always as 'financially literate' as she is, accountant Emma draws on her creativity when taking clients through the facts and figures. Holding back on the technical language, she translates information through diagrams and analogies 'so as not to bamboozle the client.'

No matter how down-to-earth our approach is, we can always expect further questions. Having deliberated for some time before presenting our clients with possible solutions, we cannot expect an instant decision. Our clients need time to review the information, give it more thought, and discuss it with others. It is a process that often raises other points of issue, which can see us revisiting aspects and fine-tuning our ideas. Recruitment consultant Steve provides information for his clients to take away and digest. At this point, he looks to direct their thinking but is not trying to steer them towards a particular course of action. He aims to raise awareness of matters his clients need to consider to make the right decision.

Before clients decide, we are responsible for ensuring they understand the issues and options available to them. If we think about it, up until this point, we have explored and analysed information on behalf of our client. All potential options are based on our interpretation and rational ways of thinking. If we are to apply good-practice principles, we need to be sure clients are not just taking what we present at face value. By providing information on each potential option, Steve offers clients the opportunity to make an informed choice. By providing guidance on what to consider, Steve is helping clients make their own choice based on their own reason and logic.

Despite our best efforts to create potential solutions, we must appreciate that some of our clients may never come to a decision. Indeed, some might choose to act against our advice. No matter;

let us stay positive and assume that our clients see an option that is best for them within the potential solutions we present. The decisions clients make may not be our preferred choice. If we are to respect clients, we must appreciate that the final decision is never ours to make.

As professionals, we are key in helping clients make choices that bring them closer to achieving their goals and aspirations. We extend clients' trust and loyalty by empowering them to be autonomous decision-makers. As decisions are made, our role changes from critical thinker to critical doer. It is an eminent position that comes with the responsibility of making things happen in line with the plan, by allocating resources and using the same careful judgement that got us and our client to this point.

CURIOSITY KEEPS THE CAT ALIVE

Decision-making starts with a conscious choice. We can either be impulsive and hope for the best or go down the more considered route, leading us to question everything. In choosing the latter, we make better decisions and achieve better outcomes. We learn in this chapter that curiosity is the spark that boosts many of our other talents and endows us with the skills necessary to be competent decision-makers. Curiosity does not kill that cat. There is no likelihood of danger in asking questions. On the contrary, curiosity is the key to unlocking our potential.

Through our inquisitiveness, we broaden our vision as to what is possible. When we are willing to ask questions, we learn and discover things. Not only do we find the answers we are looking for, but we find ourselves exposed to a world of opportunity in which our self-confidence and professional qualities continue to be developed. When it comes to being a well-rounded professional, curiosity is the one characteristic that strengthens all others.

Curiosity activates and engages our brains. It rouses our imagination and compels us to adopt exploratory patterns of behaviour that prompt us to think. Throughout this chapter, we see that, from the outset, we think and behave differently if we approach problems with a critical mindset. Our capacity for critical thought drives us to reflect on past decisions and outcomes that have previously slowed us down or held us back. With this, we become wise about what needs to change to move on and progress more pragmatically. We learn that as we adopt a critically considered approach, we improve our capacity to make logical choices that we can articulate and subsequently execute.

The examples within the chapter show us that embracing a systematic approach eases the burden, eliminates uncertainty, and introduces accountability and quality assurance into our decision-making process. Assuming we are in the right frame of mind, positively fired up, and ready to dig deeper, we can create the space to develop ideas that push boundaries and drive innovation. Quality judgements arise from our capacity to gain an informed and balanced insight, evaluate our findings, eliminate our biases, and respond to the outcomes. So as long as we are not afraid to move outside our comfort zone, are prepared to challenge our assumptions, commit to a detailed, objective analysis of the situation, and have the courage to take the more challenging path, we are all geared up for progress.

Every question we ask of ourselves or of the situation furthers our knowledge and understanding and consolidates our decision-making abilities. It is an iterative process. When we consistently adopt methods that help structure our thinking, we introduce a system of checks and balances. When we scrutinise information and consider the ethics and legalities of our ideas and standards of practice to which we aspire, alongside the effects on ourselves and our clients, we build more logic into the process. In doing so, we can take out some of the guesswork and, with it, some of the anxiety.

It takes courage to keep going until we get to a comfortable decision. Reaching the right decision demands unwavering commitment and a high level of self-discipline. It is evident from this chapter that the fewer reservations we have about our ability to come to a reasoned decision, the more likely we are to put our plans into action. Confidence allows us to express it, test it, and go for it! If we know what information to look for, know what to ask, and who else we can ask, we can see the reality of our ideas. Moreover, we get to see how strongly they hold up when viewed through the eyes of others.

As we learn that decision-making builds character by strengthening our resolve in challenging times, we discover its ability to improve our relationships. Through our competence, we can respectfully promote autonomous decision-making in others. By applying the same good-practice principles, we can help others, including our clients, to make appropriate choices that best serve their goals and aspirations.

If we want to make the right decisions and be sure our clients do, too, we must ask the right questions. However, asking questions is only part of the equation. Between the question and the answer, there is a process. Curiosity leads us to question, but it is thoroughness that steers us towards the best answers and solutions. Remove the process, and we remove the opportunity to critically reflect, think, analyse, and communicate. As a result, we side-step personal and professional growth. Only when we ask the right questions and conscientiously seek answers do we develop the proficiency and professional skill set required to be competent decision-makers.

HOLD THAT THOUGHT

Curiosity and a robust deliberation process improve our chances of consistently making judicious decisions. But, like most things, we only get out what we put in. The quality of the outcome arises from the choices and actions we make at each stage of the decision-making process.

With that in mind, we have to consider the extent to which our methods of inquiry make the grade. Without developing a deeper understanding of the situation, in line with standards, values, attitudes, motivations, assumptions, emotions and feelings, aspirations, expert opinion, and evidence, we compromise the entire process and risk making poor decisions.

One question we need to ask ourselves is: how meticulous are we when it comes to asking critical questions of ourselves and others? If we ignore the need to delve into the details, we must ask ourselves why we do this. Is it that we cannot be bothered and think we already know the answer? Or do we not want to know the answer? Or is it that we lack the skills or confidence to think critically and examine all that we see, think, feel, and hear?

Sound, logical judgements only happen with diligence. If we do not dig deep enough, we do not get the profound insight to validate our reasoning. Ultimately when we cannot make good, principled decisions, we do not get to make things happen in ways that bring satisfaction to ourselves and to our clients. Being meticulous keeps us accountable, answerable, and in business.

The fact of the matter is that no one is ever going to think of us as unprofessional if we are self-disciplined enough to take the time to examine and reflect on issues thoroughly. However, we do not just need to ask questions and do research. We need to ask the right questions and do the proper research if we want answers that direct us towards the right outcomes. When we do right throughout the process, we do right by ourselves and by our clients.

8

PROFESSIONAL EXCELLENCE

A GIFT THAT KEEPS ON GIVING

It is not possible to talk about professionalism without talking about excellence. It is our ability to perform well and exceed expectations that impresses clients and inspires our business contemporaries alike. Fundamentally, professional excellence is a measure of the quality and consistency of each aspect of our actions and endeavours. If we are to get anywhere close to being the excellent professionals we aspire to be, we need to hold ourselves accountable and take responsibility for improving the quality of our service, performance, and professional standards. Excellent professionals become visible through professional excellence. This, in turn, sets us on a path towards business excellence. Our capacity to display professional excellence builds credibility, wins clients' trust, and gives us a competitive edge.

Excellence is not about beating the competition. Yet without professional excellence, we exclude ourselves from a competitive market and if we want any chance of success, we must value and proactively pursue it. The path to excellence is, however, never-ending. Just as we think we have arrived, the goalposts shift. Invariably what we thought was the endpoint turns out to be the beginning of something else. When the world around us moves quickly, we cannot afford to stand still.

Professional excellence must forever be at the forefront of our minds if we are to stand out from the crowd and stay on top. The route to excellence comes through personal growth. If we are to adapt to change, go beyond the quality and standards our clients expect, and be the best we can be at any point in time, this must also be a priority. Professional excellence might be without end, but the learning and development that arise from it are limitless. In pursuing excellence, the outcome will always be that of improvement. The more we improve, the closer we get to achieving excellence.

In this chapter, we consider professional excellence as an aspirational goal, a professional vision that requires a continual commitment to innovation and self-improvement if we are to move forward, onward, and upward in ways that benefit ourselves and our clients. In the quest for excellence, our professionalism in managing the process of quality improvement counts for a lot.

Throughout the chapter, we examine the importance of professional excellence and its impact on our clients' overall experience. We explore how we can take control of quality and focus our efforts on personal and business growth. Emphasis is placed on the transient nature of excellence. Through this, we learn how our mindset influences our drive and commitment to continually pursue excellence. In a bid to avoid complacency and achieve our aspirations, we need to be passionate and fearless, so we can demand more of ourselves, overcome the challenges we face, and raise standards so others can follow.

Yet, much as success needs to be celebrated, we must show humility. We see that by doing so, we create greater opportunities for self-improvement. Alongside this, we discover the longer-term consequences of pursuing excellence and how our endeavours give us a gift that allows us and others to flourish as professionals.

REMEMBER, IT IS A JOURNEY, NOT A DESTINATION

What determines excellence is unclear. It is yet another critical determinant of professionalism that cannot be conclusively determined. What constitutes excellence and what it looks and feels like in practice is always open to debate. What one person sees as exceptional, another sees as unremarkable.

To Rose, a life coach, professional excellence signifies being at the 'top of your game' and having the wherewithal to be competent, efficient, and effective. For Ben, a financial advisor, it represents 'being knowledgeable and comfortable enough to talk about financial matters without making people feel uncomfortable.' To Jake, a business development manager, the idea of doing something consistently better than everyone else by 'smashing it out of the park every time' is where it is at.

There are different ways of looking at professional excellence. These few examples show how it can be related to personal competence, client satisfaction, and impressive achievement. Moreover, Ben's example underlines the role context plays in determining what professional excellence might look like, given the nature of our work and the clients we serve. No matter how we might see it in the first instance, what we find is that excellence is rarely judged on one thing alone. Instead, it is based on a combination of factors that intertwine to create an overall impression.

Taken as a whole, the service we provide is based on a series of activities that result from a combination of interactions and actions. Bearing this in mind, professional excellence is likely to be founded on the opinions of others rather than our own. Clients will judge us on many things from the first point of contact and at all other stages of their journey. They will be looking to see, for example, how empathetic and accessible we are or how compliant we are with sector standards. They will keep a close eye on the efficiency of our processes and how effectively we communicate, paying close attention to whether we fulfilled our promises and provided a service that was fit for purpose, solved their problems, and met their needs.

Our clients will predominantly base their judgements on past experiences, the results they anticipate, and the behaviours and values they expect to observe. Perceptions of excellence will vary greatly. This means there is no defined point or threshold we must pass to be recognised for our excellence. Instead, prior experiences set a precedent. Comparisons will be made on the extent to which we fall below, match, or exceed the standards of others. In essence, excellence sits on a very arbitrary scale and rests on our ability to surpass the personal expectations of clients and stakeholders.

Business excellence differs from professional excellence, although the two are not mutually exclusive. Business excellence is often defined in terms of growth, sales, profits, strategic direction, market share, cost-effectiveness, operational reliability, and efficiency. It represents the outcome of processes, procedures, systems, innovation, quality assurance, effective leadership, and good marketing campaigns.

Our drive for professional excellence serves to influence and create business excellence. Professional excellence is a measure of the type of individual we are, the values we portray, the standards we uphold, and the difference we make to others. In this context, excellence arises through the combination of our attributes and our capacity to innovate and implement good practices. It is based on our passion and commitment to quality by improving what we do to add value, inspire others, and enhance the experience for our clients and stakeholders. In this respect, professional excellence is as much about attitude as it is about action.

There is often a misguided assumption that excellence is about reaching a point of perfection. This is an unattainable goal; in seeking it, we open ourselves up to failure and put ourselves on the road to ruin. We must accept that we sit on shifting sands. The world changes in unpredictable ways. Whatever we have mastered, we will not have mastered it for long. Today's cutting edge is tomorrow's antiquity. The need to continually keep up to date and sharpen our skillfulness and expertise makes achieving perfection nigh on impossible.

Whether we care to admit it or not, as individuals we all have our flaws and imperfections. Some of these make us unique, but others make us vulnerable, particularly when we lack specialised knowledge, and social or practical business skills, for example. This threatens our business's viability, credibility, and reputation. However, no matter who we are, what we do, or how successful we feel, we can all do better and be better at what we do and how we do it. We may not be able to achieve excellence definitively, but we can aim to bring ourselves closer to it. The pursuit of excellence is about improvement and refinement. It is an aspirational intent to deliver a quality service, be our professional best, and move beyond the point at which we are now. This requires a continual commitment to enhancing the service we provide and the personal qualities we possess.

QUALITY COMES AS STANDARD

We cannot talk about excellence without talking about quality since the two are interconnected. Excellence drives quality, and quality leads to excellence. Our ambition to achieve excellence provides us with the impetus to raise our standards and the quality of our service. However, we need to subsequently meet such standards and go on to deliver a high-quality service if we are to achieve excellence.

There is no escaping the fact that clients expect quality as standard. Therefore, it makes good business sense to have quality at the forefront of our minds because it has a beneficial knock-on effect. Providing a quality service generates client satisfaction, which boosts business credibility, profits, and sustainability. Conversely, substandard practices, inefficient processes, and poor compliance limit our capacity to operate, compete, or expand within today's marketplace. So, if we are to thrive, survive and keep growing, we cannot pay lip service to quality because quality matters. It protects and strengthens our reputation and business interests and prevents us from getting left behind.

Quality is not easy to quantify. What constitutes quality of service hinges on the perceptions of our clients. Any thoughts expressed on this reflect a level of satisfaction based on the clients' overall experience, the extent to which their needs have been met, and how closely we conform to the standards and behaviours they expect.

When it comes to quality, client expectations have probably never been so high. In austere times, with limited cash to spare, clients will undoubtedly want the best value for their money. The internet makes it easier for clients to explore our services and assess our distinctive claims and unique propositions before comparing us to similar businesses. The combination of their research, budget, and previous experiences means clients arrive with clear expectations around quality and performance.

Satisfaction comes when we can deliver quality end-to-end. Every interaction or stage of the clients' journey prompts an emotional response. It is all very subjective, and we can never guarantee how clients will feel. If our actions and interactions meet our clients' expectations, they feel a sense of joy, raising their satisfaction level. The more we continue to delight them, the higher their level of satisfaction. In that sense, it has an accumulative effect. The problem comes when we fall short of meeting our clients' expectations, because this creates mixed or negative emotions. This can quickly diminish satisfaction levels and how clients rate our overall quality.

One thing for sure is that people do not settle for anything mediocre. Good is so very average and commonplace. Clients might be prepared to accept good, but good is unlikely to produce loyalty. To stand out, we must be outstanding because outstanding gets noticed. Quality is a strong differentiator that draws in crowds. A top-class individual delivering a top-quality service will outshine everyone around them because they have a wow factor. They have developed the capacity to provide a high-quality service their clients did not believe they would ever get. Their clients love them and wholeheartedly recommend them because they exceed all their expectations. They are highly rated because they have generated a positive experience with all the hallmarks of quality.

If we want to excel, surpass expectations, and keep the clients coming, we need to be alert. We need to find out what our clients' expectations are and then find out what other businesses are doing so that we can seek to do it much better. We need to know our clients' expectations to know if we are meeting them. If we are not acquainted with the things our clients value most, we will not be mindful of the need to replicate them. If we have not checked out the competition, we will never know how we measure up against them.

Anna and Ray, owners of a communications company, spend much time gathering intelligence, gaining feedback and information from clients. This gives them a sense of what excellence looks and feels like to others and how well they are keeping pace with the competition. They regularly read trade magazines, attend trade fairs, and use their contacts in the field. Through this, they discover the latest trends and how other companies innovate and adapt to change. They also conduct client satisfaction surveys and hold a quality circle, where they invite clients to join them and their team in exploring quality issues and creating solutions to problems that have arisen. This has been invaluable. Some of the best and most creative ideas have come from their clients. This has forced Anna and Ray to think differently and do things differently.

The important thing about the strategies Anna and Ray adopt is that, collectively, they help them take control of quality. In our quest for excellence, any degree of improvement is possible if we specifically identify what improvements are needed, the standards we aim for, and what needs to be done to achieve them. The insight Anna and Ray acquire provides them with the knowledge to plan and adapt effectively. It helps them focus their efforts appropriately and innovate. Innovation is the key to business success. If we want clients to want our service, we must keep pace with the times. If we stand still and let the grass grow under our feet, we lose our competitive edge and exhaust new business opportunities. We have so much more to offer when we innovate, modernise, and transform. Fresh ideas and forward ways of thinking help us build on what already exists.

However, any quality improvement brought about by innovation must be managed. Not all change results in a positive outcome. We need to monitor and evaluate the impact of any change to be sure it enhances the overall quality and does not compromise existing quality. We need to be confident that we are eliminating the problems that cause dissatisfaction, and not creating more. This means we need to continually gather data and insights to be sure of developing and sustaining high-quality performance and service delivery. There is no end to excellence because constant change necessitates constant improvement, particularly if our desire is to create a unique service that gets us noticed.

RAISE THE BAR HIGH

The first rule of professional excellence is that 'good enough' is not good enough. When we accept good enough, we impose limitations on ourselves and our expectations. This holds us back, prevents progress, and limits our potential. If we want success and the recognition that comes with it, we must raise the bar, be pioneers and demand more of ourselves. This means setting higher standards and rising to the challenge of doing whatever it takes to make it happen, even when what it takes is complex. If we are to strive for excellence, we need to lead the way by putting ourselves on a very different path from others. When we pursue and model excellence, we become trailblazers. We set the quality and standards for others to follow and raise the bar entirely.

Anyone who has ever attended a business awards ceremony knows these are auspicious occasions. Rightly so, because any success brought about by going above and beyond in terms of quality and standards deserves to be recognised and celebrated. However, excellence is not about winning awards. It is about pursuing a higher purpose: that of self-improvement, doing better, and being better. Our award winners will have challenged themselves to do just that. It is this which will have led to their success. Having already committed to pursuing excellence within practice, winning the award is like a cherry on top of the cake. This formal recognition brings the winners a more profound level of satisfaction for something they were already enthusiastic about and dedicated to.

Before anyone gets too disheartened by the absence of a gilt-edged award on the shelf, it is worth remembering that recognition of excellence comes in many ways. The certificates of achievement and accreditation we acquire attest to our compliance with industry and quality standards. The positive online client review, which describes how we delivered as promised, the recommendation that brought us new clients, and the thank you card and gift expressing gratitude for our expertise and efficiency all validate our pursuit of excellence. Any form of recognition and appreciation that recognises quality, innovation, the effectiveness of our commercial endeavours, and service to clients, is worth shouting about, not least because best practice inspires others to follow suit.

Excellence is, however, transient. Past success does not necessarily define future success. As any athlete will tell you, you are only ever as good as your last race. Their dash to the finish line in record time, lengths ahead of their fellow competitors, represents the outcome of months, maybe even years, of arduous training to achieve a much sought-after personal ambition. Throughout this process, they have challenged themselves to be better than they were the day before. It is this which has led them to achieve success. However, to stay on top of the game and keep winning, they must keep training and pushing themselves to be better, fitter, and stronger. Why? Because there are other athletes out there desperate to catch them up and pass them by.

It is the same in business. The glory of any momentous achievement will only ever be short-lived. Unless we aspire and commit to the continual pursuit of excellence, the competition will quickly muscle in to steal our glory and our clients.

NO ROOM FOR COMPLACENCY

We cannot achieve a state of excellence. We can only pursue it. Our efforts to ensure high-quality service delivery may have brought us to the point of perceived excellence, but that point is not fixed or secure. We might feel we have made it, but excellence has a shelf life. It represents a snapshot of who and where we are today, not who or where we will be tomorrow. If we want to be known and appreciated for our outstanding quality of service, adoption of best practices, and commercial effectiveness time and time again, we cannot rest on our laurels or become complacent.

The world changes rapidly, and we need to evolve with it. If we want to stay in business, we must stay ahead of the market and look for ways to improve ourselves so we can go the extra mile. If not, we fall by the wayside, sacrificing our livelihood and reputation. Our professional credibility requires us to pursue excellence. It is a quest that requires drive, dedication, and discipline.

Sometimes we need to be our own cheerleader and celebrate our achievements. However, if we stand about too long, shaking our pom-poms and hailing our triumphs, complacency soon creeps up on us. Like a pernicious weed, it roots us to the spot, blocks out the light, and inhibits our growth. Complacency affects us all from time to time. It happens because we become too comfortable and overconfident, or lose our passion. Either way, the outcome is the same: we sit back, stop trying, and stagnate.

When business is going well, and everything is running effortlessly smoothly, we feel more confident and satisfied with our performance. We can soon develop an inflated ego and let success go to our heads. Unfortunately, the confidence we feel leads us to believe we are invincible. As a result, we overestimate how good we are, becoming oblivious to our inadequacies or the need for change. As a result, we might think that we are in a strong position, particularly if sales are growing, profits are increasing, and clients are returning. The fact is, we are actually in a very vulnerable position. At this point, we are likely to take our foot off the gas and switch on the cruise control.

When we achieve success, we think we have found the winning formula. We believe we are extremely good at what we do, and what we are doing is extremely good. In this state of mind, we can easily fall into the trap of thinking there is nothing else left to learn or that we do not need to do anything more to improve ourselves or the situation. We accept the status quo, and in doing so, we do the same things in the same way. This adds to our contentment because work is easy, enjoyable, and stress-free. We sit in our comfort zone, functioning on autopilot.

However, autopilot is risky. We act unconsciously and no longer think when we operate in this mode. Our endeavours to do our best and be our best slowly decline. We stop challenging ourselves and no longer question our decisions and actions. We take risks and make bad choices. We take for granted our knowledge and skills. We no longer innovate or aim higher. We stop looking for new opportunities and ignore what is happening around us. In essence, we stop doing everything that brought us success and helped us achieve excellence in the first place.

We soon become bored when we opt to do the same thing repeatedly. Repetition is tedious; it affects our motivation and diminishes our passion. When we are no longer excited by what we do, we do not work as hard. We become apathetic and careless and no longer take pride in our work. We find ways to cut corners and become inattentive to detail. Through this, errors occur and accidents happen. At the extreme, our lives and those of others are at risk. Passion drives us to want to do our best and be our best. Without passion, there is a danger that we relinquish the professional standards we once valued, which defined us as a professional and set us apart from our competitors.

When it comes to professionalism, complacency is the enemy, a dangerous threat that turns excellence on its head. We cannot ride on the back of past achievements for long. If we do not continue to excel, accounts of how great we are soon become accounts of how great we were. Right now, we might be doing all the right things right, but our outstanding qualities will only see us into the future if we commit to the continual pursuit of excellence.

Complacency is no laughing matter. There is little to commend when knowledge and skills are outdated, quality is poor, standards slip, and best practice is not implemented. Clients want someone sharp and focused, not someone asleep on the job. To survive, we need to live up to clients' expectations. This requires us to see the bigger picture, dispense with mediocrity, and define for ourselves what is and is not acceptable. With vision and insight, we can do whatever it takes to make our goals a reality and keep clients satisfied.

LEARN TO BE HUMBLE

So, the question is, how do we pursue excellence and avoid death by complacency? Depending on where we perceive ourselves to be, we must do one of three things. We must stay grounded and continue to take control, or climb down from our cloud, tempering our excitement and euphoria as we descend. The third option is to take our head out of the sand and admit we need to change and keep pace with the times. Whichever situation we identify with most, personal growth is the route to achieving and sustaining excellence. We can only give our professional best when we are at our professional best. This requires continual self-improvement.

To grow, we must be prepared to seek and invest in opportunities to learn. Our knowledge and skills can soon become obsolete. If we are to evolve and embrace change, we need to get on top of the situation and be in control of our expertise. This not only requires time, money, and energy; it requires discipline, courage, humility, and a growth mindset. Chapter 9 focuses more specifically on how we can maximise personal and professional development opportunities. Here, we focus on exploring why discipline, courage, and humility are essential and why we must be of the mindset to seek opportunities for personal growth.

We only have so many hours in the day, and most of us do not have endless pockets of money. All the same, professionals are resourceful and proactive in seeking new opportunities in the pursuit of excellence. There are learning opportunities in everything. The secret is to adopt strategies that allow us to develop new skills, gain additional insights, remain attentive to current issues, and discover what we do not know.

Heating engineer Cameron updates his knowledge of technology, systems, and safety by accessing e-learning resources and attending training events. Anna and Ray attend network and telecommunications conferences to keep abreast of current trends. Similarly, Nicala, who provides private health insurance, reads industry-related journals and magazines each week. To develop good judgement in business, Jonty, a property developer, subscribes to a business book club. The range of books Jonty receives provide fresh ideas and the strategic insight needed to achieve his personal development and business goals. Cathryn, a public relations consultant, listens to podcasts and attends business networking events. They are, as she describes, 'entertaining ways to improve technical competence, mental health, and well-being.'

We see here that the advantages of learning new things and developing our skill set are numerous. Chapter 9 explores how informal learning methods like those adopted by Anna and Ray, Nicala, Jonty, and Cathryn are often the most effective for personal development and understanding professionalism. However, no matter how we choose to learn, learning keeps us motivated and moving forward in our pursuit of excellence. Learning and development provide the mental stimulus that improves our self-awareness and self-confidence. New knowledge, skills, and insight help us improve our efficiency, work quality, and ability to problem-solve and embrace change. What is more, they furnish us with fresh and creative ideas that are needed to innovate.

Almost any activity associated with self-improvement supports us to feel at our best and do our best. But, of course, we can only continue to improve if we are ready to challenge ourselves and be willing to learn. We must want to develop our knowledge and skills and be sufficiently motivated to move outside our comfort zone. This requires a growth mindset.

Our intelligence, talents, and standards of practice are not fixed. Thus, we can all improve and expand these if we are committed to putting the effort in. A growth mindset fuels a can-do attitude. This helps silence our inner critic and heightens our self-belief. It gives us the power to continue enhancing our performance and achieving success. If we can convince ourselves that we can achieve anything, the chances are we will, no matter how hard it first appears.

Once we believe in ourselves, we take a different approach to continuous improvement. We are less fearful of trying and more willing to give it a go. We appreciate that it may be initially challenging, but if we practise, persevere, and learn from our failures, we know we will improve in time. A growth mindset drives us towards excellence because it gives us confidence in our ability to succeed. It empowers us to continually aim higher and push ourselves that bit further. It motivates us to seek opportunities for development and put effort into achieving the desired outcome.

Pursuing excellence is not about striving to be an expert in everything. It is about having the appropriate knowledge and skills to present our best professional selves to the world and deliver the expected quality and standards. Unfortunately, we can never master it all because there is far too much to grasp, understand or be proficient at. Hence, we need to focus our development on the things that will make the most significant difference to our clients and stakeholders in terms of our relationship with them, the service we deliver, and the outcomes we achieve.

Although we might consider ourselves knowledgeable, competent, and professional, it would be arrogant to assume we have nothing left to learn. Believing there is no further scope for improvement will only isolate us, not only from people (no one likes those with a big ego) but from opportunities. Those who think this way are unlikely to defer to the opinion of others. Consequently, they close themselves off from the very conversations that expose them to new ideas and the insight needed to enhance success. By virtue of their self-importance, they become impervious and unreceptive. This means they rarely innovate, never fully reach their potential, and are left ill-equipped to deal with change.

To be at our professional best, we need to remain humble. Humility is an essential professional quality. It makes us better learners and helps us avoid complacency. In accepting that there are always new things to be learned, we continue to be curious and take responsibility for our development. Thinking and believing we can always do better ensures we remain open-minded, ask questions, seek feedback, and listen more. This means that we are not only willing to learn, but we are willing to learn from others. This makes us receptive to the knowledge and wisdom of those with more experience and we open ourselves up to endless possibilities. Without humility, we remain unimaginative, narrow-minded, and switched off to what is possible. As a result, we do no more than quash the quest for excellence.

STOP MAKING EXCUSES AND EMBRACE THE FEAR

It is all too easy to say that to be our professional best we must strive for excellence by remaining humble, keeping up to date with current trends, learning new things, and expanding our skill sets. In theory, this seems simple enough to do. The reality is that it is much more complicated. The path that leads to excellence can be an emotional journey that includes hurdles along the way. We cannot escape the existing psychological and physical barriers to learning and development. They will always be there and affect us all in some way. In addition, we will each face different challenges that potentially hold us back.

For one, our past educational experiences may not always have been positive. We have all suffered at the hands of bad trainers, emerging from conference presentations or training sessions completely bewildered and despondent, woefully aware that the last few hours of our lives are ones we will never get back! The mental image of ourselves back at school ploughing through homework does little to enhance our enthusiasm. Nor does the potential cost, because it is often hard to justify making any financial investment without knowing exactly how, and indeed whether, self-improvement will provide a return on investment and generate future revenue. Then there is that old chestnut, the issue of time, because there are never enough hours in the day to work, live a life, and learn. We may intend to set time aside, but the phone rings, the printer jams, and new clients appear. Before we know it, our schedules have changed, time has passed and, once again, personal development is shelved.

We can also easily talk ourselves out of learning something new because we fear failure. We often believe that things will be too hard to understand or that we will somehow lack the ability and skills to grasp whatever we are trying to learn. When we think our best will not be good enough, we abandon hope before we start and do not bother to try. We even convince ourselves that we are too old to learn or adapt to new ways of learning.

It takes courage to acknowledge the existence of gaps within knowledge and skill sets. The process of self-improvement requires some serious introspective analysis and reflection in relation to our knowledge, standards, and practices. When we look in the mirror, we do not always like what we see. Our vision of unblemished beauty and magnificence is tainted by reality, with the realisation that, professionally, we may not be so appealing and attractive after all.

Discovering we lack proficiency, or are no longer the expert we once were, can be unsettling. The actions we need to take to close the gaps demand a lot from us, which can be overwhelming. Once we start learning, we discover there is so much more to learn than we first anticipated. The more we know, the more we discover what we do not know. In mastering new skills, we come across stumbling blocks. We try things out, believing we understand and know what we are doing, only to discover we do not. Our independent spirit takes over and, too embarrassed to ask for help, we struggle on. With slower-than-expected progress, we feel deflated and incompetent. With this come anxiety, procrastination, and inertia, and before we know it, we are drained of our optimism and the energy we need to come out on top.

Pursuing excellence requires a fearless willingness to venture into the unknown because learning is challenging. Our professionalism is reflected in how we deal with these issues, sustain our motivation, and keep moving forward, even when it is difficult and we feel out of our depth. This is where having a growth mindset is to our advantage. Without one, we put up barriers and sabotage our success. We immediately limit our ambitions if we do not attempt to better ourselves. Any development will be haphazard and slow, and we risk becoming incompetent and obsolete and missing out on seeing the results we could have achieved if only we had tried. If we roll over and accept that we are powerless to change our attributes, abilities, and practices and do nothing to pursue excellence, we will never come close to achieving it. We cannot realistically pursue excellence without self-improvement. So, unless we are prepared to prioritise learning and development and engage in a course of action that improves us and our service, we cannot genuinely claim to be professional.

GET WITH THE PROGRAMME

To be our professional best we need to work to overcome the challenges we face and see this as part of the process of pursuing excellence. If we want to stand out as an expert with high standards, we must make it happen. As well as developing a growth mindset, we need a plan that we are prepared to commit to. Planning is pointless unless we commit to putting the plan into action. Only then will we see results. This presents another challenge, because our commitment to act requires emotional acquiescence and a robust professional identity. If we are in the right frame of mind and feel like a professional, we are more likely to commit to developing ourselves accordingly to enhance our level of professionalism. As we saw in Chapter 1, our identity gives us the passion and purpose that fuels our desire to reach our potential and strive for excellence.

However, before developing our plan, we need to acknowledge what we need to learn and how we need to develop. This is not as simple as it seems. There are times when we will have a clear understanding of our shortfalls and know exactly what improvements are needed and how to achieve them. There will be other times when we know what we need to learn or improve, but we have yet to figure out where to start or how to approach this. In contrast, we might be fully aware of the knowledge we must acquire but have no enthusiasm for it whatsoever. Then there are the times we are unaware of our lack of ability, or what it is we do not know and, therefore, oblivious to the need for self-improvement.

In the pursuit of excellence, professional development is a continuous activity. It is not something we need to do all at once. By its very nature, it allows for an incremental approach to development. A plan will enable us to take control, be strategic, and set realistically achievable goals over time.

Anna and Ray, together with their business coach, set monthly goals that support the growth of their communications company and their personal development. As well as concentrating on improving efficiency and developing new products and services, they focus on individual issues. As Anna says: 'To do things right, you need the right skills, which means that sometimes to get things off the ground and meet deadlines, we are working on the business and ourselves simultaneously.' It is a pertinent point that illustrates the integrative nature of our personal strengths, professional actions, and success.

Liam, a web developer, has created his own plan, which focuses on sharpening his work habits, business processes, and technical skills. New to the business world, Liam is keen to 'get going and move up a gear.' All credit to him for his determination. By his own admission, however, he is prone to procrastination. Planning what he wants to achieve over the next year provides structure and directs his actions. It keeps him focused and committed to improving in some way each day. Liam's plan includes regular meetings with himself to track and reflect on his progress and congratulate himself on his achievements in terms of what he has learned and what he has done subsequently.

It is a good approach because not all learning leads to action or improvement. Only when we begin to apply our knowledge and reflect on it can we say that learning has occurred. By keeping track, Liam can keep the ball rolling with current objectives and anticipate his future goals. As he says: 'It seems like once you have grasped one thing, there is always something else to conquer.' As Liam knows, it is not always easy to stay committed. Enthusiasm wanes from time to time. We want to progress quickly, and our impatience drives our focus towards how far we have left to go rather than how far we have come. Personal development is challenging and exposes us to different ways of thinking and doing, which take time to assimilate and integrate. As Liam has discovered: 'If you want success, you just have to learn to roll with the punches, appreciate setbacks, and see it through.' To excel, we must persevere. No matter the challenge, we need to stay positive because this is the very thing that helps us build and sustain momentum and raises our self-esteem, especially when we are not quite at the point we imagined we would be.

REFLECT AND ATTEND TO WHAT STARES BACK

There is a particular pleasure in personal growth and success, but we must be realistic about what we can achieve within the time we have. This has led Cameron to adopt an approach to self-improvement driven by the evidence he gathers in his work diary. He records appointments and events throughout his day and any feedback he receives. Alongside this, he records his thoughts. Then, at the end of the month, Cameron works through a series of reflective questions that help him evaluate how he is doing. He examines what is working, what he has done well, what he could do differently, what needs to change, and where improvements need to be made. This feeds into both his business and personal development plan.

In pursuing excellence, reflection is important in guiding our thoughts and actions. For Liam and Cameron, it is an active form of self-assessment that helps them process their experiences and put things into perspective. Through it, they can monitor what they do and evaluate their professional standards, and in doing so, they avoid becoming complacent.

We will never build, or indeed be confident of, our reputation unless we work towards and live up to the standards we set ourselves. Reflection helps us monitor this and puts us more firmly on a trajectory that leads to accomplishment. We understand our growth, development, and success only when we look back and examine our progress, achievements, and activities. What we learn about ourselves and our mistakes enables us to acknowledge what we need to do differently next time. Through reflection, we can hold on to our vision of excellence because the process helps us to identify success, crystallise our thoughts, clarify our goals, and recognise our priorities.

It is interesting that, for Cameron, reflection has helped him discover his natural abilities and appreciate his limitations. If he thinks things are going wrong, or his attempts are not up to scratch, he aims to learn from it and try again. When it becomes apparent that he is not improving or is not satisfied with his standards, Cameron knows it is time to get help from people who are far more capable. We learn from Cameron that when our attempts to develop ourselves take a less-than-favourable turn, our growth comes from admitting this. Having pushed on and pushed past the point at which we expect positive results and triumphant mastery, we need to concede defeat. This is not a bad thing. On the face of it, it might seem as if we have failed, but our admission has all the earmarks of a professional who knows the boundaries of their capabilities.

Discovering and acknowledging our limitations gives us the power to remedy the situation. We can make plans to do something about it, ensuring neither our clients nor our business suffer because of our lack of experience or proficiency.

We must remember that pursuing excellence is an aspirational intent. There is a professional expectation that we will have ambitions to improve. This does not mean we should be overly ambitious and expect to achieve everything we set out to accomplish. Sometimes in our pursuit of excellence, we need to free ourselves from the emotional burden of trying to get it right all by ourselves. Sometimes it is necessary to seek advice, look to those who are more capable, or even delegate tasks or outsource aspects of our work to improve our quality and service. We do not need to be good at everything ourselves; what matters is that we take responsibility by making the best use of the available resources. This way, we can channel our energy into improving ourselves and our business in other ways.

SEEK GOODWILL AND RETURN THE FAVOUR

We tend to see excellence as an individual pursuit rather than something that is built on co-operative engagement. No matter how hard we work or how talented we are, we cannot succeed without the support of others. Many individuals will have helped us become the professionals we are today. Reaching out and asking for help is often portrayed as a negative personal weakness, when in fact it is a positive way of developing excellence. No matter what line of business we are in, we each face challenges. The problems we face will by no means be unique to us; somewhere, someone will have encountered and, indeed, successfully overcome similar obstacles and setbacks. Yet we often put off asking for help and advice because we feel threatened by those who have the knowledge, skills, and insight we do not yet have. We imagine that people will assume we are unintelligent and will talk down to us. We develop an inferiority complex and fear giving power to people's egos in a way that will demean us. Yet this is rarely the case, and it often comes as a surprise that those we approach are genuinely interested in our problem and want to help us.

When we permit ourselves to reach out to others, we invite change. If we allow ourselves to build connections with those in the know and capitalise on their wisdom and experiences, we are far more likely to develop excellence and improve our service.

With additional help and support, we can often achieve far more, in less time, and to a higher standard, than we could alone. Taking time to admire the talents of others and acknowledging the impact of their help and support can be a humbling experience.

I am always struck by the humility that others have shown when I have asked for help. I feel privileged to be supported by those with proven competence, discernment, and a mind to look beyond themselves. When I have been confused, lacking in direction, or unable to think straight, the selflessness and kindness of others have been transformative. Accessing their rational insight has boosted my self-esteem and undoubtedly improved my overall success. Moreover, I have found that people are often happy to help because helping makes them happy. Doing good satisfies the soul. It boosts well-being, increases connectivity, and provides a sense of purpose.

The willingness to help others is a mark of professionalism. It reflects a genuine desire to contribute and to witness success in others. To be professional, we need to combine generosity of spirit with humility. Professional excellence is about more than just developing our qualities and practices. It is about bringing out the best in others so they can achieve the same level of excellence that we demand of ourselves. Professionals are people who give back by paying it forward. Not only should we seek to change ourselves, but we should also seek to change the world and others around us. To do this, we must be willing to share the stage and the limelight. To help others along the way, we must give our time and impart our wisdom without expecting a reward, neither resenting nor feeling threatened by subsequent success.

We all had to start somewhere. The best way to reward and thank those who have had the grace to steer us in the right direction is to help others. If we can keep sight of where we came from and the difficulties we once faced and approach assisting others with a selfless mindset, we can make a significant impact. In supporting others, it is possible to make a difference in how people feel about themselves, their success level, and the standards they adopt. Our advice provides an opportunity to demonstrate best practices and expose aspects of professional excellence that others might not otherwise get to see or experience. When we model professional excellence through our thoughts, words and deeds, we inspire others to up their game and develop excellence within themselves and in those they subsequently go on to meet.

PLANT SEEDS TO GET FLOWERS

Professional excellence is a differentiator that sets us apart and makes us commendable. When our actions, talents, and services extend beyond 'good' and bear the hallmarks of quality, we thrive. Conversely, if we drag our feet and allow ourselves to fall behind, we face an even more significant challenge when it comes to catching up. Therefore, our efforts to innovate and continually meet client expectations ensure that we do not get left behind and that we grow and flourish at a steady pace.

Professional excellence is like a special gift: one that not only keeps on giving but gives back in return. By its very nature, excellence produces gratifying results. Our clients value and appreciate an excellent standard of service. This generates high levels of satisfaction and loyalty. The rewards for our efforts are reflected in our internal feelings about a job well done and the profits we generate. They are observable, too, through the credible reputation we gain amongst clients and peers within the business community. With each new client and collaborative opportunity, there is a joy to be had over and over.

Within this chapter, we have seen that professional excellence has no defined point. If we desire something more than fleeting success, we must keep moving in a forward direction and avoid complacency at all costs. If we are to evolve and deliver a quality of service that goes beyond what clients expect, we must continually refine and improve our service. As we have seen, professional excellence depends on our capacity and willingness to assume responsibility for quality and develop ourselves accordingly. Without either, we reduce our competitive edge and limit the potential for business opportunities.

If we want flowers, we must first sow the right seeds and then keep watering them. We see that, in the pursuit of excellence, continual efforts lead to a constant pay-off. There is something of value in each of our nurturing actions that helps boost our success, enabling us to grow. The gift of excellence gives back to us before it gets passed onto our clients.

To be in control of quality, we must know what it is we are aiming for. We must understand what professional excellence means to our clients and to us personally, connect the two perspectives, and manage the improvement process. This requires us to stay alert and gather our intelligence. We must continually check out the competition, stay tuned to current trends, examine data and client feedback, and reflect on our performance and outcomes to advance. Throughout the chapter, we have seen various ways this can be achieved and how, collectively, these help us plan and hold ourselves accountable to our aspirations and vision of excellence.

What we get back from our efforts here is a sense of realisation. The reward is fresh ideas, an insight into what we have already achieved and are delivering on, and an indication of the direction we need to be heading. This insight allows us to be in control, hone our expertise, and make a difference in areas where it matters. Rather than trying to be all things to all people, we evolve according to client and industry needs and our business interests.

If we want to be the pioneering trailblazer who stands out from the crowd, we must demand more of ourselves and set our standards high. Professional excellence does not come without self-improvement. It happens when we focus on driving out complacency and prioritising learning and development. Our quality improvement plans need to include ongoing personal growth. Without personal growth, at best, we become static; at worst, we become obsolete.

However, we must be resourceful and proactive and make the most of the opportunities available to us. We must be willing to move outside our comfort zone and overcome any personal barriers to self-improvement. Professional excellence emanates from drive, determination, and discipline. Emphasis is placed on the need to work on improving ourselves and our business simultaneously. To achieve success with either, we must seek to develop a growth mindset and a can-do attitude and remain humble throughout. With the right attitude, we become teachable. We continue to be curious, self-directed, and open to the ideas and opinions of others. Our philosophy also makes it possible to put our ideas into action. It gives us the strength to persevere and see our projects and plans through to completion.

Our journey towards self-improvement allows us to grow continually. Whether we have read a book, attended a training session, or listened to a podcast, we will almost certainly come away from it enriched with knowledge, skills, and a deeper understanding of ourselves. The gift is that of transformation. We increase our expertise by knowing more and having the skills to do more. In applying what we have learned, we can give more and do better because we are better. Our sense of achievement, in line with our vision, positively affects our self-esteem and professional identity. This fuels our passion and empowers us to pursue professional excellence continually. Here, the gift is that of unwavering determination to be exceptional and outshine others.

What is apparent throughout this chapter is that through the process of self-improvement, we create professional excellence that assists in building business excellence. We achieve because of our efforts, and our clients gain because of the outcomes. Excellence has lasting consequences that are not confined to our relationship with our clients. Humility enables us to reach out to develop ourselves and others. Through our efforts to pursue excellence, we have a legacy to give. By demanding more of ourselves regarding quality and standards, we can help others do the same. Our knowledge and wisdom can inspire others to be the best, so they have something to shout about. Our humility furnishes ourselves and those we help with a more profound sense of purpose and well-being.

If we take the view that professional excellence is a measure of the values and attitudes we portray, we discover that when we value quality, client satisfaction, innovation, self-development, collaboration, and humility, and mix them with a growth mindset and a can-do attitude, we have something of a gift. This allows us to pursue professional excellence in ways that benefit ourselves, our clients, and others, time and time again. If we remain true to these values and keep moving forward in the pursuit of professional excellence, it will forever be a gift that keeps on giving.

HOLD THAT THOUGHT

To pursue professional excellence and success, we must build connections and tap into the wisdom and experiences of those who have gone before us. In business, few people ever rise to the top under their own steam. Everyone needs the help and support of someone. However, help and support only come with humility. The path to self-improvement requires us to stay grounded as we grow. The corresponding approach to professionalism demands that as we grow and improve, we empower others to do the same. The critical question arising from this is: are we humble enough to reach out to others to seek guidance and give guidance? Or are we doing more of the former at the expense of the latter?

As we begin climbing the ladder of success, we tend to look straight ahead, seeing nothing beyond our goals. Occasionally, we must stop and look back and see who else in business needs a hand-up to achieve their ambitions. Two facts need to be remembered. First, professionals are characterised by their generosity of spirit. Second, that professional excellence is about something other than beating the competition. Therefore, as we rise to the top, we need to pull people up the ladder with us and not kick it away when we get there. We need to pay forward the help and support we have received to others in equal measure.

Success is fleeting, hence the need to continually pursue excellence. Focusing on ourselves and overlooking the need to help others would be short-sighted. If we want to grow our business, we must bear in mind that the professional excellence of others is a key contributor to our success. We measure our success through business growth. As we start to expand, the strength of other people's businesses potentially affects the strength and viability of our own.

When it comes to maintaining standards, we may indeed set the bar high. However, in limiting our support, we limit our influence. With this, we break the cycle of professional excellence and by our own doing, the gift ceases to keep on giving. We need to empower others to pick up the pace, aim high, and avoid complacency, or no one benefits, least of all us. Through our actions, we restrict the number of people we can look to, be inspired by, work or collaborate with. This does nothing more than stand in the way of our efforts to pursue professional excellence. If we want to be our professional best, give our best and receive from the best, humility must be a personal strength.

9

DEVELOPING PROFESSIONALISM

TUNE IN AND TUNE UP

Have you ever wondered why some people act more professionally than others? From time to time, we come across people who are contemptuous and rude. Putting little thought into what they say and how they say it, they care nothing about those whom they offend. Occasionally, we encounter those who operate unscrupulously and adopt dodgy business practices or are utterly unmindful of their bad habits and unsafe practices. However, for every ill-mannered, dishonest, and naïve individual out there, we encounter others whose actions and words portray the very essence of professionalism. So, what leads some people to act in a conscientious, honourable, and principled way, whilst others remain seemingly oblivious to their actions and how unacceptable their behaviour is?

It is often assumed that becoming a professional is a natural process. In fact, it is anything but. Professionalism is not inherent within us; we do not enter the world of work bursting with firm and steadfast professional ideals that we instinctively put into practice. Our sense of professionalism is something we acquire and develop over time. We do not all relate to professionalism in the same way, which means that, on an imaginary scale of professionalism, we are all at different points. Where we are depends on how tuned in we are and whether we are observing, listening, and engaged enough to appreciate the need for professionalism. It depends, too, on how tuned up we are in terms of checking our performance and adjusting ourselves in line with what is expected.

As we saw in Chapter 8, when we focus on self-improvement, we put ourselves on the path to professional excellence. Here in Chapter 9, the spotlight falls on the process of self-improvement that leads to professionalism.

Becoming a professional is a complex process of transformation. How professionalism comes to be understood and incorporated within our day-to-day practice depends on the combination of internal and external factors that influence our development. The chapter explores how these collectively affect how we think, feel, and act. Throughout, we see how, as we develop, the presence or absence of certain key transformative elements impacts our level of understanding, subsequent behaviour, and response to situations.

Emphasis is placed on the need to take a strategic and self-directed approach to meet our individual development needs. As we examine the necessity for active engagement with a range of cognitive and social activities, we explore the value of critical reflection as a mechanism for self-regulation. Through this, we discover how our approach to engagement and self-assessment affects our capacity to exemplify professionalism in ways that enable us to meet the expectations of our clients and stakeholders, pursue excellence, and inspire others to follow in our footsteps.

DIFFERENT PEOPLE, DIFFERENT TRAITS

We often see professionalism as a reflection of our personality. Our distinct combination of attributes, traits, and qualities leads us to act in a particular way. How we are as people often determines how we are as professionals. If socially outgoing, we are likely to be congenial with our clients. If we have an impulsive streak, we might act in the moment without considering the consequences. When it comes to professionalism, we should not disregard our personality as an influencing factor. However, how we behave is not solely determined by our nature. It is also influenced by the ways in which we learn and how we are nurtured by others.

If we took the view that professionalism was all down to our nature, then we would have to believe that to function as a professional, we would each need to hold the same specific attributes. Conversely, if we lacked the necessary characteristics, we would have to accept that we would be somehow professionally compromised. We cannot assume that our personality predetermines our level of professionalism, yet neither can we overlook its role in developing us as professionals.

We are all unique. Our combination of qualities makes us distinctive and we each have some personality traits that work to our advantage and some that do not. In business, our personality can be a great marketing tool. However, none of us is perfect. The most successful and highly regarded professionals amongst us have personality flaws. Our personality influences the choices we make and the actions we take. Although we hold some undesirable characteristics, this does not mean we will behave in a malevolent way. It does mean, however, that we might default to bad habits, which could be detrimental to our clients, business, and reputation.

Like any other trait, our unfavourable characteristics are a part of us. We cannot ignore them or take them out of the equation. However, while inherent within us, it does not mean we are stuck with them for life, or that they will hold us back from becoming a much-admired professional. Personalities are more flexible than you might think and can change over time.

Life experiences teach us things that change us. The situations we find ourselves in lead us to adopt different patterns of behaviour. This is more of a progressive change rather than an instantaneous one, but a change nonetheless. Generally, time mellows us. With age and experience, we develop better social skills. Harsher aspects of our temperament often soften, and we become kinder, more sympathetic, and easier going.

Despite this, it would be very remiss of us to sit back and hope that life experience will positively impact and improve us. Unfortunately, while we wait, our negative qualities may have set a precedent for how we are perceived and affect our business and reputation without us knowing it. It will almost certainly be too late to respond by the time we realise this.

It matters not that we have flaws. What matters is that we address them. To develop as a professional, we need to be self-aware and critically explore aspects of our personality. If we are conscious of our characteristics, we can self-regulate and take steps to limit, improve, or strengthen these. Through our goal-setting efforts, we can initiate inner change much more quickly and set ourselves on a course that allows us to authentically display the type of professional characteristics that are desired and admired.

IT IS ALL ABOUT THE NATURE-NURTURE COMBO

As we saw in Chapter 2, our values, attitudes, and behaviours are also inextricably linked to professionalism. Our values act as guiding principles. What we consider to be important manifests through our attitude. Our attitude influences our mindset and predisposes us to think in specific ways, which as a result, influences our approach and the actions we take. Hence, if we genuinely take a particular value to our heart, it is almost impossible not to align our behaviours with it.

Our attitudes and values are not fixed constructs. They are indeed transient and can shift in any direction. As we progress through life, they develop and change as we engage with the world around us. How strongly we come to feel about specific personal and social values is open to external influences. Our family, friends, peers, social networks, life experiences, and the cultural environments we have grown up in and work in all shape our attitudes and values. All that we feel, hear, read, and observe as we experience work and engage and converse with others exposes us to and reinforces specific values, attitudes, and behaviours.

In a positive and supportive environment, when times are good, we will undoubtedly be empowered to uphold what we regard as critical professional values and standards. But find ourselves in a toxic environment, disenchanted with the world, and we risk compromise. Here, the gap between what we know to be appropriate and what we do potentially widens. Professionalism is prone to fluctuation. In the right environment, professionalism can flourish. In a less-than-favourable one, it can diminish. Circumstances can lead the most eminent and respected amongst us to lose sight of our values and act in unbecoming ways.

The erosion of our attitudes and values is something we will expand on in much more detail later in this chapter. The point is that our development as professionals stems from both nature and nurture. The combination of the two can have a powerful influence on how we live up to professional ideals. It concludes in one of three ways: we continue to grow as professionals, regress, or fail to develop as professionals. To be on an upward trajectory, we must engage with ourselves as we engage in our day-to-day activities.

There are learning opportunities in everything. However, we do not necessarily learn by the most effective and efficient means and not all learning leads to development or self-improvement. Unless we are actively engaged in the process of learning, we are unlikely to connect with what is going on in the world around us. We need to be active participants rather than passive recipients. If we want to be a professional everyone admires, we cannot expect to sit on the sidelines absorbing information that happens to come our way. We need to invest ourselves emotionally and physically in the process of learning and make the most of our experiences for the benefit of ourselves, our clients, and our stakeholders. Our ability to actively engage is central to heightening our appreciation of professional expectations. It steers us in the right direction and helps us press the reset button occasionally so we can continue to uphold, modify, and regulate our attitudes, values, and behaviours.

To self-nurture our development and, indeed, be nurtured by others, we must be sure to acquire rich experiences by engaging with a supportive community that values professionalism and provides us with opportunities for conversation, reflection, and feedback. These things raise our self-awareness, bringing insight into where we are and what we should aim for. In combination, they help us appreciate what is expected of a professional and enable us to align our personal qualities and values, attitudes, and behaviours so that we are recognised and admired as a professional ourselves.

NOT ENOUGH TO KNOW. WE NEED TO DO!

To act professionally, we need to understand what this means and how to make it a noticeable part of our day-to-day practice. In the introduction, we saw how professionalism was context-dependent. Not only do we need to understand professionalism based on the actual type of work we do, but we also need to understand it in relation to our roles and responsibilities, and understand it from the perspective of our clients and stakeholders.

Our level of knowledge and understanding drives our actions. If we are unaware of our professional obligations, we risk acting in inappropriate and unprincipled ways. First and foremost, to be professional, we must be cognisant of the principles and standards we need to achieve. This can be a challenge, given that no universal understanding of professional expectations exists. The onus is on us to discover for ourselves what these are.

By virtue of the type of industry and sector we work in, or our association with a particular professional organisation, many of us will be required to abide by a professional code of conduct. Such regulations sit alongside other organisational policies and procedures, and legislative and regulatory frameworks that relate to the nature of our business activities. Thus, reading these documents is an obvious place to start if we want to gain awareness.

Codes of conduct primarily exist to promote social values, moral qualities, and ethical principles and to endorse professional excellence. Typically, they include statements that reflect expected behaviours, values, and ideals. Essentially, they are designed to ensure we operate within the law and that the interests and welfare of the public, our clients, and others we work with are represented and upheld. We are entrusted to commit to achieving the defined standards and honour their intent. We potentially face sanctions and public shaming should we be found to fall short of meeting the required expectations.

The codes capture the fundamental constituents of professionalism. They aim to place the expectations and standards explicitly required within the context of our practice and provide us with guidance. They have the potential to influence our understanding. However, they are of limited significance in determining how we behave.

Professional behaviour is very unpredictable. Knowledge of such codes does not stop individuals from violating them and behaving in an unprofessional and unethical way. Conversely, it is perfectly possible to function without them. Indeed, not all organisations and industrial sectors have established codes of conduct. However, this does not necessarily mean an individual's behaviour will be less professional or unethical, as many other factors inform our understanding and influence our behaviour.

Several years ago, I interviewed a number of healthcare students as part of my academic research. I asked them what things influenced their professional behaviour. Very few mentioned their code of conduct. Quite a lot did, however, cite the Brownie Guide or Scout promise, whilst others quoted passages from holy books and drew on religious and spiritual teachings. Many of these principles, such as treating people with respect and being honest, kind, and considerate, are the foundations of professionalism that we see reflected within codes of conduct. This shows that our early formative years and our faith and spirituality play a significant part in establishing our professional values and how we think, feel, and act as a professional.

Nothing in business is ever simple, and our day-to-day activities can often be complex. No two clients or tasks are the same. Situations arise that challenge us and present dilemmas. To a great extent, such codes will not necessarily guide us to the answer of how to approach the matter. No doubt, if we found ourselves in a problematic situation, we would act on instinct, use our inner wisdom, or draw on our past experiences as the basis for action and moral reasoning. We would be unlikely to retrieve and consult any code before acting.

This is not to suggest that a code of conduct should be ignored. Far from it. On the contrary, it is a valuable source of information that helps raise awareness of, and reinforces, the type of obligations and standards we are expected to meet. Being acquainted with such information is a good starting point. However, we must remember that such codes provide only information. Even if they raise our awareness of professional principles, we still need to follow through and act in principled ways.

We can know all there is to know about professionalism, but it does not make us a professional. For this to happen, our learning needs to translate into action. We need to apply what we know to the real world. No amount of reading will prepare us to navigate each situation that we encounter effectively. There is not just knowledge to gain. There are mindsets to adopt, insight to be appreciated, and skills to be mastered if we are to be successful, achieve excellence, and be held in high regard.

BE DRIVEN BY REALITY AND GET OVER THE SHOCK

Professionalism only becomes a prominent part of practice with effort. It would be much easier to understand if it had an exact single meaning or a distinctive principal focus. Sadly, this is not the case; professionalism is not a single entity but a multitude of related concepts, attributes, and expectations. To develop ourselves as professionals, we must appreciate all its combined elements and their symbiotic relationship. Its multidimensional nature takes time to internalise. Not only do we have to understand every aspect, but we must also value and respond to them by developing ourselves accordingly.

It is a complicated puzzle to unravel. We must work out how to align ourselves and our services to meet and deliver to the expected standards. We are on our own with this in many ways, and it is up to us to connect the dots. This requires us to stretch ourselves beyond passive forms of learning and actively engage in the process of becoming a professional. If we are to present our best professional selves, we must learn from the world around us. We can only do this when we maximise the opportunity to learn from our experiences and social interactions. These have the potential to transform our understanding of professionalism and ourselves as professionals.

Whether starting a business, changing our services, or finding ourselves with new roles and additional responsibilities, embarking on a new venture can be exciting. However, it can also be an eye-opener. We are often naïve and unprepared for what we will encounter. We might think we know what is expected of us. However, only when we have gained sufficient experience can we fully appreciate the knowledge and skills we need to acquire or the attitudes, values, and behaviours we need to adopt.

The reality of our experience can be very different from what we initially imagined. We are often shocked and surprised by what is involved and how ill-equipped we are. Our new experiences challenge our ideas and beliefs and force us to change our perspectives on many issues, including professionalism. Emotionally it all feels a bit uncomfortable, as our inexperience leads to self-doubt and feelings of inadequacy.

Reality shock is a natural part of any transition. If we are to be successful, we must move on and shift up a gear. We can improve our confidence, competence, and capability by rolling up our sleeves and getting on with the job. It might seem complicated and demanding initially, but doing it quickly leads us to develop the knowledge and skills to cope and adapt to the new reality. Becoming a professional relies upon understanding professionalism in relation to the work we do, the roles we undertake, and the type of clients and stakeholders we serve. This only comes with experience. Professionalism is not something that can be taught. It can only be discovered and acquired over time.

Any educational or training programme we have embarked upon may have given prominence to the topic of professionalism and conveyed professional expectations. We may have role-played our way through scenarios exploring professional issues and behaviour as a means of developing our knowledge and understanding. The chances are we will have learned something, but what we learned is unlikely to have transformed us significantly. This is because the knowledge gained through instruction in a classroom can only partially expose the realities of the complex world we operate in.

Reality is a succession of unfolding events in which we see the consequences of our actions. Our performance raises emotions, which often leads us to analyse situations and reflect on influencing factors and the appropriateness of our efforts. Case studies and role-playing represent simulated activities and hypothetical situations, and are therefore unlikely to trigger the type of emotional response that would prompt evaluation of actions and circumstances. As participants in such activities, we are asked to apply what we know to what we anticipate. We do not get to see the actual outcome; hence we do not discover what we do not know, nor how real clients will respond to our words and actions. Moreover, simulated activities assume that knowledge applied in one situation can be readily used in other cases. Rarely are two situations the same, so there will always be a disparity to reconcile.

Overall, classroom-based learning is limited when it comes to developing us as professionals. Like the codes of conduct, the knowledge we acquire in the classroom will serve as a guiding principle. Consequently, with each situation we encounter, we must determine the most appropriate approach. Learning and development as a professional become much more meaningful when they are derived from personal experience. The experience exposes us to the true complexity and reality of our work. Through this, we understand ourselves and the standards we need to uphold.

LEARN THROUGH EXPERIENCE

Quite simply, we learn most by doing. But, in doing, we also learn from the interactions that transpire. Together they progressively develop our professional knowledge, skills, values, attitudes, and behaviour. As we tailor our services to meet the needs of our clients, each task or job that we do represents a unique experience. We get to apply what we know, make decisions, and solve problems through the process. Each time we will learn something new, refine our skills, acquire new ideas, or understand ourselves better. Numerous activities and interactions inform and transform. What might seem insignificant at the time works to change and develop us over time and, in combination, provides a holistic experience that brings contextual coherence that connects us with our work in a way that helps us do our job better and be better professionals.

In terms of professional development, experience represents more than a hands-on approach. Experience equates to things we engage with or participate in as we go about our day-to-day lives. Whether it is a conversation we have had, something we have observed, read, watched, or listened to, each incident or interaction has the potential to influence us in some way. However, the impact on our development as professionals will be minimal if we choose to be passive consumers. We need to engage actively. This starts when we consider how all we have learned from the experience can be applied in a way that elevates our potential and extends our level of professionalism.

Frank, a musician, starts each day by listening to motivational podcasts. These inspire him to believe in himself and give everything his best shot. Frank makes the interesting observation that people often listen to podcasts because it seems a trendy and impressive thing to do. He says he is 'more impressed when people are capable of actually listening, and curious enough to try it out.' Frank is right. If it has captured our attention, we should delve deeper, look for a connection, and seek opportunities to learn from it, apply it, and develop through it. We must put it all into practice and make it real for it to have any impact.

Without practical application, anything we come to learn about professional behaviours and expectations is abstract information. For example, make-up artist Alannah always knew that she had to be a team player to collaborate. However, it was only when she began to work on film sets alongside special effects teams that she came to appreciate how much her personal qualities and contributions affected the creativity and outcomes of various projects.

As a young journalist, Andreas thought he knew all there was to know about pitching an idea to publishers. Only after several rejections did he realise how inexperienced he was. While he did not initially get it right, he did improve because, for him, 'practice made perfect.' Feedback and a better understanding of the publishing industry came with each rejection letter. By applying this knowledge and insight to each new pitch, Andreas sharpened his approach, which led to him getting work writing human interest stories. Having got the job, Andreas soon realised how much he needed to develop empathy.

Part of Andreas's professional development was learning to accept rejection respectfully. Although Andreas appreciated the need to accept the outcome with good grace, it was largely down to him to find a way of managing the process and his own emotions. In his words: 'It is not something they teach you at journalism school. Over time, I stopped gnashing my teeth and came to respect people more for their honest insights and opinions.'

We learn from Alannah and Andreas that it is only when we begin to apply our knowledge and skills during our working activities that we get to appreciate their effect and impact on outcomes. As well as competence, we develop a range of other attributes needed to carry out our work professionally. Without experience, we have no context. The context in which we work provides the scaffold that strengthens our understanding, allowing us to see the significance of specific qualities and behaviours.

MAKE THE TRANSITION

Whatever we do, there will always be some element of change. As we innovate, grow, and expand our business, new systems, additional contracts, and up-to-the-minute directives create distinctive experiences that bring fresh challenges. As a result, we need to revise our skill set to adjust to unique circumstances and situations. This might seem daunting, but from a professional development perspective, it is a big plus. Restricted experience confines professionalism to one context. This narrows our views and can prevent us from appreciating professionalism in its entirety. As we set out on a different path, taking on new roles and responsibilities, we are often forced to challenge our thoughts and ideas about professionalism and alter our perspectives. In whatever way we need to modify ourselves or accommodate new obligations, the ultimate goal is to be the best professional we can be.

Steve, a recruitment consultant, recalls how his ideas of professionalism changed when he set up his own business. Coming from a corporate world, he had always taken time to dress smartly, be punctual, and arrive prepared. Since setting up his business and becoming an employer, he has taken a different view. Experiences of dealing directly with clients led him to appreciate how much of his professionalism is portrayed through his actions rather than his appearance. It is not that the significance of dress, punctuality, and expertise is dismissed. It is just that Steve's attention is more focused on his internal ways of being in order to achieve success for his clients, himself, and, more recently, his employees. For Steve, building trusting relationships has taken on a new significance. Through trust, Steve can lay the foundations for timely, open, honest client conversations and give his employees the confidence to make decisions on the company's behalf.

Steve's example illustrates that engagement and interactions with clients and employees create a sense of purpose and heighten the relevance of certain professional behaviours. The relationships we form assist in developing us. Through the content and language used in the conversations that materialise, it is possible to bring meaning to the word professionalism. The connective relationships we build with others expose and reinforce humanistic and social values. These have a positive impact on the way we come to embed these values in practice and intensify the relationships we have with our clients and others.

The context and nature of the work we do, and the conversations we have, combine to create a holistic experience. This is particularly significant because it goes beyond the acquisition of factual knowledge. It takes us into a place where we can develop broader practical knowledge and skills, define and refine our values, attitudes, and behaviours, respond to different situations, and continually learn and improve.

This all-inclusive experience grants us a depth of understanding that allows us to develop in accordance with the professional expectations of all stakeholders. As we embrace the necessary changes, we are transformed emotionally, psychologically, and intellectually. This transformation alters our understanding of what it means to be a professional and how we perform as a professional ourselves.

EXPERIENCE IS NOTHING WITHOUT REFLECTION

Our experiences are only the starting point for professional development. Unless we respond somehow to what we feel, read, see, and hear, or to what transpires because of our actions, there is little chance of self-improvement. To achieve personal growth, change needs to occur in how we feel, think, and act. However, change only happens when we actively engage in reflective learning. It is this which transforms our insight and understanding of professionalism. Only by looking back on our experiences with a critical eye do we gain clarity on our abilities, where we need to improve, and what to do next. This clarity leads us to act differently to become better professionals. Without action, we are unlikely to develop in ways that help us meet the needs of our clients and stakeholders.

In essence, reflection on our experiences assists in building our expertise and strengthening our values and competence. In Chapter 8 we saw how Cameron, a heating engineer, and Liam, a web developer, adopted a formal approach to reflection, in which they analysed the factors which influenced their actions and outcomes. As a self-evaluation process, this enabled Cameron and Liam to become more self-aware of their standards and performance and initiate and flexibly structure development in line with their aspirational goals.

We do not necessarily need to formally reflect to improve ourselves and the quality of our service. Almost every day, in our heads, we will press the rewind button and play back some of the day's events. Andy, a marketing consultant, reflects as he walks his dog, whilst Sarah, a personal stylist, takes time out with a coffee to quietly consider the week's events. On the other hand, Rose, a life coach, engages in encouraging self-talk because, as she says: 'We all have the ability to change, but sometimes we have to hear it before we can see it.' The methods might differ, but the purpose is the same for Andy, Sarah and Rose: to understand their practice and the decisions they have made or the actions they have taken. In doing so, they come to appreciate what needs to stay the same, what needs to be done differently, and what potential options are available to them going forward.

Experiences represent a series of often unique, complex, and extraordinary events. These events often raise emotions. What we feel inside can unexpectedly prompt the process of reflection. When something goes well, we get excited and feel proud of ourselves. On the other hand, frustration sets in when we have made a mistake, or things do not seem to be going our way. Either way, we are prompted to revisit our experiences, which either reinforces our sense of professionalism or exposes things we did not previously appreciate.

New to self-employment, Andy, a marketing consultant, reflects a lot. After 30 years of working in a corporate environment, he has become aware of how the transition accentuated his strengths and weaknesses. As an employee in a large organisation, he notes: 'Personal weaknesses were less of an issue as you always had a cushion to fall back on.' With plenty of people around possessing the correct skill set needed to complete the work, Andy could learn from them at his own pace. Now that he is freelance, those weaknesses, by his own admission, 'stand out like a sore thumb.' Conscious of addressing such shortfalls, Andy uses reflection to sharpen his skills. It has been a steep learning curve for Andy, but a positive opportunity to learn and 'become a more complete professional by filling in the gaps and being more self-directed and resourceful.'

In a different way, Sarah, a personal stylist, uses reflection to ensure she provides an all-inclusive service and effectively applies the knowledge and skills she's gained through various training programmes. By reflecting, Sarah explores how different style methods associated with colour, shape, fabrics, and lifestyle translate into practice. It allows her to question her effectiveness in collectively implementing these principles to meet individual client needs. Her range of options allows her to experiment with ideas and prompts her to try different things and adopt new approaches. These various applications bring different experiences and other opportunities to reflect on the actions taken. For Sarah, it is a way of assessing her ability to integrate and apply her knowledge to deliver a comprehensive service. We learn from Andy and Sarah that reflection helps us respond to new situations, develop the skills needed to adapt, and experiment until we get the right outcome.

SHARED REFLECTION, SHARED BONUS

Of course, reflection does not have to be a solo activity. We benefit more when we make it a social process and reflect alongside others, not least because we can access alternative perspectives and eliminate personal bias that can hinder self-reflection.

Recruitment consultants Steve and Georgina facilitate reflective discussions at their team meetings. As a group, they revisit testimonials, explore feedback, and review cases and situations that have arisen. It is an opportunity to consider events and the approach they have taken. Working together to solve universal problems or individual challenges allows them to pool their collective wisdom, share their differing perspectives, and pick up on things they might otherwise have overlooked.

As employers, Steve and Georgina observe how these exploratory conversations have helped the team understand that there is value in what they do and how they do it. With shared understanding comes the harmonisation of professional expectations and ideals. For Steve and Georgina, engaging in the process of reflection has reinforced the value of reflection as a tool for learning and improvement. The collective attempt to analyse has led to new ideas and created opportunities to implement change. Moreover, shared reflection has helped the team bond by removing some of the fear associated with reflection and by building honest and supportive relationships. In addition to creating ownership of aspirational goals and achievement standards, it has enabled staff to contribute to the development of others and the business. Here we see how collective reflection broadens insight and develops a better working environment that leads to professional development at all levels, converting personal and business limitations into strengths.

If we are serious about ensuring that our practices and services are up to date and that we can fulfil our roles and responsibilities, then we must put time aside to reflect. It matters not where, with whom, or how often, we reflect. What matters is that we do more than think about experiences. To be professional, we must regard reflection as something more purposeful. We need to see reflection as the route to becoming a self-directed learner, reactive to change and uncertainty, and capable of continued learning and self-regulation.

To benefit from reflective practice, we must be effective in our endeavours. This means being committed to adopting an analytical approach and developing the skills that allow us to have in-depth critical conversations with ourselves or others. We must remain objective, unbiased, and honest in our appraisal of ourselves and our situations. We must learn to question our thoughts and actions positively, raising our self-esteem and inspiring us to further our development.

We need to critically reflect on our experiences to bring our thoughts and feelings to the surface and gain the insight and understanding needed to raise our self-awareness. Without deeper knowledge of ourselves and how we practise, we cannot consciously consider our level of professionalism and the extent to which we meet standards and progressively develop ourselves and our business. This leaves us ill-equipped to deal with changing landscapes and the challenging situations we may face. Moreover, it leaves us ignorant about our competence and the appropriateness of our actions, and thus ignorant about the need to improve our future selves. Just as experience is nothing without reflection, reflection is nothing without action. Having reflected, we need to accept everything we discover and commit to doing something about it.

CONNECT WITH PEOPLE AND THEIR IDEAS

To be our professional best, we need to learn from the best and position ourselves within a community that will nurture our development and further our success. Networking events are often marketed on the premise of the opportunity they bring to promote ourselves and our business rather than on the prospect of self-development. But we should never underestimate how much mixing socially with a broader community of business owners or members of industry-specific organisations aids our progressive development as professionals.

A common purpose often unites people that come together as part of a group. In the case of business networks, there is a shared interest in wanting to be successful. Within industry-specific organisations, there is an aspiration to pursue professionalisation with an underlying desire to raise the sector's profile, improve standards and reputation, and enhance career development opportunities for its members. These networks and organisations represent a community of practice where diverse individuals gather to interact, advance, and collaborate. They include people from various sectors with differing roles and responsibilities and years of experience and expertise. This makes members of those communities a rich and accessible resource for developing ourselves as professionals.

Jonathan, who runs a business network, puts a lot of effort into getting the right people into his network. He wants to add value to people's networking experience by ensuring his members are the type who are resourceful and can positively contribute to the success of other businesses. Jonathan believes that networking is not just about connecting people. It is about connecting people with those who have knowledge, skills, and ideas. Every network co-ordinates its activities differently but, typically, networking centres around some form of social activity. When networks such as Jonathan's champion the ethos of support, the encouragement we feel can uplift us and enrich the entire experience. This opens our minds to fresh perspectives and creative ideas and motivates us to develop ourselves and get things done. We do not have to be listening to guest speakers to learn or be enthused. We simply need to be chatting with others. Conversations are a powerful tool for personal development. If we can avoid the hard sell, and engage in thoughtful discussion, there are no limits to the amount of information and insight we can share and obtain.

As business development manager Jake says: 'It is not always easy to start that conversation when you are a networking novice.' Jake admits it is something he initially had to work at. He was inspired by those whom others would naturally drift towards. Wanting to be similarly successful in the art of engaging others, he took time to observe what it was that made the difference. The lightbulb moment came when he realised he needed to dispense with formality, be himself, and let his human side and personality shine through. Seeing best practice in action, Jake found the confidence to 'go for it' and model himself on the way others acted and conversed. The thing is, once we start those conversations, we immediately enhance our social and communication skills. Jake discovered how to present himself and chat in ways others could relate to. This was something that also resonated with Sarah, a personal stylist. She found that by listening more, she improved her ability to engage with others on a deeper level.

For Emma, an accountant, conversations keep her informed. They allow her to update her knowledge and tune in to what is happening in other business sectors, locally and nationally. It helps her avoid the tunnel vision that arises when we work with the same people. In such cases, we can often think and feel the same things. Conversations with owners of larger businesses have broadened Emma's insight and helped to develop and expand her services to match what companies expect and require. Through discussions, she gets to hear how people feel about particular issues and how the changes in tax legislation impact them. Through this, Emma has become aware of the need to develop herself to be able to give practical and emotional support.

If we are not part of the conversation, we are on the periphery, away from all the action. As a result, the benefits that come with social connectivity pass us by, and we remain unaware of the opportunities to add value and make a difference.

LISTEN UP!

Networking is an opportunity to hear about what is happening in the real world and where businesses are heading. Adam, who repairs computers, finds hearing about people's new ventures and initiatives exciting. His fascination lies in the fact that behind success there are always problems to solve, solutions to be found, and mistakes to correct. This gives us a platform on which we get to question people, explore their rationale, examine the challenges they have faced, and appreciate what it is that has brought them success. Through this, we get to understand the world of business better. We learn what qualities, skills, and resources are required to get us where we want to be. What is more, we discover whom we can turn to for advice when we are facing similar issues.

To me, conversations that start with the words: 'Oh, you will never guess what happened the other day!' are always thrilling because suddenly, we are vicariously re-living someone else's journey of success, adversity, or disaster. No matter the circumstances, the outcome will always be learning and development. There will always be a take-home message to reflect on. We get to learn from the lessons learned by others. We discover things to avoid and the things we should do. We discover how to reconcile dilemmas, become aware of the significance of professionalism, standards, and responsibility, and consider how we would match up to those challenges and expectations. Through other people's spontaneous narrative, we receive guidance and get to access ideas and insight and reflect on things that would not otherwise be apparent to us.

Of course, we do not have to network face-to-face physically. Digital technology allows us to interact with others on a global scale. So it is no surprise that social media communications manager Simone uses various social media platforms and applications to engage with other like-minded individuals. For her, online networking is beneficial in supporting her development. She gets to make friends and watch live videos that enable her to advance her skills, and by engaging in group chat, she can share her experiences and learn from others.

How we choose to network is neither here nor there. What matters is how we are prepared to engage and connect with others. If we are of a mindset to connect and communicate on a deeper level, we optimise our opportunity to strengthen our professional identity and develop as professionals who can achieve professional excellence. Networking brings development through socialisation. If we can sustain it, we find it has all the elements of a good education. Meaningful participation within a supportive practising community brings progressive and continuous development of skills, attitudes, and behaviours. Observing, talking, and listening facilitate active discovery, and we develop a deeper understanding of all that is around us. The exchange of information raises our consciousness of expectations and standards of practice. Through this, we can seek the support that helps us respond to professional requirements and meet the demands of our business. The fact that all of this happens over a computer keyboard, breakfast, lunch, or dinner, is something quite amazing.

GET WITH THE RIGHT PEOPLE WHO HAVE THE RIGHT VALUES

The environment we are in can either enhance or erode professional values, attitudes, behaviours, and standards. To flourish professionally and develop positively, we must be in the right place with the right people. While spaces, places, and communities with which we engage will differ, several elements critical to professional development need to be visibly present to sustain and enhance our professionalism.

Fundamentally, we need to be within a supportive and nurturing environment that accepts us as a legitimate part of that community and permits our active involvement in various activities that bring to life and reinforce aspects of professionalism. In addition, there must be access to role models, people with different expertise and experience, and opportunities for dialogue, reflection, and feedback. These are the things that help to transform us and determine the type of professional we come to be. However, these variables can also fluctuate. Thus, professionalism is not a definite outcome.

When new to an organisation or network, we sometimes feel pressured to fit in and impress others. It is a natural state of self-preseveration. We all want to be liked. However, social acceptance can take time, particularly if our association with a community is brief. Showing compliance with expected group norms and behaviours is what usually gets us accepted into the fold. The need to survive and be accepted leads us to follow the crowd and display affiliative behaviours. Here we risk sacrificing our standards without question just to fit in. Rather than being seen to belong, we need to feel an inner sense of belonging with the power to remain true to ourselves and our values.

Electrician Iain set up his own business after being made redundant. The company he worked for had ceased trading quite quickly and there was much controversy and speculation amongst the business community as to why it closed the way it had. As he describes it, Iain found himself amongst a group of networkers who wanted him to 'dish the dirt.' Iain expresses how the stigma of redundancy can make it harder to engage with others. Iain felt he was being coerced and pushed towards a series of actions he did not want to take. Feeling uneasy about this, Iain knew he needed to find a network with people genuinely interested in helping him make a fresh start.

As soon as we start to modify our behaviour, our actions can drift towards meeting the expectations of others rather than the expectations we have of ourselves. Phil, who owns a cleaning company, can also relate to this. He once worked in an environment where speed and efficiency became a top priority. As a result, Phil noted how colleagues stopped communicating, interactions declined and, in time, group actions failed to portray humanistic values, respect, or collaboration.

The question is, how could fundamental social principles such as these become so devalued so quickly? The answer lies in the level of encouragement and reinforcement we get. It is not always what is being said or done that leads us to behave unprofessionally. Often, what is not being said or done leads us to disregard the significance of particular professional practices. Without constant reminders through visual or verbal stimuli, or other methods of communication, it slips off our radar, and so does our concern for it.

We can unconsciously replicate, reconcile, and normalise deviant practices and inappropriate actions. In an environment where we are exposed to frequent incidences of unprofessional behaviour, for example, we can unwittingly find ourselves becoming tolerant of other people's actions. We often accept unprofessional behaviour rather than contest it, to maintain the status quo and avoid marginalisation. No matter when we replicate and excuse unprofessional behaviour or renounce our values and standards, we thrust our reputation into reverse. Get with the right people, and we stand a better chance of doing what is right.

BE PART OF SOMETHING BIGGER

Good practice and humanistic values must be constantly demonstrated and reinforced to build and sustain professionalism. If we can find people with exemplary virtues and values who care enough to want to develop a relationship with us, we have found a good role model. Role models are central to influencing our behaviour and standards and to developing our professional identity.

When Phil found himself amongst people he describes as 'well-rounded professionals', it was not just the advice they gave that influenced his actions, but the way they gave it. The open discussions intensified the strength of the relationships they formed. This made Phil aware of the need for connection and participation, making interpersonal aspects of his working practices evermore salient. Through his own experiences, Phil was motivated to change his approach. Malinka, who provides home care to older people, on the other hand, notes how networking alongside a group of nutritional therapists reinforced her way of thinking and behaving with regard to dietary requirements of her clients. She came to appreciate why what she did mattered and the difference it made. This strengthened her belief that she was acting in the best interest of her clients and doing all she could to prevent them from becoming malnourished.

As we bond with people, we form friendships. As friendships grow, so do we. If we can build a trusting relationship with inspiring role models who are kind, empathetic, and willing to share their wisdom and expertise, then we are well on the road to increasing our potential and reaching a new level of understanding, like Phil. Or, in the case of Malinka, a renewed sense of her professional practice.

Of course, we cannot overlook the fact that amongst the role models we encounter, there will be anti-role models. These are the kind of people who embody traits we should avoid if we want to be admired and respected. Anti-role models can be a positive influence as observing unprofessionalism in others can motivate and inspire us to be better professionals. However, anti-role models will only be a positive influence if we have progressed in our development as a professional to such a level that we can recognise deficiencies in others. If we cannot distinguish patterns of behaviour, we have little control over how we come to be influenced by others.

Professionalism is not something that happens by accident. We must be sure we are continually moving in a positive direction. If we want to be admired as a professional, the best place to be is among those who are professionally admired. If we pay close enough attention, their professional values and virtues will become exemplified within us. We, too, can become role models who inspire others to be strong, principled professionals.

We can create change in ourselves and others if we take the time to be part of something bigger and take a more active role within the networks and organisations to which we belong. Human resources manager Niamh co-ordinates training events for other HR professionals in her region. This has enabled her to get to know more people in her sector. We often shy away from engaging with people in the same line of work. We tend to think of them as competitors rather than collaborators. Yet for Niamh, other HR professionals have become a channel for support in tackling present-day challenges. As Niamh explains: 'Although on a day-to-day basis we often face the same issues, it seems pointless trying to out-rival one another, when they can be overcome by helping one another.' Niamh's active involvement in the group has meant she has become a prominent figure and a key connector. As a 'go-to person,' she finds that 'people with so much talent want to talk,' and Niamh learns things when they do, a reminder that by developing connections, we build knowledge.

Similarly, Jaime also plays an active part in an organisation for administrators. They voluntarily sit on a board that peer-reviews applications of those members wishing to gain accreditation for their professional standards, values, and practices. To make fair and reasoned judgements, Jaime must be conversant with a series of benchmarks and standards. There is no doubt in Jaime's mind that this role has broadened their understanding of professional expectations and enhanced their practice as an administrator as they have adopted some of the good practices they have encountered within the applications.

Jaime's role means they move from a position of being someone who adopts those standards to someone who is a guardian of those standards. It is a pretty responsible position to be in, and a transformational one at that. When we sit on external panels, boards, or committees, we get exposed to, and become more conscious of, professional issues and how they play out in practice. These types of roles typically focus on safeguarding standards and maintaining the reputation of the organisation and its members. So, through our involvement, not only do we create our own vision of professionalism, but we also get to create an inspiring vision for others to follow.

Niamh's and Jaime's experiences show us that we can improve when we become part of something bigger. A deeper level of involvement furthers our connection to matters of professionalism. Through that exposure, we can drive up our own standards and guide others across a whole sector to reach their full professional potential. In doing so, we become role models, developing future role models.

FOREVER FINE-TUNE

No matter how distinctive we are as individuals or how different our work, roles, and responsibilities are, we all have the potential to be admired as professionals. The underlying issue is not where we start but where we end up, because the path to developing professionalism is uncertain and ambiguous. To be professional, we cannot remain motionless in a world that does not stand still. To survive, we have to adapt and realign ourselves to changing expectations. What this means is that professional transition and transformation are never-ending. This requires us to retain a sense of the professional we aspire to be and continually develop ourselves accordingly.

We have seen in this chapter that, without much to guide us, we have to guide ourselves. This requires us to be self-directed in our approach to learning and development, as well as self-regulating. Self-direction leads us to the point at which we think and act as a professional. It helps us to tune in to what is expected, so that we develop an applied understanding of professionalism. The discussion and illustrative examples in the chapter highlight that if we use our initiative, and are motivated enough to actively engage with a broad range of cognitive and social processes, we can benefit in many ways.

As we read, observe, listen, and converse, we learn. Our experiences expand our knowledge and skill sets. We become more self-aware of our own development needs. We get to focus on the things that matter to us. Whether vicarious or direct, we acquire insight into standards, gain new ideas, and access alternative perspectives. We get to see professionalism played out in the words and actions of others within different settings and fields of practice. Moreover, we get to see how others react to our professional intentions. What we learn transforms us emotionally, psychologically, and intellectually. Acquiring a broader overview of professionalism changes our perspective and we begin to think, act, and behave in informed ways. We begin to internalise all we know such that we naturally incorporate it into what we do.

If we are to pursue professionalism, we have to develop the capacity for self-regulation. We cannot assume that our approach to professional development will be effective. Although we might be adopting the right strategies, there are no guarantees that all the reading we do, the training we undertake, or the networking events we attend will enhance our level of professionalism. This chapter shows examples of how cultural environments, interactions, and circumstances do not always change us for the better. We can unintentionally tune in to the wrong things and unconsciously adopt behaviours that fall below expectations. This makes the need for self-regulation even more critical. Self-regulation allows us to tune up and check in with ourselves, so we can be sure of developing, improving, and performing well. It is a way of quality-assuring our excellence regarding our attributes and practices.

If we consider self-direction to be the process that moves us towards thinking and acting as a professional, then self-regulation is the process that leads us to contemplate if how we think, feel, and act is leading us to be better professionals. Through self-regulation, we allow ourselves to press pause and assess how well we are doing.

Reflection is central to the process of self-regulation and primarily the only way we can control our development and steer ourselves in the right direction. Within the chapter, we have gained much insight into the benefits of reflection, both to ourselves and to those we might work alongside, particularly when achieving personal growth. When we have a critical conversation with ourselves or others, we get to synthesise information and evaluate our performance. In combination, this brings clarity, deepens our understanding of our attitudes, values, and behaviours, and prompts us to try new things or change our existing approach.

Using reflection as the basis for self-regulation places us in a better position to assess how we respond to change, if we are doing the right things in the right way, and if we are amongst the right community that provides the right level of support. It allows us to assess if the outcomes match the benchmarks and expectations we had in mind. If so, we get to pat ourselves on the back. If not, then we get the opportunity to press the reset button and try again. Through the process, we can fine-tune our development strategies, plans, and goals as we go along. This allows us to learn from our mistakes, make better choices, and direct our actions towards maintaining and developing our professionalism.

We can only continue to positively develop ourselves if we regularly stop and recalibrate. Each time we tune in, tune up, and fine-tune our thoughts and actions, we align ourselves more closely to our professional ideals. Each small change creates a big difference in the way we perceive ourselves and the way others perceive us. If we can be self-disciplined enough to be both self-directing and self-regulating, we enhance our capacity to meet professional expectations and demonstrate excellence even in times of change. This generates external admiration and inspires others to adopt the qualities and good practices we portray. Self-direction and self-regulation are mechanisms of constructive control that bring practical benefits at every stage of our development. If we do not take control, we end up being controlled or constrained by a multitude of internal and external factors, which stifles our development and limits our potential to exemplify professionalism.

HOLD THAT THOUGHT

Professionals are situationally responsive and repeatedly seek to enhance their professionalism in ways that confidently reassure themselves and others of their capacity to live up to professional expectations and pursue professional excellence. This requires us to be professional pioneers, aspiring individuals, confident in our potential to achieve, and strategically purposeful in our approach to continuous self-improvement.

If we want to transform ourselves as professionals and transform our future and that of others, we must first put our house in order. We can only be professional pioneers if we are sufficiently tuned in to what guides us and what is expected in terms of values, personal qualities, and standards of competence. Moreover, we must be tuned up enough to know that professionalism manifests in our approach to better ourselves, and deal with the uncertainty and unpredictability of our working practices. Unless we stop and take time to reflect effectively, with purpose and focused analytical intent, we can soon end up off track.

With this in mind, let us pause for a moment and consider this fact. We cannot exemplify professionalism when we have an incomplete or fragmented understanding of the concept, or fail to actively boost our opportunities for learning and development. Neither will bring about transformation. Primarily when we focus on developing ourselves as a professional, we become self-nurturing agents of change. To achieve this, we must ask: to what extent do we tune in, tune up, and fine-tune? Moreover, how effective are our strategies in ensuring we actively create and protect our vision of the professional we want to be? These are pertinent points to consider because these processes push us towards being better professionals. In terms of professionalism, they are a leap forward. Here, we progress from being a professional pioneer to being a pioneering success.

10

PASSION AND PURPOSE

LIVE TO GIVE AND GIVE TO LIVE

Two things that stand between us and a fulfilling life are passion and purpose. It is never too late to discover either. In our younger years, we probably sat around wondering what to do with our lives. One day we might have toyed with the idea of being an alpine ski racer, the next day, a zookeeper. Finding a sense of purpose is never easy in a world that offers unlimited career choices. For some of us, it is still a mystery how we ended up doing what we do, even though we enjoy it.

Long before I went to university, I worked in a petrol station. Bored with that, I then got a job in a pharmacy. Both provided me with a source of income, but I never felt truly content. Without purpose, I drifted along with no clear sense of direction. Without passion, I was not motivated to excel. Then, suddenly out of the blue, I discovered a fascination for anatomy and physiology. Learning how the body works led to an enjoyable and rewarding career as a radiographer and lecturer in medical imaging and clinical practice research, a career that saw me teaching and researching concepts of professionalism, through which I discovered a love of writing. Here ends the story so far. The moral of this is that, in discovering what we enjoy, we not only find ourselves but also find happiness and success. Passion and purpose change us. We evolve to become better versions of ourselves.

Central to this chapter, therefore, is the idea that professionalism is fuelled by passion and purpose. When we do what we love and love what we do, we become better professionals by default.

The delight and excitement that come from discovering what ignites the spark in our hearts make all we do more pleasurable and meaningful. As a result, we are driven to achieve in ways that make life better for ourselves, for our clients, and for those around us.

No surprise, therefore, that within this chapter we focus on the extent to which passion builds connections and influences ambition, professional excellence, and our ability to impassion others. As we progress, we discover what it takes to be a broadly developed, passionate professional. Emphasis is placed on the need for interaction, visibility, and a strong sense of self-belief, alongside a requirement to leverage our talents for the good of society. As we explore the benefits of giving our time and energy to others, we also consider the significance of receiving what others offer.

Not overlooking the fact that passion requires commitment, we examine the importance of establishing boundaries and adopting strategies that help sustain our activity level and enthusiasm, health, and well-being. In the final concluding section, we consider the need to reframe the meaning of altruism to avoid self-sacrifice, enabling us to give and continually live a life full of passion and purpose.

FIND A SENSE OF PURPOSE

Everyone needs a purpose and a reason to get out of bed in the morning. Julie, a voluntary fundraiser, wakes up 'fully charged,' knowing all she does makes a difference in the lives of sick children. Life coach Rose is equally enthusiastic. Her mission is to help others navigate through tough times and appreciate their potential to grow. Patrick, a Methodist minister in a large inner-city area, answers the call of God to interact with those on the edge of society: the vulnerable, dispossessed, lonely, and poor. Meanwhile, Jason, a partner in a multi-service utility organisation, is dedicated to reducing energy costs for his older clients so they have more money to spend on life's little luxuries.

With a sense of purpose, Julie, Rose, Patrick, and Jason wake each day knowing what they want to achieve and accomplish. Their aspiration to do good in the world seemingly galvanises them into action. Our desire to do something meaningful and feel fulfilled is a basic instinct. We have an innate desire to be happy and make others happy by being helpful. Whatever we perceive to be our purpose, we are often motivated to serve our interests by doing something that adds value to our own lives, alongside doing something that adds value to others. It is born out of the need to grow as individuals, connect with others, and be part of something much bigger than ourselves.

We all have a strong desire to provide for ourselves and our families and build a thriving business. However, our success in achieving this long-term economic objective will only be accomplished when we do what we do best. For this to happen, we must understand and appreciate our talents, what we value the most, and what we love to do. We can define our purpose if we can discover where we stand, what we enjoy, and how we can make the most of our knowledge and skills. Without a sense of purpose, we become lost. If we do not know what makes us tick and what makes us content, we drift along wondering what to do with our lives.

Our sense of purpose is very personal. There is always an interesting backstory of how it came to be. Exactly how we discover our sense of purpose is somewhat enigmatic. It tends to find us rather than us finding it. Business advisor Clayton is committed to helping less experienced entrepreneurs build successful business careers. His purpose emerged as a result of his experiences working in the corporate world. Having come through the ranks, being mentored and coached himself, and then doing the same for others, his sense of purpose materialised naturally. Patrick's purpose evolved as a consequence of something he already valued and was committed to. Being a Christian and a lay preacher, ordination had always been in his mind. It took a sabbatical from his retail job to reawaken the idea. With renewed intensity of purpose, he felt it was a path he had to follow. Julie has a very different story to tell: she found her purpose as she navigated her way through a tragic situation. After the devastating loss of a child to cancer, she set about raising money to buy vital hospital equipment. Wanting to give something back to those who had cared for her daughter, she describes how everything snowballed. Approached to raise more money, Julie set up a charity in her daughter's name. Three decades later, it is still going strong.

Our sense of purpose is by no means fixed. It changes and evolves. Major life events, changes in employment, the activities we pursue, and our experiences, can shift our focus. We become inspired and stirred for different reasons and in different ways. It is common to have more than one purpose. We can find meaning through many things unconnected to our work. By day, insurance broker Colin is dedicated to protecting clients from life's uncertainties. Yet, in his spare time, he participates in a local initiative. Colin recalls how his happy childhood gave him the impetus to mentor displaced young people, many of whom find themselves in difficult circumstances through no fault of their own, without the support to make appropriate life choices.

Discovering our sense of purpose gives clarity and guides our decisions. It provides us with greater awareness, control, and direction. We become conscious of what is important and where we need to invest our time and energy in ways that make a difference to our lives, our experiences, and those of others. However, only when we connect with our work emotionally and have human objectives within sight do we derive the greatest level of satisfaction. Our sense of purpose is not so much grounded in what we do as in why and for whom we do it. Knowing this shifts our motivation from what we want to achieve for ourselves to what we wish for others.

ADD VALUE AND MAKE IT WORTHWHILE

A sense of purpose is nothing without a sense of satisfaction. Personal satisfaction only comes when we firmly believe that what we do is worthwhile. There is a cyclical element to it all. Finding value in what we do motivates us to do something constructive. When we do it consistently well and with professionalism, we see things happen due to our input and influence. The reward we get is the satisfaction of knowing we have value, enhancing our sense of self-worth and purpose. This strengthens the belief we have in ourselves and all that we do. Value comes from knowing what we want to achieve through our work. Business advisor Clayton wants his clients to experience the pleasure of running a business without stress. He wants to see his clients happy, enjoying a better work-life balance, and taking great delight in what they have created. To Clayton, nothing is more satisfying than seeing others succeed and sharing in that success. Experiencing unemployment, and a relationship breakdown, Rose sought clarity through a series of coaching sessions, which provided the opportunity to repurpose her life. Now a life coach herself, Rose feels she has the chance to help others repurpose theirs. Her goal is to help clients see life differently and appreciate the greatness within them. She wants them to understand that 'there is more to them than where they are now.' To Rose, satisfaction comes from seeing her clients' faces light up when they recognise they have potential. It is gratifying when clients tell her how 'things suddenly do not seem as bad as they were before.'

We learn from Clayton and Rose that finding our true value requires us to be something of a visionary. For our purpose to be beneficial, we need to know what the endpoint looks and feels like to ourselves and to our clients and what we need to do to get there. Jake, a business development manager for a company that provides printer services, explains how technical problems generate a lot of stress and anxiety. When a client reports a fault, Jake already knows they are having a bad day, so he does his best to turn the situation around quickly. Jake is humbled to know that clients think he is 'amazing.' He goes on to say: 'When you hold the solution, it does not seem such a big deal. Yet for a company reliant upon technology, it is, because downtime costs money and reputation.' Although it might seem as if we are just doing our job, we add value when we care about what matters most to our clients.

Knowing our value and purpose changes how we connect with ourselves and others and we become more engaged personally and professionally. It influences our identity, values, attitudes, and behaviours. Purpose leads us to care about the job and care about our clients. We become more proactive and enjoy putting the effort in because we find fulfilment. The positive emotions we feel keep us motivated to the cause. When we have a stronger sense of purpose, we can connect what we do to the impact it has. When our actions have significant outcomes for people, our worth becomes visible to us. Knowing we have enriched people's lives or made a positive difference makes what we do more meaningful. Positive affirmations that what we do is valued by others leave us feeling happy, fulfilled, and proud. This reinforces our understanding of why we do what we do in the way we do it and motivates us to carry on in a similar way.

It is purpose that helps us find our place in the world. Yet our purpose is nothing without passion. Passion underpins professionalism. To deliver a quality service, we have to be motivated. Passion creates the energy that drives us to give it our all. When we have enthusiasm, quality comes as standard. When we follow our heart, we find ourselves pursuing professional excellence.

PROFESSIONALISM IS NOTHING WITHOUT PASSION

When we are passionate about what we do, we have a zest for work. Not only are we committed to doing our best, but we are also committed to being our best, and when these combine, we get the best results. Jason describes it as 'working hard in a happy way.' Enthusiasm trounces drudgery and makes everything seem so much easier. It uplifts our spirits and makes us want to go on forever and ever.

As Jake neatly puts it: 'Work will never be all rainbows and sunshine.' Our work can be rewarding and frustrating in equal measure, and aspects will always seem incredibly mundane. Churning out the paperwork can be tedious, and no one leaps out of bed to deliver bad news. But, as Jake points out: 'The world is full of people drained by life, with no fire in them, and who wants to be like that?' With this in mind, we all need something that ignites a spark, energises us, and creates an equilibrium. Finding something that enlivens us will make our days more interesting. It makes our work enjoyable and sustains us through the peaks and the troughs, the highs and the lows.

Patrick is passionate about supporting others who do not have a sense of spirituality but are in need. He devotes time to a job training and enterprise hub that helps the long-term unemployed overcome the challenges and prejudices they may face. Clayton delights in running workshops for young entrepreneurs; he is helping them get their businesses off to a positive start by removing some of the angst that comes with the unknown. Jake is unique in his love for printers and photocopiers. By his own admission, it is not a passion he ever thought he would hold, which demonstrates that our passions grow with time. It is not so much the machines he enthuses about; it is the impact of their functionality and how they make the world of business go round. More than this, what really excites Jake are installations. Here he gets to talk and bond with clients. For Jake, it is a critical moment. It represents the start of a very different relationship, one that sees him making someone else's business successful as well as his own.

Interestingly, Jake describes himself as a 'people person'. Before becoming a minister, Patrick was an employer within the retail sector. Clayton was a managing director of a corporate organisation, who had run a business for years. We see in these few examples that we are often passionate about things we have, over time, come to experience and value, which plays to our strengths. That is good. Our strengths and experience equip us with the attitudes, beliefs, skills, and authoritative expertise needed to keep our passions alive. Moreover, they help us to remain authentic and true to ourselves.

Passion gets us results, but it also brings enrichment. We are much more proactive, spirited, and enterprising when we are excited about something. We are naturally driven to do our best and keen to gain as much knowledge and experience as possible. Jake is in no doubt that his love of the job leaves him 'hungry, ambitious, keen to move onto bigger things and extract as much out of the day as possible.' Chef Dominic, determined to own a restaurant, wants to 'soak up' all the experience he can get. When we are impassioned, we develop ambition and a growth mindset. We take pleasure in acquiring new knowledge and skills, and as you would expect, we engage in activities that support our growth as professionals.

Dominic's passion for food means he reads cuisine-related publications. He's part of a supportive hospitality network and is 'forever experimenting and trying out new ideas.' Frank, a musician, is passionate about using music to bring about social change. He is part of a community arts network that connects him with like-minded people across the music industry. Excited about her theatre work, make-up artist Alannah describes herself as a 'body art cosmoholic.' This sees her 'glued to experts online' and attending webinars and workshops because, in her words, she 'wants to be bang on trend and the best by miles.'

Whether we are conscious of it or not, engagement helps us pursue professional excellence and keep our passion alive. What we see in these few examples is how our interests expose us to fresh and creative ideas, which leads us to innovate. We learn from experts and build relationships and systems of support with equally passionate people. We become part of a community that gives us an identity, promotes a sense of belonging, and keeps us up to date. We become inspired by others and share what we know. So keen are we to get it right, we practise. We never give up because we are prepared to try, fail, and try again. Through this, we build resilience and set the standards by which we judge ourselves. No matter the challenge, we are ready to give it a go and see it through simply because we care and are inspired and dedicated enough to be the best we can be.

Passion instinctively leads us to be self-directed learners. As we engage in various activities, the knowledge, skills, attitudes, and behaviours required to be a professional are continually acquired and reinforced. Personal development allows us to pursue professional excellence. As we do, we avoid complacency and keep ourselves in the game ahead of the competition. To be better professionals, we must discover what we are passionate about and why. We have nothing to fuel our aspirations if we cannot get excited. This renders us incapable of accomplishing our own goals and meeting the needs and expectations of our clients or the community we serve.

SPREAD THE WORD, SPREAD THE LOVE

Passionate people are instantly recognisable because they exude confidence and talk about what they do in an enthusiastic and engaging way. In fact, they never stop talking about it, but rather than turning people off, people tune in. Passionate people can command our attention. We are drawn to their energy and actively listen because what they say inspires us. If we are blessed with an inner passion, the last thing we should do is keep quiet about it. Much good comes to pass when we follow our heart, even more so when we can find it within us to tell the rest of the world.

Professionalism has no room for arrogance, false modesty, or servility. Still, there is room for a humble appreciation of all we care about alongside a momentary celebration of what we have achieved. We have every reason to be proud of ourselves. Through pride, we internally acknowledge our interests, abilities, and success, and we validate our endeavours.

In pronouncing our passions, we remind ourselves, our clients, and our business associates how much we love what we do and what drives us to succeed. It is an excellent platform to gain external recognition, glean support, and encourage others to similarly get on board. As professionals, we are not here to share our passion solely out of self-interest. We are here to feed the minds of others and help them think positively about their work or future. Through passion, we show leadership and build stronger social connections, inspiring confidence and trust.

Dynamic interactions with people who are full of life are always pleasurable. Passion is a good foundation on which to build relationships. Excitement and enthusiasm change how we connect. Those who display a genuine passion for something are usually successful and popular amongst their peers. It would be erroneous to assume any causal relationship between passion and success, but passion invariably leads us to take actions that are likely to bring success. When people are both passionate and successful, they have always got something to give that we can learn and benefit from. This draws us in and motivates us to acquaint ourselves with them.

Passionate people stand out from the crowd and are taken seriously. Notably, they convey their message well because they have developed characteristics and skills that allow their passion to shine through. Moreover, they have come to value themselves, disregard negative self-talk, and leverage their talents well. Therefore, knowing our strengths and capabilities is significant because it influences how we exhibit our passion.

It goes without saying that we need to build passion in our working relationships. The level of help and support we provide is often a good indication of our enthusiasm. For example, Jake spends a lot of time on the telephone. He enjoys answering questions and giving advice. He notes how sometimes he can be 'quite giddy.' If we believe what we do is worth doing, we have every reason to sound lively and cheerful. Positive emotions set the wheels of business in motion.

If we are of the mindset to deliver good customer service, we can exude passion with each and every action. Clayton notes how, when advising his clients, he can get quite animated as he draws diagrams to illustrate his points. This might look as if Clayton is simply shining a light on an issue in a better way. However, when we unpack this, we see that through his passion, Clayton is creating a level of understanding that takes away the stress and reignites his clients' passion for their own business.

We can stimulate interest, whip up support, and fill others with our enthusiasm in many ways. Jason is a passionate conversationalist and networker. As a result, he can express his love for his job, his latest projects, and his charity work with relative ease. Jason also regularly shares exciting thoughts and opinions on LinkedIn. By posting purposeful questions and points to ponder, we can channel people's curiosity and create opportunities for people to engage with us.

To pique interest, we do not have to be physically in each other's company, but we do need to be communicating. We add value when we find words that capture the attention of those who share our passions or want to know more. Through this, we enrich other people's understanding of what we know and do, and who we are, boosting our credibility and personal influence. In making our deepest interests known, we build social capital. Whether we share information in person or online via videos, blogs, or social media, we can connect with people who are valuable resources for sustaining our interests and fulfilling our ambitions.

As a former teacher, Julie is no stranger to public speaking. In her spare time, she plays the saxophone. As an entertainer, she knows how to read the room and engage people. They are good skills to have when it comes to demonstrating the impact of her fundraising efforts. One thing Julie has come to appreciate is that to rally support, we need to tell a good story that entertains, hooks people in, and leaves a long-lasting, memorable impression.

When we communicate our passion and demonstrate impact, we enhance our ability to inspire and influence others to be impassioned about something just as much as we are. Passion stirs up passion. However, to enthuse others, we have to be visible, which means we need to be comfortable and confident in how we present ourselves to be sure of showing our best selves. We also need to believe in what we do and in ourselves. Only with high self-esteem and a strong sense of self-worth can we stay true to what we believe in and keep our passion alive.

BLOCK OUT THE NOISE AND ALL THOSE DOUBTERS

Earlier, we noted how passionate professionals keep on growing. Our enthusiasm drives us to discover more, try new things, and innovate. Following our heart can lead us to dream big. There is no limit to our ideas. We have grand visions and high aspirations and set our sights on achieving things others consider impossible. Success only comes when we are prepared to rise to the challenge, move out of our comfort zone, and take a few risks. It emanates from our courage to set ourselves apart and from our determination to stay focused and never give up. Our hopes and dreams are well within our reach, provided we do not allow negative self-talk or the acerbic opinions of others to stifle our success. To accomplish our aspirations, we must be confident in our ability to achieve from the outset.

Self-confidence serves us well because it leads to action. If we believe in our capabilities, personal qualities, and judgement, we can be out there doing what we want and being the person we want to be. Confidence gives us the drive needed to succeed; it prompts us to try, and in doing so we show ourselves and others what is possible. Conversely, a lack of confidence befalls us when we start to doubt ourselves, compare ourselves to others, or become absorbed in what others might think.

If we fear failure, we set ourselves up to fail, mainly because we never begin to try. Whatever our ambitions, we are always going to be tested. There are elements of uncertainty in every situation. If we want success, we have to start believing that we can see it through. Gaps in our knowledge and skill set can easily be filled. We can always do some research, get advice, develop skills through practice, or even outsource.

Rose offers us a delightful analogy: noting how the endpoint always stems from the beginning, she likens it to an apple seed. The apple seed will always be an apple seed. Its growth into an apple requires some good fertile soil, water, and sunshine. Rose's point is that what we want to achieve is already within us. We just need to be in the right frame of mind, amongst the right people, with the right strategy, in the right environment. Rose goes on to explain that, although we might be apprehensive, 'nothing is wrong, we do not need fixing, we just need to realise we have potential.' Whatever we want to achieve, somewhere, someone will already have achieved it, so it is not impossible. It is not that we cannot do it; it is simply that something is currently missing. Whether that is knowledge, skills, willpower, or something else, we need to find out what it is and do something about it.

One thing for sure is that we have to learn to run our own race and avoid comparing ourselves to others. Julie and Rose think that the only person we should be competing with is ourselves. We have to keep a positive frame of mind and quash feelings of inadequacy. People around us often put on a show for appearances' sake. Social media makes it easy for us to develop imposter syndrome. As we falsely judge others to be better than us, we get to think that we somehow fall short of other people's expectations. Paying too much attention can seriously damage our self-esteem.

Things might move more slowly than we would like, but if we remain committed, we will always progress forward. Small actions have an accumulative effect that leads to big changes over time. All it takes is to be a little better than we were the day before. Whatever stage we are at, we will always be learning and making an impact in our own way. The secret is to value ourselves until we get external validation. We must learn to be our own cheerleader until we can find a supportive, vocal crowd to do some cheering for us. A strong sense of self-worth enables us to confidently show our best selves as we progress and embrace every challenge.

Like myself, Rose is an aspiring author. We often compare notes on how we feel and how we are progressing. Since we work, have family commitments, and other interests, we each individually developed our action plan and determined our markers for success. Life events stall progress occasionally, but we celebrate small milestones and take inspiration from each other as and when we can. We do our best to remain optimistic and focused, but some people are always ready to rain on our parade. Whatever their reason, they remain disparaging and fall over themselves to criticise. Sometimes it can be demotivating, but rather than dislike these people, we choose the alternative and pride ourselves on our creativity and what we have to offer others.

Jason believes that we do not need to be liked by everyone to achieve. On being bullied at school, Jason recalls that his father once told him: 'Whatever anyone thinks of you is never your business.' Wise words indeed, because our critics do not know us enough to judge us or our capabilities. Worrying about what others think when they know so little about us has a negative psychological effect. No matter who we are or what our aspirations might be, we are all deserving of success. We learn from Jason and his father that personal dreams and ambitions do not need anyone's approval. By paying little attention to the unsolicited advice and opinions of others, we can free ourselves of worry and get on with enjoying all that we do, from start to finish.

Fundraiser Julie notes how her plans to raise £500,000 in one year 'raised a few eyebrows'. She aims to fund the employment of a hospital-based psychologist for ten years. It is an enormous appeal and something of a swansong: a final tribute in honour of the daughter she lost before she embraces retirement. Julie has every confidence in herself. By drawing on her past successes, she has hope for the future. She recalls how in running a marathon, it was not her legs that got her across the finishing line but her positive mental attitude. Recognising the need to similarly 'dig deep and keep going', Julie took time to prepare physically and emotionally, drawing inspiration from motivational books. Through the act of self-nurturing, we can train our brains to think positively. This strengthens our resolve. The more self-belief we have, the less stress we feel and the more productive we will be. When we silence our inner critic and cease listening to the cynics, we become self-confident enough to challenge ourselves by dreaming big and making it happen.

MAKE TIME TO DO GOOD

We will have acquired vast knowledge and experience and developed a broad skill set throughout our lives. Our wisdom, proficiency, and acumen are central to success. Our expertise has the potential to make us distinctive and boosts our capacity to fulfil our ambitions and achieve professional excellence. It is true: knowledge gives us power. However, shared knowledge is more powerful and has a more significant impact. Sharing is never a one-way street. Whenever we give, we gain. As we proficiently apply our knowledge and skills in the interest of clients, we earn both an income and a reputation.

Yet professionals are characterised by their generosity of spirit. There are times when we need to act benevolently, without payment, for the sake of humanity. As talented and unique individuals with a passion, there is a social need for us to help people other than our clients. Some call this professional citizenship. Others call it civic professionalism. Either way, the main objective is that we voluntarily use our energy and talents to benefit wider society. By having the will to help others in our community, we make the world a better place. Our contribution, however small, can have a big impact. Whatever drives our motivation, as we channel our passion into sector-specific or community-based activities, we positively change the lives of others and ourselves.

A gifted saxophonist, Julie uses entertainment as a vehicle to fundraise. Helping others makes a difference in the way Julie feels about herself. Seeing children, parents, and hospital staff happy due to her efforts fires her up. Every event she organises, be it a quiz, a concert, a junior aquathlon, or a classic car show, creates a sense of achievement.

However, we do not have to organise events or raise money to do good. Property lawyer Alasdair offers his time and services pro bono to two small charities. He serves as a trustee for a charity that provides support to children with special needs and another that feeds people experiencing homelessness. These charities do not have the financial means to access legal and conveyancing services, or the human resources to oversee governance and facilities management. Alasdair has selected to do good, within his working day, by applying his skills to causes close to his heart. In doing so, he notes its impact on his practice as a property lawyer. His broader knowledge of operations within the charitable sector means Alasdair can deliver better service to paying clients in similar situations. Insurance broker Colin similarly notes how volunteering influences his practice. Conversations with the young adults Colin mentors have enhanced his capacity to listen without judgement, a vital skill in the insurance industry.

We do not have to go overboard or burden ourselves to help others. Alasdair has shown us that we can use our day-to-day skills in mutually beneficial and satisfying ways. Nor do we have to feel the need to get involved with external organisations. Instead, we can do good for people in places closer to home. At work, Alasdair mentors trainees and newly qualified lawyers, helping them build the confidence and discipline to apply what they have learned in training to the real world. In doing so, Alasdair becomes part of a learning community. As he works to enhance the qualities and practices of others, he broadens his repertoire of interpersonal, supervisory, and managerial skills.

Jaime voluntarily takes an active role as a member of an organisation for administrators. Jaime delights in the fact that they have 'found a whole new family.' Their role on a board of accreditors connects them to different people, with different roles, in different environments. Jaime explains how suddenly they discovered a supportive network to which they would otherwise not have had access, a network that has helped them make better career choices and has also enabled them to rediscover their '*joie de vivre*', boosting job satisfaction and professional identity.

For Nancy, who supports vulnerable adults to access health and social care services, doing good has given her a new identity. The death of her parents left a void in her life, and with time on her hands, she became a Brownie Guide leader. It gave her a new sense of purpose that became a passion. Being a Tawny Owl is now part of who she is. In organising and leading activities, she feels useful and has gained new skills, including recently becoming a first aider. It keeps her fit and makes life fun. Above all else, she feels a sense of accomplishment.

These few examples tell us so much about giving ourselves and our time to others, not least because no matter what we do, there is always something to learn or appreciate. Our contributions and interactions with others deepen our understanding of society and enhance our ability to perform and live up to professional expectations. Being part of something else enriches our lives. We experience pleasurable and exciting rewards that strengthen our professional identity and develop our emotional intelligence. Amid all the fun, we find contentment, cultivate self-belief, expand our skill set, and find new friends. Doing good does us good. It provides a platform on which we can nurture ourselves as individuals and as professionals.

GIVE, BUT KNOW HOW AND WHEN TO RECEIVE

When we give something of ourselves and give our time to others, we often do so with altruistic intent. Most of us are used to being of service, so when people ask for help, we are there, ready to give them and the matter in hand our full attention. We get involved because not only are we passionate, but we also like the idea of doing things. By and large, we feel in an excellent position to be doing good and wanting nothing ourselves. Hence, we do it out of joy rather than need. We rise to the challenge because we want to be helpful and make a difference. Although we stand to gain in some way, we do not consciously think about it. It is usually the furthest thing from our minds, because we believe it is better to give than it is to receive.

In giving, our passion intensifies. However, if we are constantly giving, we will soon run out of energy. Professionalism requires us to be ready to give and receive in equal measure. In creating a balance, the benefits to us and others escalate. If we are genuinely making a difference in the lives of others, they will naturally want to thank us and credit us for the part we played throughout their experience. The first rule of giving states that we must also do some appreciative receiving.

We never really see ourselves as others do. Since we love what we do, and do it with effortless skill, it always feels that we are doing very little in the grand scheme of things; we often underestimate the impact we make and the value we bring. As a consequence, we do not feel worthy. This often makes it hard to accept kind words and flattering remarks with grace and gratitude. On top of this, we never know what to say in response when people express their appreciation. We prefer to be caught up in the doing rather than the emotion that transpires.

Yet we cannot make light of it because, in doing so, we show disrespect. In discounting our effort, we devalue the judgement of those who like and admire us enough to convey their appreciation openly. Professionals are those who are ready to respond to others. The most gracious thing to do is to thank people for thanking us. Nancy has an interesting perspective. She likens each thank you she receives to a gift. She notes how it is often the only sincere way for young children and vulnerable adults to express their gratitude. In her view, dismissing a thank you with a statement like 'oh, it was nothing' is an insult. 'It is like saying no to a present,' she says. Appreciative receiving is thus central to building and sustaining relationships.

Of course, no one will expect a gushing Hollywood-style Oscar speech, but people will expect us to accept their thanks with humility and take context into account. Methodist minister Patrick recognises that many of those he serves often express their gratitude in difficult circumstances when they lack inner strength in other ways. For Patrick, that in itself needs to be acknowledged. Lawyer Alasdair favours a reciprocal compliment. The legalities of purchasing a property can take time, so he credits clients for their patience and understanding.

There is more to be gained if we can be inwardly thankful for the praise, tributes, and gratitude we receive. Jason loves organising charity quizzes and golf days. He gets a real buzz out of the congratulations he receives because he gets to feel the pleasure and excitement that others feel having participated. Personal recognition affirms Patrick's calling to the ministry and rids him of self-doubt. Julie received what could be described as the ultimate public recognition, receiving a Member of the Order of the British Empire (MBE) medal for her services to the community, representing years of dedication to fundraising. Naturally, this boosted her confidence. But, in a bizarre way, she has achieved a lot more since the award. It keeps her productive. Holding an award is an honour, but it is something Julie feels she has to live up to, which keeps her doing more of the same.

Whether we receive personal or public recognition, it is recognition all the same. Patrick equates it to a 'recharging process' that validates our existence and all that we strive to achieve. Recognition is instrumental in developing our self-worth and helping us overcome negative self-talk. It fuels our passion and keeps us actively engaged with the things we love to do. In a self-gratifying way, it helps us appreciate our qualities and capabilities.

Other people often spark the things we are most passionate about. Rarely do we get to accomplish great things without the help of others. Thus, we must be thankful for the friendship, love, help, and support we receive as we progress towards our goals and ambitions. Julie feels blessed that she is surrounded by a loving family and has good health. Dominic is indebted to those who helped him get to where he is today. At the same time, Patrick appreciates the support he receives from his local community and those who accept him as an individual, as well as their minister, recognising who he is rather than what he does.

To fulfil our purpose with passion, we have no choice but to receive. We cannot give unless we open ourselves to those who want to help us. What others have to give provides us with the knowledge, skills, resources, and strength to grow and continue to be of service, to do good, and act with passion. Rarely does receiving stand in the way of pride, admiration, or acceptance by others. By humbly accepting help and support, we provide an opportunity for others to share their expertise and create a space for them to shine. In letting others step in we validate their qualities and abilities. Moreover, in doing so, we lay the foundation for a relationship built on trust and assist others to develop self-confidence and self-belief, and find their passion and purpose. In the broader scheme of things, accepting help allows others to be active participants in society, enabling them to enhance their level of professionalism, meet the expectations of professional citizenship, and gain from all that comes with it.

WAKE UP WITH ENERGY

Passionate people wake up refreshed, looking forward to the day ahead. Passion demands a lot of positive energy. Expend too much of our reserve, and we find ourselves without the motivation to get things done and make the best of every opportunity. It is a delicate balance. Our passion can lead us to great things, but if we are not careful, it leads to exhaustion and stress. In all the excitement, our determination to be of service can see us taking on too much. We can soon become obsessive to the point that we make sacrifices and forgo time with family and friends. In not wanting to miss an opportunity, we can ignore the fact that we have allowed ourselves to be complacent, distracted, and unreliable.

To be professional, we have to be fit for practice. As well as having all the right personal qualities, we must be able to do our job proficiently. We cannot expect to provide a professional service unless we look after our needs first. Business would not be business without some level of stress. There are periods when stress can be a great motivator. However, stress only brings success if it is managed effectively. Too much stress over prolonged periods diminishes our interest and level of engagement and affects our health. As we know from Chapter 2, how we think, feel, and act has a powerful impact on our mindset, our level of professionalism, and how others perceive us. The secret to sustaining passion and professionalism lies in the practice of self-care. To do our utmost best and live every moment, we need a plentiful supply of energy. Self-care allows us to create the time and space to nurture our health and mental well-being so that we can consistently give something of ourselves to others.

For Jason, self-care starts by ensuring he has a good work-life balance. Making time for everything he is passionate about ensures he does not have to prioritise one thing over another. This allows Jason to combine his love for his family with his love for his job and his passion for golf. Self-employment gives Jason the flexibility to play golf whenever he chooses. He notes how he initially felt guilty and feared that people would think he was not dedicated to his work. Then he realised that because he did not follow convention, it did not mean his approach was wrong. Maintaining the right balance often comes when we stop looking at what others are doing and find our own way of working.

Taking time out to relax, or to pursue hobbies and interests, refreshes and revitalises us. We get to enjoy time by ourselves or with others. Either way, we get to do things that broaden our outlook and make us happy. Julie enjoys holidays where she 'does nothing other than lie down on a sun lounger, being treated like a queen.' Alasdair enjoys walking in the countryside with his brother and his dogs. Musician Frank likes to play bridge, while human resources manager Niamh likes to sew. Creating boundaries between work and pleasure ensures we get much-needed time out.

Self-care is not something we should do every once in a while. If we genuinely value our physical and mental health, we must be sure that we top up our energy levels daily. To stay switched on, we need to know how to switch off. Whether we opt for a long soak in a bath, do a crossword, meditate, exercise, or spend time with friends, these daily acts of self-kindness are vital. Whichever way we choose to relax, we should never underestimate how much it replenishes our energy.

We might be forgiven for thinking that there is a mixed message here. The need to make time for others seems in direct conflict with the need to make time for ourselves. The former requires us to be selfless. The latter requires us to be selfish. Professionalism is expressed in how we manage what seems like two extremes: there is a balance to be struck. If we are to be fit for practice, we must consider the impact our state of health and mind has on our clients and others.

Professionalism requires consistency. Varying behaviours and levels of enthusiasm leave others confused about who we are and what we feel. This undermines the extent to which our passion and dedication are taken seriously. Professionalism requires us to be emotionally and physically in the right space. We will never be emotionally invested in what we do, keen to learn, or go the extra mile if we are worn out and weary. With good physical and mental health and an optimistic mindset, we add more value than we subtract.

To strike a happy medium, we must learn to be adaptive and address any imbalance. We have to allow ourselves to be vulnerable and take steps to look after ourselves. It is the give and take that will enable us to survive. Time out doing the things we enjoy is a way of giving something back to ourselves that allows us to continue to grow as passionate professionals. Through these self-nurturing activities, we find the get-up-and-go that gets us results, and we gain the energy to perform in extraordinary ways. It gives us the strength and discipline to meet expected standards, be our best, and do our best. With the right strategy, we wake up with the energy required to fulfil our role with passion and purpose.

KEEP THE ENERGY FLOWING AND BUILD MOMENTUM

If we can find a meaningful purpose that plays to our strengths, excites, and motivates us, then we are well on the road to finding fulfilment. Having a clear sense of purpose moves us in the right direction: we look to the future, focusing on what we want to achieve for ourselves and others. Discover our purpose, and passion soon follows. Enthusiasm strikes at the heart of ambition and, armed with an enterprising spirit, we stop at nothing short of professional excellence. Purpose gives rise to passion, and passion gives rise to professionalism. It would be a reasonably straightforward process were it not for the fact that passion is something of an animal, prone to fear, that needs to be nurtured and kept alive.

It is evident throughout this chapter that passion is necessary for professionalism to thrive. We need a steady flow of energy to achieve our ambitions and live up to professional expectations. To feed our passion, we have to feed ourselves. The onus is on us to manage the process and create a healthy equilibrium that ensures we are fit for practice. We need to continuously work to address any imbalance in the interest of progress, professional development, health, and well-being.

The energy coming in needs to equate with the energy going out. In using that energy, we must ensure the benefits extend to us, our clients, and wider society. With so many competing demands, we must seek to create a balanced lifestyle that enables us to make time for others and ourselves. Moreover, we must learn to accept the prudent advice and well-intentioned support of others, and unashamedly take time out to reduce stress and strengthen our expertise, health, and well-being.

It seems a tall order and takes some discipline. Yet, if we can find the inner strength to draw on resources that sustain our energy and dispense with all that saps it, maintaining that equilibrium becomes less problematic. Moreover, by keeping our energy flowing, we can live to give in ways that enable and inspire others to do the same.

If we want to have an impact, our passion must be consistently visible. We have to be out there loud and proud, attracting attention. Through some of the illustrative examples, we gain a sense of how passion manifests in our everyday work. We also see that we widen our visibility by channelling our enthusiasm into building social capital and doing good in society. The various avenues through which we communicate our passion lead us to an audience that shares our passion. Here we find people ready to listen in the hope of being inspired, individuals who have ideas and insights all of their own that fuel our interest and give us strength to dream big.

Of course, dreams only come true if we make them happen. Energy and enthusiasm are wasted without effort. Within this chapter, emphasis has been placed on the need for self-belief. None of us are without ability. We are perfectly capable of applying the knowledge and skills we have, as long as we do not allow personal insecurities to hold us back. We learn that the only thing that matters is the opinion we have of ourselves. When we waste time feeling inadequate, we waste the opportunity to prove to ourselves and others that we can do good and achieve great things. Our capacity to self-nurture will stem the negative energy flow that drains us of potential.

With passion and purpose comes the strong desire to give everything our best shot. Through our quest to be the best, we learn, develop, interact, and lead from the front. So, not only do we become passionate professionals, but we also become passionate leaders. This places us in a strong position to embrace professional citizenship by directing our enthusiasm, expertise, and business acumen in ways that help build a better society.

We discover that as we expend energy, we gain more energy. Enthusiastic engagement boosts proficiency and self-belief and secures external admiration. Through the qualities we possess, we prove ourselves fit for practice. In doing so, we build momentum in others. As we give in ways that help others live and achieve their ambitions, we leave something of a legacy. We get to be remembered for the value we added because of our skills and the advice and time we offered. With this, we are reminded that giving also means receiving. By accepting compliments with gratitude and grace, we allow others to feel good. Humble in obtaining help and support, we enable others to do good and nurture professional citizenship.

If we get the balance right, we can consistently exude passion. By continually giving and taking, we extend our opportunity to personally flourish and motivate and inspire others. Giving and taking enriches every experience. We get to feed our interests and nurture our ambitions, personal development, and well-being. More importantly, we get to live a better life personally and professionally.

HOLD THAT THOUGHT

Professionalism is grounded in the concept of altruism. The idea is that we give something of ourselves to others without expectation. It is underpinned by notions of self-sacrifice: that we put our interests before our own, regardless of the consequences and exclusive of any personal benefit. As we have come to appreciate, professionalism is built on peak performance. Furthermore, greater emphasis is being placed on achieving optimum physical and mental health throughout society. The question is: have we got our work-life balance right? Are we living in a way that allows us to give while protecting our need for growth alongside our own health and well-being?

If we are to be passionate professionals, fit for practice, and capable of leadership, we need to subscribe to a different view: one that focuses on altruism as a set of personal characteristics rather than a philosophy to abide by. If we see altruism as a series of attributes centred around kindness, thoughtfulness, and generosity of spirit, we get to take responsibility for them. We get to develop them through our experiences and personal interests. Moreover, we get to manage the balance between giving to others and giving to ourselves in ways that show us to be proactive and civic-minded professionals admired for our passion.

The truth is that, as professionals, we can never expect to have an endless supply of energy and enthusiasm. What we do have, however, is the potential to set boundaries that allow us to consistently share our time and expertise without self-sacrifice. Through self-regulation, it is possible to be self-regarding, self-respecting, ambitious, and altruistic, all at the same time. This turns the idea of living to give on its head. As professionals, we should give to live, not give and give up all that we hold dear to our hearts.

CONCLUSION
LOOK BACK, MOVE FORWARD

We often get a greater sense of meaning when we reflect on events. Exploring the past helps us face the future with optimism. No experience is ever complete until we reflect on our learning and development; we need to make sense of the insight we have gained and think about where we go from here. If we want to move forward, it is worth looking back on where we have been to know the direction we should be heading.

We started the book by acknowledging our diversity of opinion when determining what constitutes professionalism. This will not have changed and diverse opinions will always exist. However, as we read each chapter, we will all have responded differently to the points raised and in this respect, our point of view will have changed. In some way, shape, or form, we will have come to appreciate particular aspects of professionalism with greater clarity. We will have reached a new level of understanding that has the potential to change the way we act.

As we know, professionalism requires us to evidence our appreciation through application. Applying all that we know sounds relatively straightforward. It looks as if the only thing we need to embed our learning in practice is a good level of understanding. This is true. But as we no doubt realise, it is not that simple. Professionalism is a complex concept with many interrelating aspects. Providing a quality service that leaves clients satisfied relies upon us bringing a whole range of ideologies and best practices coherently together.

So far, we have explored several significant aspects of professionalism in isolation. Each chapter offered an insight into critical issues associated with the subject, and the potential internal and external influences likely to intensify or diminish our commitment to acting with professionalism. Yet, even within these chapters, we have acknowledged co-existing relationships and interdependencies. For example, in Chapter 3, we saw that trust depends on our ability to be competent decision-makers who are respectful, honest, transparent, reliable, and consistent. In discovering these connections, we also learn that should we fall short of being any one of these things, distrust ensues. The secret to professionalism lies in the effortless integration of each aspect within our day-to-day business activities. Here, we make the kind of impact that gets everyone talking. If we are to up our game, raise our sights and standards, and become the successful, well-rounded professional everyone admires, we must know how to join it all together.

Several chapters emphasise the need for synchronicity. Until now, we have yet to explore the powerful effect of alignment. The combination of our character, values, attitudes, skill sets, behaviour, and mindset puts us on a very different professional level: a cut above the rest. The book would not be complete without giving this some consideration.

So far, we have come to appreciate that professionalism flourishes because of many factors. What is evident is that to achieve success, the groundwork starts with us. Professionalism is rooted in concepts of self. With this in mind, we turn our thoughts away from the insight and opinions of others and turn our attention towards ourselves. For all the new knowledge and ideas we gained through our reading, self-improvement does not happen unless we set the wheels in motion. Professionalism comes from owning how we develop, adapt, and manage ourselves. As we look back on all we have learned, we also look forward to the future. Before we continue our professional journey, we consider the attributes and proficiencies needed to identify our needs, implement our ideas, and achieve our goals, so we can become the professional everyone admires.

GET THE SHOW ON THE ROAD

When it comes to coherently applying every good-practice principle, the stars rarely align to make our endeavours effortless. We have learned so far that although our core values and attitudes serve as a frame of reference that guides our actions, we cannot function in a prescribed way. We live in a changing world, in which there is diversity among stakeholder needs. Meeting their expectations requires us not only to be orientated towards professionalism but also to be situationally responsive. This itself relies on us understanding the intricacies of professionalism and having the personal capacity to manage unpredictability and uncertainty and continually adapt to every situation.

Circumstances often dictate the professional we are or become. Internal and external influences can fluctuate, varying our levels of commitment. The integration of our professional ideals is thus not absolute: it relies upon enthusiasm, understanding, opportunity, self-belief, and professional identity. There are many aspects of professionalism that we need to control, simply because positively influencing factors are not always there, and we will not always be physically and mentally in the right place.

Our level of engagement with cognitive and social processes is what orientates us towards professionalism. Experiences, interactions, critical thought, and reflection help transform us, empowering us to keep pace with change, rationalise our decisions, and reconcile all we encounter. These processes are inseparable from the process of learning and it is through these that we develop as professionals. When we are intellectually engaged, we gain a deeper insight into everything happening around us. As a result, we become inquisitive, join in with meaningful intent, and listen to understand ourselves and others. Unless we seek to raise our consciousness of professional expectations and are receptive to thinking and acting as professionals, we are pretty much doomed. Apathy pushes us into the realm of unprofessionalism – a void that anyone with any sense would avoid.

Professionalism is no more than a journey of transformation. The will to begin that journey is the point at which we see success. Having got this far in the book, we are already steps closer to achieving our aspirations. The debates, observations, and illustrative examples have given us plenty to digest. In addition to the things we already knew, new insights and ideas have changed our perspective. No doubt, as we read, we will, in part, have been reassured by how close we come to meeting particular professional expectations. There will have been points where we could truly relate to the experiences and opinions of those who have contributed and shared their stories, and are comforted to know we are not alone in our struggles and quest for excellence. We will almost certainly have recognised aspects of ourselves, the qualities we possess, our strengths and skills, and the excellent practice we currently employ. Equally, we will have identified points where there is scope for improvement.

In reading, we have learned things from others and, in doing so, learned something about ourselves. In a short time, we have come to credit ourselves for all that we are and have become through our efforts so far. At the same time, we have become cognisant of what is required to be the professional we aspire to be and remain active in that pursuit. Now, we need to be out there doing it, because this is the only way we are likely to benefit and make any significant impact.

The thought of habitually incorporating each professional expectation into every aspect of our practice might seem overwhelming, particularly if we are new to the business world. Yet we must remember that professionalism is a journey without end. It develops with time, much of it through incremental personal development. Version one is always better than version nought. No one raises their sights by lying low and it is always better to grow slowly than to not grow at all.

Let us remember that we are all capable individuals. Whatever our aspirational intent, getting the show on the road is all it takes. Contrary to what we believe, it does not take the level of courage we think it might; it simply requires engagement with the activities we already do and the people we already do them with. There is nothing to fear. We just have to be a bit more actively involved than we were yesterday and more cognisant about what is happening around us. It is an ordinary process in which something quite delightful and extraordinary happens.

Engagement acts like a portal. Through it, we are transported into a different world. It changes the way we interact and alters the way we think. All in all, it advances our level of understanding, transforms our perspectives, and accelerates our development. As we are about to see, engagement is the catalyst that takes us to a different professional place where all the many facets of professionalism finally come together. It is not as if we are rolling dice. There is nothing risky about engaging with what is already familiar to us. It is simply a matter of engaging with an enquiring mind and a keenness to pick up on and process all we observe and hear.

MOVE UP A GEAR

Chapters 1, 9 and 10 emphasised experience and social interaction with clients and the wider business community to progressively develop our identity, passion, and purpose, together with our professional knowledge and skills. The combination of our experiences and interactions alone has a huge transformative effect. As we hit the engagement button, the succession of events that follows carries us into a place where we get to see for ourselves what is happening within and around us, and we also get to be seen. As the bigger picture unfolds, we move from a place of obscurity to one of visibility, which is essential if we want to be respectfully admired.

Before exploring how engagement leads to visibility, we should explore how connections are created between what we see and do, so that we can coherently bring together the different aspects of professionalism. It is worth noting that there is nothing new in what we are about to read. Every point has already been considered somewhere in the book. By itself, it represents a neat summary of all that is expected of us as professionals. This aside, we get to see the relationships that exist and how powerful and influential our experiences and interactions can be when it comes to being a professional. Here then, in an ideal world, is how it works.

The more we engage, the more we connect, and the more meaningful everything seems. In finding meaning, we find passion and purpose. These strengthen our inner beliefs, sharpening our values and professional identity. We feel professional, look professional, and are committed to executing our duties and serving the interests of our stakeholders in a professional manner. With a professional mindset, we take our obligations seriously and are prompted to adopt strategies that will keep us moving in the right direction. We invest in social relationships and work to develop mutual trust based on honesty and transparency. As we strengthen connections, we secure co-operative engagement with due regard for our differences. And in knowing people better, we get to know their circumstances; we learn through them and with them.

The emotional connection we make leads us to care for the way we do things. By working in partnership, we become conscientious and are driven to do our best. We communicate sensitively, treat people respectfully, and preserve their dignity. We put extra thought into treating people fairly and looking after their happiness, safety, and welfare. We extend that care by caring, too, about the type of people we collaborate with. In wanting to attend to our clients' needs and deliver as promised, we look to invest in systems that help us manage our time and resources and consistently replicate our standards. The desire to get the right outcome, achieve client satisfaction, remain accountable, and strengthen our reputation prompts us to act ethically and go above and beyond. By acquiring a can-do attitude, we invest in critical thought to overcome the most challenging problems. As we innovate, we break new ground and, in doing so, we move out of our comfort zone, building resilience and expertise as we go.

The positive outcomes we achieve confirm that we have something of value to offer. With greater self-confidence, we step into the business arena happy, knowing our abilities and worth. As we continue to engage, we build connections. In acquainting ourselves with knowledgeable and inspiring people who offer the hand of friendship, humanistic aspects become reinforced. We continue to learn and develop. Through support, we become receptive to fresh ideas and feedback. Feedback provides us with something concrete on which we can reflect. Here, we get to re-evaluate our goals and reframe our perspectives. We become mindful of the things that help us prioritise our development and positively manage our emotional, physical, and mental state. Positive in our outlook, energised by passion, self-belief, and a growth mindset, we are ready to aim higher and achieve our aspirations, affording time to help others along the way.

We see here that with each professional action, we get an outcome that orientates us towards another aspect of professionalism. In reality, the system is not as linear as it is presented here. Nonetheless, this illustrates that each action is like a connecting gateway that transforms us and places us in a different professional world where we perform better and more effectively. As soon as we become more attentive we enhance our level of understanding, which helps us establish, reinforce, and strengthen connections. We see our obligations and expectations differently, and because of that, we think and act differently. As we pass through several gateways, we change. Professionally we mature and move up a gear.

ASSEMBLE IT TO CREATE IT

We can liken the transformation process to collecting pieces of a jigsaw puzzle. As we pass through each connecting gateway, we collect individual pieces of the puzzle. Then, with enough positive momentum, we quickly advance, collecting more pieces as we go. Since each piece accords with a professional ideal that is inextricably linked to another one, it becomes easier to connect the pieces. Thus, we can see more precisely what the bigger picture looks and feels like. In time, we find that not only do we have a holistic overview of professionalism, but we also find our values, attitudes, behaviours, and practices are coherently aligned with expectations because in connecting pieces, we get to develop an integrated way of operating and thinking.

What starts small gets bigger, stronger, and more powerful. Proactive engagement helps us link the various aspects of professionalism together, such that we are guided towards doing the right things right. In doing so, we evidence our integrity and people can see that we are authentic and that we carry our credibility. We visibly stand out if clients, stakeholders, or business associates can see and feel what they expect. If we can combine passion, expertise, and a positive attitude with the confidence to achieve excellence consistently and effectively, with practices firmly grounded in professional principles, we show ourselves to be well-rounded, authentic professionals. When people can positively relate to the collective qualities of our character, competence, values, attitudes, behaviours, mindset, and benevolent intentions, we offer all-encompassing proof that we have integrity. When people see this, they trust us, believe in us, and admire us. If we can establish ourselves as professionals in the eyes of others, we are winning at life.

Of course, we have to remember that success is fleeting, and complacency lies in wait. We must keep collecting pieces and moving through the gateways if we are to remain at our professional best. As we know, change constantly changes the picture. With insufficient pieces, the complete picture of what it means to be a professional is never revealed. We need to maintain the momentum and work to fill in the gaps to avoid disconnecting ourselves from a transitional process. Without it, we are left incomplete, vulnerable and, all too often, stuck. From time to time, we will all arrive at this point. It is okay if it is a temporary stop, but hanging around for any length of time would be unwise.

Throughout the book, we have explored the need for positive influencing factors to be synchronised. A smooth and effective transformation relies on this. For everything to fall into place, we need to continually heighten the positive influences and adopt strategies that help us develop and limit the negative ones that only hold us back and make our endeavours ineffective. Get the balance wrong, and we find ourselves drifting along a path that sees us compromising on standards and giving up on ourselves, our clients, and our ambitions. We get closer to achieving synchronisation when we create continuity. For this to happen, we must value accountability and check in on ourselves to ensure we forge and maintain strong and stable connections that enlighten our understanding.

Pursuing professionalism will never be a walk in the park, and the landscape will constantly alter. There will be hoops to jump through, bridges to cross, holes we must dig ourselves out of, and obstacles that stand in our way. Some of these will be of our own creation because of how we feel or the choices we have made. Others will not be. No matter what, we cannot pursue professionalism unless we overcome them.

If we believe that professionalism is built on the notion that our attitudes, values, and behaviours are integral to what we do, and that we will act in diligent and principled ways, any gap that exists in our knowledge or skill set will challenge our capacity to live up to these professional expectations. Our ability to build and sustain our level of professionalism depends on our strength of character to deal with the challenges and changes that come our way. The onus is on us to collect the missing pieces and fill in the gaps. Otherwise, we potentially stall our development. By now, we will appreciate professionalism as a composite construct. Yet it is about more than just understanding the underlying concepts and principles and pulling them together. It is also about understanding ourselves, so we can well and truly get our professional act together.

FORGET THE PAST. IT IS WHAT HAPPENS NOW THAT MATTERS

Having got this far, we will have identified several aspects of our practice or attributes we would like to improve. This is great. With a renewed sense of purpose, knowing what we are about to do will make an impact and difference to our clients and ourselves, we are keen to get going. Let us take a moment to remind ourselves about the purpose of self-improvement in this context.

A thriving business and a strong reputation are only ever built on the back of satisfied clients. Since every client is unique, each with their own needs and aspirations, the purpose of our development has to be focused on our ability to remain situationally responsive. Professionalism is built on our ability to deliver excellent service through which we confidently and consistently model professional behaviours. We cannot afford to be reactive if we want satisfying and successful outcomes for ourselves and for our clients. When we take this approach, we bumble our way through. When we bumble, we stumble. We are inadequately prepared and lack the capacity to adapt and remain consistent.

To appreciate just how situationally responsive we are, we must be self-assured enough to know we live up to professional expectations. In addition, we must be self-disciplined enough to regularly look back at ourselves to be assured of that. Only by reflecting on feedback and undertaking self-evaluation do we become sufficiently self-aware and understand our self-perception and how this aligns with the views held by others.

If we want to be that situationally responsive professional, we must question our assumptions about who we think we are, based on who we really are. We must remember that professionalism is built on authenticity. We cannot be lacking in sincerity and substance; nor can we afford to be self-deceiving. Instead, we must be sure that we are genuinely the person we claim to be. If we are not, we need to set about changing things. Either way, the truth brings us closer to securing our reputation.

This brings us to the short sections at the end of each chapter, where we were asked to 'hold that thought'. Each of these sections prompts us to reflect and examine our motives, intellectual engagement, attitudes, and strength of character. This encourages us to be clear on where we stand in relation to specific values. In terms of understanding ourselves as professionals, they are a good starting point for self-discovery and a way of holding ourselves to account. The insight and questions offered encourage us to rationalise our actions and think about what might differentiate us from others. After all we have read, they are there to help us face the truth about ourselves. Whether the outcome of our reflections is confidence-boosting or a change-initiating call to action, it provides us with insight into who we are and what needs to change for us to become our professional best. Moreover, it gives us a clearer idea of where to invest our time and energy. We must never forget that if we do not know where our strengths lie, we do not know where we add value. If we do not know where to improve, we cannot make the right choices and develop and implement strategies that will make us effective in our professional endeavours.

What comes through loud and clear within each 'hold that thought' is that we cannot begin to enhance our level of professionalism without being self-reflective, self-disciplined, self-aware, and self-regulating. Whether we possess these skills or not is not a big issue; they are all skills that can be nurtured. Remember that we develop as professionals when we change our habits of mind and adopt specific patterns of behaviour. If we learn to be self-reflective, self-disciplined, self-aware, and self-regulating, we have this fantastic superpower.

This incredible quartet of skills strengthens our self-efficacy to succeed in being situationally responsive professionals who act in principled ways. These skills prompt us to aim high, set expectations, and strive for quality. They help us get creative, think critically, evaluate, and manage risk. They ensure we push ourselves, listen, express ourselves, treat ourselves and others kindly, and remain honest, curious, and humble. In effect, they help us cognitively organise ourselves and set boundaries to control some of our professional frailties.

When we are self-reflective, self-disciplined, self-aware, and self-regulating, we boost our capacity to think and act as professionals day in and day out for the entire duration of our careers. Collectively these skills keep us committed to thinking and acting as a professional. They keep us engaged, responsive to the needs of ourselves and others, and honourable in our intent. Each plays a part in helping us pull it all together. By developing and applying these skills, we gain the self-assurance needed to know we are living up to professional expectations in ways that differentiate us from others.

Whatever professional aspirations we have, they need to translate into meaningful actions. Nothing about us will change unless we are honest about our capacity to be all four of these things. To pursue professionalism, a certain amount of our developmental energy needs to be channelled here. Since there is no road map for professionalism, self-reflection, self-discipline, self-awareness, and self-regulation are really the only things that will keep us accountable and moving in the right direction.

Looking back on our thoughts and actions, we see who we are. Yet we have to remember that the past is done. The purpose of looking back is to gain clarity, vision, and a sense of possibility. This allows us to see and create our professional future. When it comes to pursuing professionalism, there is no doubt we are in it for the long haul. It might be the end of the book, but it is by no means the end of our professional journey. All that we have learned so far is just the beginning. If we want the story to have a happy ending, we must actively craft it for ourselves, leaving nothing to chance. The future belongs to those of us prepared to positively manage our professional destinies. The outcome of our efforts is, at this point, unknown. Yet the professional that sits within us knows it would be most unprofessional not to try.

ABOUT THE AUTHOR

Cheryl Whiting has been writing, teaching, and researching the subject of professionalism for more than 20 years. After starting her career as a diagnostic radiographer within the National Health Service, she entered academia, becoming an Associate Professor in Medical Imaging and Clinical Practice Research at Kingston University. Her role in training healthcare students to deliver and advance effective patient-centred care sparked her interest in the topic of professional excellence.

In 2009 Cheryl was awarded a Doctorate in Education from the Open University for her research into professional development through workplace socialisation – research which revealed the complex nature of professionalism and highlighted the challenges people face in developing professional attributes. This led Cheryl to develop a series of workshops that support trainers to maximise the professional potential of others. In 2017, Cheryl became a freelance education and training consultant, spanning clinical, academic, and commercial sectors. Using her extensive leadership, team building, and teaching skills, Cheryl builds positive professional cultures by developing a shared understanding of professional values and standards of practice.

When not writing or delivering training, Cheryl can be found out and about enjoying the beauty of the Cotswolds and promoting the work of Cheltenham Open Door, a charity that supports vulnerable adults and those experiencing homelessness. If you want to learn more about Cheryl and the training and development opportunities she offers, visit www.drcherylwhiting.com. Alternatively, you can engage with her (Dr Cheryl E Whiting) on LinkedIn.

Printed in Great Britain
by Amazon

31234999R00239